REACHING A
VERDICT

Reviewing The Bill: 1990-1992

EDWARD KELLETT

DEVONFIRE

REACHING A VERDICT: Reviewing The Bill (1990-1992)

By Edward Kellett

First edition published March 2024 by Devonfire Books

Cover and spine design by Oliver Crocker

Project editor and internal design by Oliver Crocker

Proofread by Tessa Crocker

ISBN 978-1-8382819-5-3

Printed and bound by 4edge Limited, UK.

AUTHOR INTRODUCTION

Part of the reason that TV develops into an obsession for some is that it contains little-known byways that take time to explore. The period of *The Bill* covered by this book was one of the last that I experienced, thanks to the random way in which episodes were available fifteen years ago. With official UK DVD releases only covering up until the turn of the Nineties, YouTube supplied a steady trickle of off-air recordings from the middle of the decade onwards. But of the early Nineties there was virtually nothing, save a few fragments from very well-worn tapes. That it should now be my favourite era of the show is perhaps a testament to the power of delayed gratification. One can hardly call it an obscure time when *The Bill* was a massive mainstream hit in those years, its viewing figures steadily increasing towards a peak. And yet it strikes me that, when online surveys seek the opinion of fans about favourite characters, few in number are the nominations for DCIs Wray and Reid, Sgts Maitland and Corrie, PCs Smollett and French. These short-lived figures never broke out of this era, like others before and after them. But if there is any phase of the programme that fine tunes its ingredients, offering stories big and small, edgy and playful, it is this one. This second volume of *Reaching a Verdict* explores how *The Bill* became not just a series of one-hit wonders but a continuing saga that ventured into ambitious and dark territory.

It feels strange to turn an introduction into a eulogy, but here it's important to acknowledge my route into the show. Had I not picked up the DVD releases of the three hour-long series, a passing curiosity would never have become a fixation. Like countless other gems they were the product of Network, the distributor of archive film and TV that was without parallel. My shelves, like some of yours no doubt, groan from the weight of its output. It came as quite a surprise, then, to discover in June of last year that Network had gone into liquidation, its stock now fetching inflated prices wherever it can be found. The history and standing of vintage television are hugely dented without it, and make books like this more important. We should be aware of and treasure the great things in our lives, for we never know when they will come to an abrupt end; only that we will not see their like again.

Edward Kellett, March 2024.

For
MARILYN KELLETT
Greatest of all the Greats
A woman of infinite kindness, patience and generosity
Not lost, never forgotten

CONTENTS

FOREWORD
By Tony Virgo
Producer, *The Bill* (1990-1992)

I first met Michael Chapman a long time ago at the BBC, when as a first assistant director I worked with him on the BAFTA winning drama series *Secret Army*. By the time I went freelance as a producer, *The Bill* was already an iconic show and one that everyone wanted to work on. When Michael was looking for someone to come in and take over from outgoing producer Geraint Morris, he gave me a chance.

The Bill production team was split into two units making episodes simultaneously. I was responsible for the Red unit, which tended to get all the action scripts, while Pat Sandys was responsible for the Blue unit, which focused on the more human stories. By the time we read the scripts, they were already in good order, thanks to the work done by script editors Tim Vaughan and Gina Cronk, two very clever and decisive people who were both fantastic at their jobs.

I hadn't been working at Barlby Road for very long when the script for *Trojan Horse* landed on my desk. This ambitious story was going to see Sun Hill station devastated by a car bomb that would result in PC Ken Melvin, played by the very popular Mark Powley, literally go out with a bang! I remember the only instruction that Michael gave me during planning was, "This is going to cost a lot of money Tony, so whatever you do, don't screw this up!" I assigned the story to Graham Theakston, a bold and very stylish director who always knew what he wanted to achieve. Revisiting *Trojan Horse* again over three decades later, I think Graham and his cast and crew all did an amazing job.

The explosion was helping to mask the fact that we were moving from Barlby Road to Merton, a brilliant idea only made practically possible by the efforts of many people, including production coordinator Nigel Wilson and designer Bill Palmer, who grappled with the organisation and creation of the new Sun Hill at a former bonded warehouse on

7

Windsor Avenue. Filming began at Bosun House, named after Michael's faithful black labrador, on Sunday 8th April 1990.

The Bill was not an easy show to produce. I remember one day very early on at Merton crouching on the floor of my little office, literally on my knees feeling the pressure of our rigorous production schedule. Michael looked through the window and sensed there was a problem. He banged on the door and said, "Come and see me in my office." I thought "Oh God, he's going to fire me…" Michael had served in the Navy and he ran *The Bill* like a battleship. In his office, he poured me a rather large glass of Glenmorangie and we talked about politics and life in general. As I was walking to the door and thinking I'd got away with it, Michael said "Tony… don't think about things for too long."

Michael once told me how much of the budget was spent on writing off scripts every year. They would pay writers to develop storylines, but if in the end they weren't going to work for *The Bill*, Michael wasn't going to let us shoot them. Today that wouldn't happen, you would have to make it work because you had spent money on the script. But Michael had very strict rules and a clear vision about what was right for *The Bill* and he was absolutely adamant on maintaining the reality of a police procedural. He gave us so much freedom as producers, though woe betide you if you broke those rules.

In Edward Kellett's book, you will read about episodes that we should all feel very proud of. Scripts from the imaginations of Russell Lewis, Christopher Russell and J.C. Wilsher were brought to life by a team helmed by ambitious directors like David Hayman, Nick Laughland and Stuart Urban. The groundbreaking results still stand up today.

Of all the television I've made, *The Bill* is the series that will always be imprinted on my mind the most. I loved the way Michael ran the show, it was not one actor's show nor one producer's show, it was a team effort and a show for everyone. I feel very fortunate that Michael gave me a chance to work with all those brilliant people.

Tony Virgo, March 2024.

REVIEWING THE BILL: 1990

First Broadcast 2 January – 27 December 1990

Script Editors: Zanna Beswick, Barbara Cox, Gina Cronk, Peter Eyers-Hill, Mark Lyons, Tim Vaughan. Producers: Brenda Ennis, Pat Sandys, Michael Simpson, Tony Virgo, Peter Wolfes. Executive Producer: Michael Chapman.

Key Exhibits:

1. *I Thought You'd Gone*
Written by J.C. Wilsher. Directed by Nicholas Laughland.

2. *Close Co-Operation*
Written by Garry Lyons. Directed by Michael Simpson.

3. *Middleman / Corkscrew*
Written by J.C. Wilsher. Directed by Michael Simpson.

4. *Victims / Somebody's Husband*
Written by Jonathan Rich. Directed by Derek Lister.

5. *Trojan Horse*
Written by Pat Dunlop. Directed by Graham Theakston.

6. *Rites*
Written by Jonathan Rich. Directed by Derek Lister.

7. *Witch Hunt*
Written by Christopher Russell. Directed by Derek Lister.

8. *Something to Remember*
Written by Christopher Russell. Directed by Laura Sims.

9. *Effective Persuaders*
Written by J.C. Wilsher. Directed by Nicholas Laughland.

10. *A Sense of Duty*
Written by Julian Jones. Directed by Bill Hays.

11. *Start With the Whistle*
Written by J.C. Wilsher. Directed by John Strickland.

12. *Out of the Blue*
Written by J.C. Wilsher. Directed by Moira Armstrong.

CASTLES ON THE GROUND

The last in a series of upheavals for *The Bill* was also to be its most lasting. Having been forced into one move across London by outside forces, a second rapidly followed when the owners of the Barlby Road site decided to redevelop it. What would turn out to be the show's final resting place in Merton, south-west London, was a further experiment in state-of-the-art programme making. Not content with hiring a building, the production team took over a warehouse and turned it into an entire TV complex, with standing courtroom and hospital sets that had years of mileage built into them. A third shooting unit joined the existing two, to capture as much footage as possible; this would become a permanent feature when the show went thrice-weekly. Script editor Tim Vaughan has observed that in the rush to scrape material together to cover the transition, "The pips did squeak... You could feel it rocking a little bit."[1] But however fraught things were behind the scenes, in front of the camera there's no appreciable dip in quality. The necessary economies show in other ways. It can be no coincidence that, throughout 1990, the show leans into serialised stories more than at any other time in the half-hour era. Proving that the best work is often forged in adversity, these two-parters – and one six-part storyline spread out over several months – not only give the programme a new feel, but push it to new heights.

The ground is cleared with the removal of two standout characters from the Barlby Road era, Taffy Edwards and Christine Frazer. Both are dispatched in *I Thought You'd Gone* – the first offering of the year from the man who is indivisible from this early Nineties era, J.C. Wilsher. The previous volume of *Reaching a Verdict* spoke of the difficulties he and other writers had in overcoming the commissioning hurdle. Some, like Nicholas McInerny, succeeded early on but took longer to get the green light again. But for others, once you were in you were in, as seen in the sudden explosion of work by Wilsher, *The Bill*'s new Most Valuable Player: of his fifty-plus episodes, over a quarter hail from 1990. Like Christopher Russell, he is entrusted with the bigger storylines, sending two more regulars on their way at the

---

[1] *The Bill Podcast: Homes and Gardens* Patreon Commentary, 2020

other end of the year. On the day of her departure, Frazer's bosses have no more idea what to make of her than they ever did. Choosing a farewell card, Chief Superintendent Brownlow hands Derek Conway one from the Police Horse Benevolent Fund. "Very fine-looking stallion, sir." "Do you think a mare would be more appropriate?" "Depends what you're trying to say." They share a schoolboy giggle. Having failed to tackle workplace sexism from the practical end, Christine is taking the theoretical route. Drawing on his own background in higher education, Wilsher salutes the ivory towers with help from one Frank Burnside DI (DisHons.) "So, you're getting all this time off to write a book." "A thesis, Frank." "All right, a book without pictures. What's it in aid of again?" "The topic is, 'A Comparative Study of Women's Career Patterns in the Police Force and Private Industry and Commerce.'" "You'll get bored. I got bored while you were telling me the title." "As a matter of fact, I'm looking forward to spending time in an academic environment with people who can offer me some intellectual stimulation." "Poofs."

Burnside sets his department straight on Frazer's book – "Thesis, you dickhead!" he berates the ignorant Tosh – before heading to a leaving do of "dry wine and dead things on toast." Rumour has spread that Frazer is going to use the occasion to speak out. Assured that Brownlow will defuse any tension in his speech, Conway heads hastily to the bar to fortify himself. "The thing is Frank, you're a lecherous conniving bastard with a vicious streak, but at least I know where I stand with you," she concedes. She stands poker-faced alongside her uniformly male uniforms while they endure the Chief Super's tribute, in which he manages to make a sexist quote about WPCs sound even worse through his wooden recital and equally wooden refuting of it. When applause breaks out around her, Frazer offers no more than an enigmatic smile, but she does manage to lob a grenade at the Dynamic Duo in her own speech. "Your senior officers say such kind and encouraging things about you; if they'd only said them earlier you wouldn't have wanted to leave." Conway glowers at her as she goes on to voice the usual platitudes, averting any controversy. Meeting June Ackland in the ladies', she observes that "you've found a way to survive, haven't you? You haven't let them put you down, they haven't stuck one of their labels on you, like the relief bicycle, or the ballbreaker, or the bull dyke. And you haven't quit." June reminds her that she hasn't

11

either – but Frazer is not so sure. "I really don't know. Maybe this is their world, and maybe they're welcome to it."

Her fellow escapee is even keener to let the party go on without him. Ordering Taff not to fall into any trouble on his last day, Bob Cryer agrees he can trust him: "I mean you have done your best to stay out of harm's way all the time you've been here." In his final meeting with Brownlow, he is as much of an afterthought as he always was. "Well Edwards, or Taff as you prefer to be called..." "As a matter of fact, I prefer to be called Francis" – not a tune he was singing when the name first became public knowledge in Series 3's *Domestics*. "I get called Taff here on account of being Welsh. It's a bit ironical really isn't it; spent all that time at Hendon being taught not to treat people like stereotypes, and I found out I was one." This barb is aimed at the show as much as the officers, highlighting a quaint era of TV in which people from 'the regions' were defined solely by them, like the other man from that wasteland beyond the North Circular, 'Yorkie' Smith.

Taff's story is also a prolonged comment on the troubles of being an outsider and how one point of difference can multiply into many. Brownlow wishes him good luck for his transfer to Cardiff – "I'm not going to Cardiff, sir" – and happiness for him and "Megan..." "Mary." "...Mrs Edwards. Oh, and thank you for your dedicated and sportsmanlike captaincy of the badminton team." A baffled Edwards is sent to his next meeting with a terse Conway, who hands him the exit questionnaire Met leavers have to fill out, stating their reasons and comments on potential improvements; he knows full well Taff will use it to take the almighty dump on the service he has longed for. But Cryer chips in his own word of warning: "Don't criticise. Don't burn bridges, you never know in this life. Wales might not suit you after all. The sheep might bite you, or the Sons of Glendower might decide you're a traitor and set light to your house! However you feel now, you might want to come back. And if you slag off the Metropolitan Police in writing you'll never darken our door again, and that's a promise!"

Cryer changes tack a little, acknowledging that they have "had their ups and downs" and he's spoken to him harshly, but all for his own benefit. Taff offers him a handshake. His biggest enemy is the only man to acknowledge him, unlike the parade of people he meets who remark, "I thought you'd gone!" He pauses as he reaches the question on change in the Met, full of thoughts that will probably go unrecorded. Clearing out his locker, he takes a final look around the room, trying and failing to summon the emotion that Yorkie felt six months earlier in his place. Life, unlike drama, often lacks a sense of occasion; that is Taff in a nutshell. He is late for his own leaving do, a stingy affair just like his engagement do was. "He's a short streak of Welsh misery; I'll still have a drink off him," says Stamp once the bar opens. The party is in full swing when Taff arrives, the strippergram calling out his name. He takes one look at the doors, one listen to the carousing inside – and heads on his way. Minutes later, Ackland and Frazer turn up, only to meet the stripper as she leaves. With one look at Christine's uniform, she exclaims, "Not another double booking, I just done the gig love!" If that valediction for Frazer tells you all kinds of queasy things, even as a joke, then the final sweeping crane shot of Taffy as he heads into the sunset is a wonderfully epic way to sign off this smaller than life figure. His is a tale without sound and fury, signifying plenty; the kind that is only possible in a show telling the stories of twenty people, rather than one or two. Not all hit the mark, but this is one that rings true to the experiences of thousands of people and, most likely, hundreds of police officers: those who don't get the book deals once they hang up their uniforms.

The refurbishment of Sun Hill becomes official in Wilsher's *Citadel*. For a while the station is a hive of activity, surveyors wandering into offices and shoving tape measures in people's faces. But then Brownlow is summoned to a meeting with the Commander and is introduced to a Home Office man and a security consultant. The latter, an enthusiastic bow-tied boffin, explains that if Brownlow is expected to meet the policing challenges of the future with reduced manpower, the solutions must be technological. Attention switches to the scale model nearby, of "a divisional police station for the twenty-first century": a toy of little interest to the Super until he learns that it's going to be built at Sun Hill. The officials boast that for low running costs it will combine "user friendliness and combat survivability", with an optimism that shows no-one in the Met saw the Paul Marquess era coming. The new open-plan front office "constitutes defensible space. Your lines of sight are much more comprehensive, and you can drop an armoured shutter over the front door that can stand up to an RPG-7 rocket attack!" "I'm not expecting a rocket attack," Brownlow replies drolly. "Yes, well that's what they'd have said in Belfast in 1969." He is reminded of his own complaints about having to transfer prisoners into the custody area via the rear entrance, which feels like the show highlighting a flaw in the Barlby Road design, and told that a new secure yard will enable him to "process busloads of detainees... None of this business of driving armoured personnel carriers against the gates when the hooligans are revving at the base!" "We don't operate armoured personnel carriers," he points out gently. "No, but the security forces would." The Chief Super looks disturbed at the notion of police stations becoming army barracks in this dystopian view of the inner-city future; already the authorities are prepared to transplant the way they handle the Troubles to the mainland.

Picking up where he left off in *Street Games and Board Games*, Wilsher dives further into what we might call the police-industrial complex. A decade of social and political strife has caused misery for many, but opened new markets for some, including contractors from the world of private security, courting a public service desperate for answers. The planning for doomsday scenarios has become an industry in its own right, addressing the symptom rather than the disease. On Brownlow's doubting face is written the question: can a gulf in trust with the public be plugged with steel and concrete rather than real ideas, from real people? Like dozens of issues raised by *The Bill* over the years, and especially those by Wilsher, this one sounds at us loud and clear in the present. Of all the handicaps to a revival of the show, one of the most profound is that the community police station itself has receded from use; if not turned into fortresses, many have been anonymised, reduced to office blocks. That the police now need to disguise rather than advertise their presence is testament to a world filled with more random dangers and axes to grind than ever. Whatever his own feelings, Brownlow puts a brave face on it, leaving all the qualms to Doubting Derek. "We mustn't start off with a negative attitude," he insists as they step out of the front entrance to examine the new design. "I'm going to get enough carping from certain quarters without you adding to it as well." We are given a rare view of the street outside as they wander round examining the changes that need to be made – all of which were implemented miles away in Merton. Brownlow gives Conway "a token that I have every confidence in your abilities" by landing him with the day-to-day running of the building works. "The last thing I want to be is a barrack room lawyer," he protests, "but strictly speaking I am in charge of operations. This does strike me as a classic example of admin." "Oh no, I see it very much as an operation – a heart and lung transplant. With a bit of brain surgery thrown in."

As resignation sinks into Conway, the show's most enduring duet takes flight. How best to define the decade-long feud between Sun Hill's Lemmon and Matthau is tricky. At times it resembles an overlong car journey, harassed father trying to quell the endless whining in the back. But it's also a masochistic relationship, in which Conway endures any amount of pain in return for the rare moments of pleasure when Brownlow falls on his face. Arthur McKenzie's *Full House* begins the renovation work, the yard transformed into a chaotic landscape of building materials and debris. Officers are shunted out into Portacabins in rotating groups, an idea which by accident or design mirrors the early years in Wapping where production staff had to vacate offices to make way for filming. "These places really are like the TARDIS, aren't they?" Brownlow notes approvingly of his own cabin – only for his smile to vanish when he realises that it's Conway's too. "Look, this isn't a question of rank," he insists sheepishly to the Commander over the phone. "I'm talking about efficiency, and simply that we must at all costs retain our public character... It's just that a separate Portacabin for me would... I see, sir. And that's your final word, is it?" When it turns out that they will have to keep the work going and their prisoners transferred to Barton Street for two more weeks, Conway gossips gleefully with Cryer and Monroe about Brownlow's sudden interest in keeping the Super there happy: "He thinks he's trying to make friends... Brown stuff – you could go into business with the amount he's going to produce at Barton Street!" These small victories are what sustain him.

Saddled with the nightmare of cowboy builders, Conway's persecution complex rears its head. He begins to suspect them of fraud, charging excessive amounts for substandard materials and pocketing the difference. He tells Tosh to "look into" window-frames – "Where's he gonna stick the Fraud Squad, in the portaloo?" asks

Burnside – and when word gets back to Brownlow, he politely suggests that Conway should take some gardening leave. "I can't leave everybody in this mess," he replies, as the point sails way over his head. Both his paranoia and his superior's hissy fit about the cost of the work seem ungrateful when, as far as the viewer in 1990 is concerned, it's done and dusted in less than two months: a timescale of the wildest dreams for any building job you or I have ever been close to. *A Fresh Start*, in which the new station is unveiled, feels like the moment at which the whole of *The Bill* tips on its axis. How fitting that the same episode that poses Brownlow in front of the new Merton entrance also sees the debut of then-Detective Superintendent Jack Meadows – who, twenty years later, closes the show by driving away from that same entrance, having regained his rank and taken Brownlow's job in the end. Unaware of the shelf life his work would enjoy, Christopher Russell marks the momentous occasion with the sound of one hand clicking a camera shutter. "Could we have one next to the scaffolding?" asks the bored photographer. "Gives us a before and after story: shows the public what they're really getting for their £1.5 million." "£1.3 million," he is corrected sharply. "Whatever." "I was expecting a reporter as well," the Chief Super adds hopefully as the man leaves. "She had to cover a story over at Barton Street. There'll be a press release later, won't there? I expect they'll cobble together something from that."

Inspecting the list of VIPs, Conway notes dismally that the loony-left MP Annie Donovan is "bound to be a vegan", an option that hasn't been catered for. After being humiliated in a wind-up by Ted Roach, who has told him not to salute DAC Jago because "he hates formality", the hapless George Garfield greets his local, black MP with the words, "You can't come in here, it's official visitors only," and insists on seeing her ID. Tony once nicked her for breach of the peace on a demo: "She didn't half kick. Got off and all. But she's a lawyer, so she would. I wouldn't nick her on a demo now she's an MP though. It's what they want, innit? To be martyred." The dignitaries embark on their tour as Tom Penny admires his new custody area, unhappy that "the scrotes and slags have to come in again tomorrow and spoil it." He notes that everyone wants to see the cells: "It's like visiting a castle. The only bit people are really interested in is the dungeons." Anticipating criticism from Ms Donovan, Brownlow says she'll be pleased to note the number of cells has not been expanded, but she flips this on its head: "Doesn't that lack a certain logic? If £1.3 million is being spent on increasing your efficiency, how come you're not expecting to arrest more criminals?" With Brownlow stuck for an answer, it's Penny who rides to the rescue, assuring her that they have an above average number of cells but "the only problem has been their use for remand prisoner overspill. We're assured that is a thing of the past." "By the government? Then it must be true," she smiles sweetly. Penny is left beaming in triumph, which is swiftly negated outside. Brownlow's anger at the heap of rubbish by CID's Portacabin – "Shouldn't this have gone by now, Derek?" – is nothing to the sight within. The PR nightmare that the Super prophesied the moment he set eyes on Tosh Lines comes true when the big man turns to face them on his knees, apple wedged in his jaw: the hog roast of the day.

What the saga of the new station achieves is to bind the fiction of the programme closer together, into a more unified whole. The ability of the half-hours to press the reset button at the end of each story was a strength, but a certain amount of continuity is also rewarding for the long-term viewer. Seeing the officers huddled inside freezing Portacabins for weeks on end helps to reinforce the sense of time passing, and of a new hurdle that these seasoned characters are having to face. That feeling of greater cohesion is apparent throughout this year. Themes echo back and forth along it, one episode's events commenting on and expanding another, issues joined up in satisfying circles. Evidently this amount of serialisation, a little bit but not too much, hits my own sweet spot with regard to *The Bill*. At this point it treads a fine line, a high-volume drama series rather than a procession of single plays: before the move to thrice-weekly made each episode more self-contained than ever, and the return to the hourly format swung the pendulum back again, eventually turning the show into one huge serial.

The disruption of the building work serves to remind us that Sun Hill doesn't exist in a vacuum. We don't just hear about its rival stations, Barton Street and Stafford Row, we get to see inside them and see how they tackle the problems that occupy our heroes. The latter have a squeaky-clean nick to go with an increasingly clean image, the extremists like Pete Muswell having been phased out. Instead, the show uses its visits to other stations to be more overtly critical of the police than it could be on 'home ground'. The regulars are suddenly outsiders, the environment around them strange and threatening as it would be to a prisoner. The sets are as cramped and gloomy as they were in the Artichoke Hill days; the officers less photogenic, presenting an unknown, disturbing quantity.

First up is Stafford Row, when Burnside returns to his old fiddling ground in Julian Jones's *A Clean Division*. On the way in with Alistair Greig, he sums up the brick monstrosity that towers above the landscape: "That building represents us, Alistair. It's modern, clean, efficient – and has precisely no relationship to the buildings in the area around it." After greeting two old unloved colleagues, he remarks, "All the good officers are gone. That's why they brought in that pair of foot and mouth." Battling to stay awake during a conference on managerial co-operation, he is brought to life by the news that Jim Carver has been arrested by the fanatically by-the-book PC Horden for drink driving. Having left his broken-down car to visit an informant at a pub, Jim returns to it and steers it off the road at Horden's instruction. Then the latter smells alcohol on his breath, and the test is positive. "I would have stuck out like a white zit drinking Britvic 55... I was working for us!" "Oh, 'I was out of my brain for Sun Hill' – that's going to sound good." Burnside embarks on a quest to 'sort it' and discovers the limits of his power. Horden, the purest of choirboys, offers the DI his notebook but insists he will have to say he did so. Once they realise who made the arrest, his senior officers are terrified of crossing him and being accused of wrongdoing too. Told what has happened, Brownlow naturally assumes it was his *bête noire* Roach and is surprised to learn it is Carver. While sympathetic, he can't square it away because of his rank: "It hits me just as hard as it does you. It's every officer's nightmare, being breathalysed... This is not an internal disciplinary matter! Carver has broken the law of the land."

Jim finds a crucial ally in a young and hirsute Mark Strong, playing a custody PC who takes him for a toilet break and allows him an extended mouthwash. After giving a second sample he storms out, almost crippling Burnside with a traffic cone he hurls in his wake. "I tripped, over one of your bollards," the DI tells Horden. "You want to get those *bollards* sorted out!" "Is it cracked?" adds Greig, in an endearingly feeble effort to match the macho banter. "They didn't let me off," says Jim, "I hadn't done anything, I was under the limit! Come here, you *cretin!*" His teammates sensibly drag him away. But, ever the optimist, Burnside invites Greig and Carver for a celebratory drink and they hastily cry off as one. This is not the last we will see of the intoximeter, and the groundwork for its return is laid in our next trip to an oppressive rival nick. The extent to which each station is a tribe of its own, determined to close ranks when one of their number is threatened, is more apparent at Barton Street in *Close Co-Operation*, writer Garry Lyons's final script for the series. Fed up with housing Sun Hill's clientele, their message is delivered loud and clear by the terrifyingly abrasive Inspector Twist, later to be remodelled as Chief Inspector Cato. The "Bald Headed Bastard from Barton Street" is already in fine form. Of the clear-ups Burnside is expecting from the burglar he's arrested, Twist asks, "What do you want, congratulations as well? We'll put up with you, that doesn't mean to say we have to like you, all right?" The only Sun Hill man who does feel welcome is Tom Penny, who has struck up a friendship with his opposite number, the blokey Sgt. Terry Coles. He offers Penny a good deal on a motor: "You know what they say, keep the old lady sweet, then you can concentrate on the crumpet!" "Leave it out Alec, it's just a bit of fun," Penny tells a disapproving Peters after he has chatted up a woman in the canteen and arranged a night out at the dog track.

But Penny goes to the dogs earlier than expected when a dealer, brought in with a bleeding nose from an escape attempt, is found badly beaten in his cell after Tom was absent from his desk. Realising the Barton Street officers are keen to play it down, Penny points out that he's a Sun Hill prisoner. "Then he's a Sun Hill problem, isn't he?" It's clear that Coles is responsible, but Penny thinks he can keep it quiet, insisting he must have had a reason. "Just listen to yourself," says the disgusted Peters, who gets on his back and won't let go. Hearing the observation that it "puts you back twenty years", Alec muses sadly, "I thought those days were dead and gone", of the same era that Penny has recalled wistfully in the canteen. Twist is dismissive; the facts show an assault committed by Sun Hill during the arrest. In the end Penny cracks, his voice faltering as he admits that

"The prisoner was beaten, sir." The story reveals an extra layer when Peters, the voice of conscience, talks to the suspect in his cell. Terrified, he doesn't want to make a complaint, but Alec announces cheerfully that he's done so on his behalf: "Basically mate, no can do. It's my back I'm covering – not yours." In the era of PACE, all that really matters is being able to distance yourself from the brown stuff. But we also see how those like Penny who tread the middle ground, never taking a stand on anything, pay dearly for it in the end. Trying to keep everyone happy, he ends up friendless, despised for his inaction and for ratting out one of Barton Street's own. Instead, it's the sanguine but principled Peters who triumphs at the end, walking away from a poster on railway safety that declares: 'Game Over'.

ONE TEAM, TWO GUVNORS

Barton Street is crucial again as we are introduced to a short-lived but important figure: Gordon Wray, first Detective Chief Inspector to grace Sun Hill and the man tasked with dragging Burnside kicking and screaming into the Nineties. Following on from *Close Co-Operation*, J.C. Wilsher's two-parter *Middleman/Corkscrew* turns the latter on Frank Burnside. Authorised to run Operation Middleman, targeting overlooked wholesale suppliers of crack, he is unhappy to be saddled with Wray, a fellow DI from the Drugs Squad acting as liaison. The latter deduces that Burnside's plan is dependent on a snout, but Frank has a strategy in mind: "Get hold of young kids, still wet behind the ears, bust 'em, turn 'em, put them straight back out on the street and say, 'Who are you scoring off tonight?'" "To make that work you've got to play your informants very carefully." "You've either got it or you haven't." "I look forward to seeing how it's done." Wray's caution is well-founded; a raid on a squat doubling as a crack factory produces a covert haul of talcum powder, and it becomes clear someone tipped off the suppliers. Greig is called in to give his version of events, armed with advice from Dashwood: "You know what they say about resisting interrogation, Alistair – just imagine Brownlow and Conway stark naked." It doesn't pay off, and he admits that Burnside gave his source, the weaselly burglar Kenny Stoller, a lift home before the raid. Asked to account for himself, the man who doesn't play by the rules comes running home to them crying once his interest is threatened: "If I'm under investigation, I want a Form 163 laying out the charges against me. No Form 163 – no comment."

With Wray leading the enquiry as a safe figure from outside, Burnside is suddenly *persona non grata* among his own team. Pressing Tosh for info, he gets 'no comment' thrown back at him: "This whole deal smells of bent coppers, and I'm watching my back, 'cos when a diarrhoea bomb like that goes off, everybody gets splattered!" By keeping his troops permanently in the dark in order to hog all the glory, he has left them unable to trust him. But when Wray visits Barton Street to question Mark Duggan, a squatter who tried to take his head off with a machete, the latter gives him the score: "Whatever you want me to say... I can't say it here." Shuttled into hospital with a bogus ailment, he insists, "It's well known, isn't it? There's a sergeant there doing the business... Coles." The bully boy is also bent, passing on warning from Stoller about the police raid to the suppliers. Catching up with Kenny, Burnside puts the boot in before declaring that "he made a sudden movement, so I struck him in self-defence. Write that down Alistair, they believe your log sheets." Stoller is wired and sent to entrap Coles, who twigs what is going on, drops a knife in his lap and uses the same excuse of "self-defence" to lay into him. "You *scumbag*, Coles!" yells Burnside, the script highlighting his hypocrisy without beating us over the head with it. The villain is confident he said nothing incriminating, but the attack has also been caught on videotape: "You're dead, Coles." Burnside's good mood at being cleared is short-lived; over a drink, Wray announces he's been made up to DCI. "Oh yeah, whereabouts?" "Sun Hill, Frank. I'm your new guvnor."

The Gordon Wray we see in his first two episodes is cut from the same blokey cloth as Burnside: delivering Cockney lingo in a macho growl, swaggering about in a long coat and grabbing slags for a quiet word in an alley. Had the character been nothing but a Burnside clone he would have worn thin, but the show performs something of a bait and switch. When Wray arrives for his first day in charge of CID, his ambitions have broadened. He wants people "to understand I'm in the business of crime management", and the glow of approval from Brownlow positively radiates off the screen. "We'll be talking manpower, resources, budgeting, public relations, and looking after the needs of the victims. The days of Jack the Lad doing the business on the streets and in the boozers, out of all control and supervision, are definitely numbered." Burnside tries to fob him off with a rundown of cases and figures, only to be told, "I don't want to pick over the nuts and bolts, Frank; I wanna talk philosophy." Wray soon gets ammunition when he finds Tosh asleep at his desk, flat out after working thirty-six hours straight. With a priceless 'I told you so' look from Greig in his best Val Doonican sweater, Tosh is summoned to Wray's office. He explains that the DI wants him on a job: "I don't care if Jesus wants you for a sunbeam, book off!" A dismayed Burnside claims that "Tosh loves the old overtime; he can't get enough of it!" to feed his six kids (an error caused by counting Kevin Lloyd's actual offspring!). Wray points out that Tosh won't have a family much longer if he never sees them. He wants to end the pursuit of vendettas against 'overdue' crooks and focus on delivering a service instead. Burnside answers a phone and clarifies where he stands on victim support: "Salvation Army, Sister Anna speaking. No, you pillock, this is Burnside."

By this point St. Francis is well established as a quote machine. A sergeant who breaks the news that uniform have lost his prisoner is aware he's annoyed. "First class passengers on the *Titanic* were annoyed – what I'm feeling now goes beyond that!" "Act natural," he tells a man opening his front door to a villain. "What if he's armed?" "Act scared." Visiting a hardened thug in prison, Burnside restates his view on academia when told the man is now reformed and wants letters after his name. "He's got letters after his name – Ralph Pender, GBH." My all-time favourite hails from *University Challenge*, in which Burnside pursues ex-con Joey Buchan for a robbery, only for his timid girlfriend to give him an alibi. "Nice lady," Burnside remarks at the door. "The mysteries of human attraction," smirks Buchan. "Where's the mystery?" asks the DI coldly. "You've seen one robber's dog, you've seen 'em all."

But it's not just the police serving up quotes this time. Buchan, played with louche swagger by George Irving, has become an Open University-educated scholar who gives interviews in which he holds forth about police malpractice. "PACE was brought in to help bridge the credibility gap that I was referring to, as was the Crown Prosecution Service. And yet – and this is my point – something like half the population still believe that the police will lie under oath in order to get the job done. Now he can smile," Buchan adds as he looks at Burnside, "but this is not just paranoia or some popular urban mythology. It's a widely held and deeply rooted perception of the modern British police force, and it's justified. George Dixon does not flex his calves under the blue lamp anymore; he flexes his knuckles behind a riot shield before leading a baton charge." Urging his team to "forget the psychology degree, the letters to the press and the articles none of us read", Burnside has Carver follow the girlfriend without being discreet about it. She is reduced to tears, and Carver has another of his classic eruptions at Burnside: "I've waded through sewers, I've collected pieces of people who've been hit by trains, I've had a crossbow bolt miss me by that much, I don't mind that – but hassling some innocent woman...!" "Don't come to me for back-up on some iffy arrest like you have done in the past, like everyone else in this department has!" Buchan complains to Conway, but tellingly, Jim stays loyal to his boss, insisting he was merely careless, not brazen, in his snooping.

Jim is the DI's bagman again in *Once a Copper* when another raid falls through, this time on a local crime boss, Speers. "The last CID golden boy to raid Speers ended up in Her Majesty's Prison," notes Jim. He and Burnside visit Cooper, a former DI convicted of taking bribes. The increase in out-and-out bent coppers is no coincidence; while they are outsiders, they throw Burnside's shady character into relief. The snarling, silver-haired cadaver they meet is showing the effects of prison life. "Do you know what it's like in here? 'Once a copper...' That's what they say. Like it was some incurable disease. Maybe it is. For six months I couldn't go to the khazi without a chorus of 'nick-nick' seeping out of the sewers. What you staring at?" he asks a silent Carver. "Never seen a bent copper? Never knowingly, son." Offered help in his upcoming parole in return for info on Speers, he declares, "What really makes me puke, Burnside, is I used to be like you!" Returning his gaze to Jim, he quips, "You never think you'll end up back in uniform" – a line more clairvoyant than it could possibly know. Cooper outlines how easy it is to slide into corruption, receiving favours from crooks that lead to good results. "Then you find he's paid off your car." "Then he's paid off your career." "We all smell a little – you more than most, Burnside. What you don't like about me is looking in the mirror." Burnside learns that Cooper's history of bribes can be traced back to Speers, and realises the latter is holding the other convicts at bay in return for his silence. "He's the only thing keeping you alive." Cooper agrees to a deal, giving other leads on condition Speers is left alone. But Burnside wants to make sure that in pursuing them, he doesn't 'accidentally' fall on Speers. He has a line in smuggling art from the Continent, using a Docklands warehouse. "We go there sometimes... so we need to avoid it," Burnside hints. As Cooper writes the name down, there is a silent understanding between them: that he will give Burnside exactly what he wants, while keeping up the pretence that he hasn't. Having crossed the line, he can be used and discarded, by a younger, more ruthless version of himself. Burnside spells it out to Jim once they have left: "Let's go and get Speers." "I thought you'd done a deal?" "I only do deals with people that matter."

All the while, the power struggles and controversies of CID drift past Michael Dashwood as he continues on his heedless path. On the face of it Mike should be the least interesting character because he is the most content with his lot. Jon Iles observed that Mike was a "dry old sot" with "quite an impenetrable sense of humour."[2] But underlying Dashwood's every scene is the funniest thing about him: the faint disdain of someone who knows he's way too good for his surroundings. When he turns up in what Iles called his 'country squire' outfit, a picture in brown tweed, Burnside is lost for words. Mike bears the funny looks with dignity, even when his suit is ruined in a chase. But if he is the country squire, then Carver is his imposed guest: the feral evacuee from the inner cities who has never seen a tree before. On obbo in a car, Jim passes a burger to Mike, who sniffs, "I don't like relish." Realising he's swapped them by mistake, Jim hands over his half-eaten one. More a Fairtrade quinoa man at heart, Mike takes one look and passes. Later Jim chucks a Coke can out of the window, hooligan-style, prompting a pained, "Do you have to?" Funnier still than what Iles achieves in the role is the loathing the real police had for Mike, questions asked in print about how a mere DC could afford his lavish lifestyle. The show addresses this when he's given a hard time about his plan to buy a weekend cottage in

---

2 *The Bill Podcast* 01: Jon Iles, 2017

Wiltshire, while living in a police-subsidised home. "Ah, moral scruples Jim, that's what the force needs more of." Pressed for details of his "personal finance plan", he explains, "A bit of saving, a bit of investment... I'll tell you something about the class system, Jim. You think you're working class because your dad was. In fact, you're sitting in a comfortable middle-class job. What about the eighty per cent of your time that is spent filling in paperwork? You are treated as an employee, aren't you? Now what happens when you retire? You're out of your police flat and onto the street."

When not baiting Carver, Mike is sniping at Roach. The two old hands of CID, bickering brothers in the early years, are now a married couple who have been together far too long. Dealing with a giddy, wisecracking Ted, Mike looks irritably at the SOCO: "I hate it when he's in this mood." She thinks they are after a criminal with a blue jumper. "Well, that rules out Rupert Bear, doesn't it?" notes a sage Edward. On a surveillance job, Roach spies a couple across the street snogging each other's faces off. "That takes me back," he daydreams. "When to, last night?" asks Mike. Yearning for the finer things in life, he knows they will not be found close to home. "Yes, I'm a snob," a burglary victim admits to him as she describes the vulgar couple who turned up to view her house. "That's all right, Mrs Fillery – so am I." In *Unsocial Hours*, Burnside learns that a complainant who has hung over him for years and held up his promotion to DI has dropped dead. He does the only decent thing: invite his team for a celebration piss-up. Corralled into joining them, Greig, the innocent abroad, looks on in helpless stupor as the air grows thick with smoke and ancient anecdotes from the booze cruisers, Tosh and Jim. Finally, his head reeling, he asks Mike how he copes with these lunchtime sessions. The answer is simple, but comes with plenty of shade attached: "I've been drinking low-calorie tonic water. I don't want to end up a pickled-livered tosspot like that mob. I'm surprised at you." Greig pays for his lack of resistance when he returns to the office and Tosh appears with two buckets of KFC, to act as "ballast." He runs out in a vomiting fit, leaving Derbyshire's hardiest to finish them all by himself. Small wonder that the show's technical adviser, the ex-chief inspector Brian Hart, observed sceptically that if you tried to get a bunch of CID men out on a night-time enquiry, "They'd be pissed out of their minds anyway."[3]

Mike would be insufferable if his greatest issue was simply being stuck with the wrong crowd; but that is only one side of the story. "And what about you, Mike?" asks the eponymous hero of *Greig Versus Taylor*, after Dashwood has chipped in his usual two penn'orth from the sidelines. "Me? Well, I'm in the middle, aren't I?" "Good for you." When he later sounds off about their flimsy evidence, he is startled to find he has poked the bear. "'Even if, even if', what's your problem Mike? Shall I get someone else to sit in for the rest of the day, would that be less tedious for you? Start being a bit more positive, right?" As Oliver Crocker noted of this episode, Greig is what Dashwood never tried hard enough to be.[4] In theory they are a breed apart from the rest of CID, but instead of emulating Greig's fastidious approach, Mike is still enamoured with the hardman act. "Boys like this want us to give 'em a good hiding," he says of his teenage suspect in *Bad Faith*. "Gives them status; martyrdom." "You're even beginning to sound like Burnside," says a disappointed Cryer. In a rare insight into his past, Mike tells his old skipper how much harder the job becomes in CID. "You were a good PC in uniform, remember that," he is told. We see his ruthless streak in *The Strong Survive*, when he has a drug-addled teen tailed from Sun Hill by a group of officers who see his condition get worse and worse. But Mike insists they follow him all the way to his rendezvous with his boss; he and Jim later find him lying on rubble with his neck broken, his usefulness over. Mike calmly radios in the death, seemingly unmoved by his culpability for it. Jon Iles is superb in bringing out the character's inner doubt whenever Mike suspects he has gone too far. In contrast to the volcanic eruptions of Ted Roach, Dashwood's failings are buried deep within: an anxious look behind the eyes, betraying a concern for himself but also a lingering morality, whatever he may claim.

---

[3] *The Bill Podcast: Canley Fields* Patreon Commentary, 2019

[4] *The Bill Podcast: Greig Versus Taylor* Patreon Commentary, 2020

Dashwood and Greig come to blows a second time in *Against the Odds*, when the latter is Acting DI. CID trainee Viv Martella wants to get stuck into something juicy and is read the Book of Alistair in all its unsexy glory: "In my experience, big cases bring nothing but grief and frustration. Consistent work, well presented, is far more effective in your career." Mike is of course taking option A, in a covert chat with Burnside's hapless snout Alfie Dobbs. In his second full year on the show, Arthur McKenzie's dialogue feels a bit less like carrying a horizontal pole up a spiral staircase, but still has a unique timbre. "Dennis Wheatley'd lose his bottle down here," says Mike of the disused Tube station where they meet. Greig is horrified to learn he met a snout alone and took no notes or recordings. "I was using my initiative! Why don't we just go out with Brownlow and play golf all day?" Urged on by Jim, Mike doesn't wait for Greig to make a decision: "He'll want a conference, then he'll ask for an agenda... coffee, biscuits." He pulls in a suspect for an assault, but the latter claims to suffer from tinnitus – which means that under PACE rules he can't be interviewed without an interpreter. "It's a perfectly legal delaying tactic," Conway tells Mike, "He knows we can't get the evidence in time; you're stymied!" McKenzie, knowing all the tricks in the old book, points out there are plenty in the new one for the crooks to exploit. But as the man's possessions are returned, Mike recognises a watch taken during the assault. Later, he and Greig celebrate their result – only for the latter to suggest they should inform the authorities of the outstanding tax owed by the victim, which Mike promised would be dropped in exchange for his co-operation. "If we stand him up in court, he'll be discredited... I'm just dotting the Is and crossing the Ts." "Just so long as you're enjoying yourself," says Mike as he walks out, confirmed in his view that playing by the rules is a mug's game.

KNOCKED INTO SHAPE

While fighting a rearguard action in CID, Burnside has a bigger adversary to contend with. 1990 sees the debut of his opposite number, in every sense: the staunch disciplinarian that is 'Andy' Monroe. His arrival signifies the start of the Nineties *Bill*, just as much as Sun Hill's new facade. Both would remain in place for the entire decade, equally firm and impervious to the elements; both would need a firebomb to displace them. The third uniformed inspector in as many years is the first to assume control of the relief, becoming both their leader and representative. The baton is handed over at his predecessor's leaving do, when he is glimpsed among the guests, stating his emphatic views on police misconduct. "You're going to have a lot to say to him and all," Cryer, up to now the real power in Sun Hill, tells his fellow sergeants. "He's our new guvnor." "Strewth, didn't know when we were well off!" says an alarmed Peters. "At least Frazer had legs." Monroe is quick to stamp his authority, telling the troops they may have to stay on for a missing child enquiry, despite their grumbling. "Between ourselves," he tells Conway, "A Relief could do with a bit more 'by the book' and a bit less 'as you please.'" He is warned to keep Bob Cryer onside but makes it clear to the latter that while he values his advice, "I'll make the decisions." Bob is put out by the veiled criticism that things have become too soft. The only man singing a welcoming tune is Tom Penny: "Monroe suits me. He's rock hard, he's dead straight. My idea of a copper. He'll do our relief a lot of good." Cryer warns him that he hasn't been targeted yet: "You wait till he does, you'll see what I mean."

The moment soon arrives in *Roger and Out*, when Penny's snide streak bubbles to the surface again. He summons Tosh Lines to custody to meet "a friend of yours": Roger Collins, arrested for drunken behaviour, with Tosh's address on his student card. "Nice to have some manners wouldn't you say, in the circumstances? 'What's the charge, Sergeant?'" Milking the situation for all it's worth, he gets an admission that Collins is lodging with Tosh: staying *and* paying, without approval from above. "Anybody else would have ignored it or had a quiet word, but not you, Penny!" He sends a report upstairs to Conway and Tosh faces losing his job. "Once the word gets round the top brass, they'll be wetting themselves," Roach tells Carver. "Brownlow gargles with mouthwash before he picks up the phone to the DAC." "It's a shame Penny went into print," Monroe tells Conway, pointing out the standard method to handle Tosh would be to "kick his backside and be done with it." Lines is saved when Burnside marches into Brownlow's office and performs the 'I'm Spartacus' routine to the hilt, insisting that he okayed the lodger and must therefore be punished too. The furious Super must resolve the matter in-house rather than passing it to Area. Penny then learns to his discomfort that he can't out-pedant the ultimate pedant. By informing Tosh of his error, announces Monroe, "You acted, Penny, as an accessory to a disciplinary offence." Worse, he bypassed the chain of command: "I don't like underhand dealings. My reports go to the chief inspector. Your reports come to me. If this goes further, that's how I shall deal with it, sergeant – correctly." This is the template for the Lectures of Monroe down the years: the folded arms, the quietly hectoring tone and the undercurrent of menace in his soft Derbyshire voice. The poignancy of watching Colin Tarrant in his pomp is magnified in this episode, which showcases the talents of three men who were all lost far too soon.

As Cryer found before him, Monroe is unpopular above as well as below for being the nagging voice of truth. In *Ground Rules*, his last script for the show that made his name, Geoff McQueen highlights the bureaucracy that has overwhelmed the service in the six years since the freewheeling days of *Funny Ol' Business – Cops and Robbers*. At a meeting to discuss a forthcoming inspection, Monroe cuts through the optimism by producing a report on areas in which he feels Sun Hill is procedurally under-par. An angry Conway thinks he went behind his back to score points with Brownlow: "There are bound to be one or two minor problems regarding procedure, we're constantly being subjected to rule and procedural changes, almost on a daily basis!" One can sense the real reason for his insecurity: the fanaticism of Monroe makes him look like the cigarette-dragging slob he really is. "It's going to take me some time to forget about this," he warns him ominously. McQueen calls on the familiar trappings of the early days; besides the eye-catching work of Christopher Ellison's stunt double, as Burnside dives out of the path of a fleeing van, the inevitable "sweet F.A." makes a return visit. So too does the release of a uniform prisoner on the DI's authority, to deliver the goods for him. But they are also used to prove how things have changed. McQueen's guiding idea for the show was the clash between uniform and CID. In these two inspectors, that divide reaches its full expression: Monroe the rock-solid martinet, Burnside the ultimate fruit salesman. The latter's approach hits troubled waters when Roach and Dashwood, the other survivors from the class of '84, have an off the record chat with a suspect in their car and he tape records it. In this new era of accountability, the criminals are learning fast. It's Monroe who bails them out when he hands Burnside a tape recorder from a stolen batch found in a warehouse, of the same unusual make. "I think you'll find your Mr Kenning has some explaining to do." The DI is startled to realise he has an ally of sorts; however much the show may hero-worship him, with *The Bill*'s focus on the unglamorous realities of policing, McQueen observes that it's the nitpickers like Monroe who will inherit the future.

Unhappy that Burnside's methods have landed the undercover Dave Quinnan with a beating, Monroe issues a warning: "If you ever set up my blokes again, I will come after you like a bat out of hell." In Arthur McKenzie's *Angles*, they clash over the familiar subject of overtime. Monroe insists that any uniformed officers supplied to CID operations must come out of the latter's budget. He wonders how Burnside manages to get "sixty hours a month allocation more than any other inspector", which the DI freely admits is him playing the system: "If uniform haven't got the nous to ask for twice what they need in order to get half, tough! You continue giving overtime back to Brownlow, you get your allocation chopped." Warning Monroe he'll face rebellion in the ranks if there is no overtime on offer, he declares, "Ovies is the sweetener. I didn't learn that on a course." Through Burnside, McKenzie comments further on the lies, damned lies and statistics that now dominate policing in *Tactics*. At a weekly crime meeting, Brownlow brings up CID's detection rates of twenty per cent. "Of all crime reported at Sun Hill," the DI points out, "eighty per cent is screened out, filed, dead. Yet I'm supposed to wave a magic wand and come up with forty per cent – unless we're talking about forty per cent of the twenty per cent left, in which case our figures are some of the best, pound for pound, in the force. I might be old-fashioned, but I think effectiveness should be measured by quality." In another episode, anxious not to go to Area with poor clear-up figures, Brownlow advises that "if massaging is what is needed, I suggest you stick your thumbs in good and deep." Burnside explains to Conway the trick that has yielded Stafford Row's supposed improvements: "They've got a bloke almost permanent on prison visits, doing deals to clear up cases. Any snot-nosed juvenile they nick down there is leant on to cough for TICs." "Well get some in!" the Chief Inspector demands. "*You* get some in! I'm looking to nick serious villains, not toddlers."

In his defence of CID, Burnside has one obvious weak spot to cover; and sure enough, Monroe homes in on it near the end of the year. His hopes of promotion now abandoned for good, Ted Roach seems a little more at peace with himself. But in Julian Jones's *A Sense of Duty*, the fire is ignited again when he makes a new enemy, who will ultimately do for him at Sun Hill. Dining with a lady friend in a restaurant, Roach has to subdue a drunk who kicks off. He calls in uniform and Stamp and Garfield bring the man in. However, when Ted hands him over on the street outside, he doesn't make it clear that they are the arresting officers, given that he is off duty. Had there been a more intuitive sergeant in custody there would be no problem, but unfortunately, it's Penny, who wants to know where Roach is. "He's with this woman – she is *gorgeous*, like a model." "Oh, all right then, that's what I'll put down on the custody record: arresting officer, Jerry Hall. You go down the CAD room, contact Roach and tell him to get himself in here." The restaurant informs them that Ted has already left with her in a cab. Covering his own back, Penny informs Monroe, who begins a relentless crusade to get Roach in. He is located at a nightclub, ignores the request to return and heads home. Realising this is part of a wider beef with CID, Penny tells Peters that "Monroe's out for blood, the longer this night goes on, the less he cares whose it is. Look out, here's Count Dracula," he adds hastily, and Peters makes a crucifix sign once he's gone. The bolshie streak that surfaces in Alec from time to time prompts him to march into Monroe's office and suggest a caution. Instead, he is tasked with bringing in Roach himself, and gets the crucifix sign thrown back at him by a gleeful Penny.

When Roach finally arrives, the spectators have assembled to watch the show, and not for the last time. Monroe orders Roach to hand over his pocketbook so he can issue him with an official caution. "That's ridiculous!" The magic of Tony Scannell re-emerges as Roach's disbelief turns to fury. His eyes blaze accusingly at Penny, who looks away in shame; again, by trying to dodge trouble, Tom only invites contempt. "Would you like to see me salute, sir?" demands Roach, before delivering the two-fisted version. "It's prats like you that make this job not worth doing any more! I'm going to Brownlow, this is victimisation!" he roars as he storms out. There is always something childlike about Ted, in that everything must revolve around his needs. Penny and Peters usher him to an interview room and try fearfully to ease him out of his tantrum. As he rants and raves it's clear his pride is hurt above all else, after such a calculated humiliation. "I've been in the job twice as long as he has! What does he think he's *doing?* An official caution in front of everyone in the custody area? I don't get promotion because of tykes like him!" "You'll come out of this all right, Ted," Peters assures him. "Everyone's going to think Monroe is a jerk." "Monroe *is* a jerk," adds Penny. Reg Hollis reveals that Monroe is going to release the drunk at the bottom of all this. "So help me," growls Ted, "I will smack that man in the mouth!" The tramlines are neatly laid down for Roach's exit; unlike the threat he once made about Galloway, this one is going to stick, in every sense.

Monroe's principal antagonist over this year, however, is his fellow new boy on the relief, Dave Quinnan. When he and Burnside argue over Quinnan being seconded for a CID job, it's easy to be put in mind of Cryer and Galloway battling over the rookie Carver years earlier. But whereas Jim was an idealist whose true calling was uniform, yet who ended up going to the dark side, Dave – or at least this early wide-boy version of him – is the reverse: a dodgy operator whose natural environment is CID but who has somehow ended up on the beat. Andrew Paul arguably has a literal character arc: Dave starts out as a slippery geezer, becomes the loved mainstay of the relief, and ends up in shadowy territory again. In the same way Arthur McKenzie focused on Tosh during 1989, his scripts this year concentrate largely on the ongoing feud between Quinnan and Monroe. In *Full House*, Brownlow informs Monroe of a complaint over an assault case that has not been followed up: "PC Quinnan." "A name which crops up with depressing regularity." When Dave is radioed and told to see Monroe, he gives his present whereabouts in exact detail: "Just about to flush the pan, Sarge." He responds to the order with that very sound, finding it a useful metaphor when asked to account for his failings: "I'm always in the sh... mire, sir, it's only the depth that varies." Monroe frogmarches him to the scene of the crime so he can make an arrest, coaching him in the basics of policework like a parent helping their child. But they also let a man walk away who they don't realise is a suspected child molester, because Dave was late for parade and missed the briefing. When

Monroe sees the photo fit, he realises the error and tears into Quinnan for his sloppiness.

Relations get steadily worse, Dave whinging, "Old Marilyn's definitely got it in for me." His main grievance is the lack of overtime. A freelancer at heart, he is always on the lookout for extra income: "I'm talking about real bunse – paid rest days, football matches, demonstrations." After an operation on a gang of car thieves goes wrong in *Angles*, he argues the case for more overtime, to which Monroe insists sternly, "It's a concession, not a right." Highlighting the mercenary bottom line that preoccupies most officers, the same way it does people in other jobs, McKenzie again composes verse the likes of which would never return, even when the show had more room to indulge in its dialogue. "Fed Rep?" Dave jibes at Reg after they emerge from Monroe's office. "You stood there like a tin of milk." "Dave! Softly softly, catchee monkey; Monroe's attitude will be thrashed out at the next conference." "Cobblers." Matters come to a head in *My Favourite Things*, when Dave borrows a jemmy from the property store to break into the flat of an old lady who has locked herself out. On one of his morale-collapsing tours of the station, Conway realises that it is missing. In Monroe's mind there is only one suspect, and he sets out to prove it. He orders every PC's locker to be searched, sure he will find the offending item in Dave's. Reg adopts his Federation guise, insisting he will advise his members to say nothing. We get some interesting glimpses into their lives: Reg has absolutely nothing in his locker, pointing out that there's nothing in regulations to say he must, while Tony Stamp's has the priceless motto 'Those of you who think you know everything are annoying to those of us who do' engraved on the front.

When the search extends to the female lockers, the bad feeling intensifies. "He's got no right to read my private letters," declares an outraged Norika Datta. June tries to placate her: "Look, if I'd wanted a private life, I wouldn't have joined this one." But she gets roped in when Norika insists on a female officer being present for the search; and when it's June's turn, she is not immune from Monroe's relentless drive for perfection. "Urgent paperwork not completed," he scolds her, brandishing it in her face. June leaves in disgust, and the increasingly worried Peters tries to tell him the damage he is doing:

"She's the best policewoman we've got." When Dave returns, the padlock on his locker turns out to have been broken all along. The farce is brought to an end by Conway, who declares, "This place gets more like an overgrown crèche every day." The jemmy turns up magically in the property store and Monroe wants it forensically checked. "Oh no you're not," Conway overrules him, wiping his fingers on it. As per tradition, the last word goes to Cryer, who tells Monroe some home truths: "I often wonder, if I was a kid again, whether I'd still join... When I ask them to do a job, it's Bob Cryer asking. The day I have to cling to my rank for respect – well, that's the day I've lost." "Stuck with each other, aren't we?" says a defiant Monroe. Though he remained a stickler for the rules, he would never be quite as tyrannical as in this first year. The change in his persona from outright dictator to fussy stick in the mud is typical of the gradual softening in long-running characters.

Such a pattern can also be observed in the development of what would become Sun Hill's greatest bromance. In *Watching*, Dave Quinnan and George Garfield are called out to a school by its caretaker to investigate the sighting of an intruder. As the two men wander the premises, the show delivers another pure form of the mini stage play that came into vogue the previous year. We learn a little about Dave, but a great deal more about George, one of the show's most useful characters during the Nineties – and a man full of strong opinions, and hang-ups, about the job. He says of Norman Rossington's cheerful caretaker, "He's one of them berks who try to make a friend of you – 'George' this, 'George' that. If I'm in civvies down the pub then fair enough, I'm George to anybody. But if I'm in uniform it's different. I don't want kids and dossers pulling at me sleeve calling me George. There's got to be some distance, otherwise it don't work... Popularity brings contempt in my book, not respect. Like we're soft teachers. And I'm not – soft." Touring the school brings back plenty of bad memories for George, teased all the while by a grinning Dave. "They messed me up – teachers. I never rated 'em, see. I could see straight through them and they knew it. They're all talk, all sarcasm. Even then I could spot a phoney." He fantasises about being able to nick a few of them now. Dave is keen to hang around, rather than getting back on watch. "You're not a copper, Quinnan," George sneers. "Why join if you don't want the hassle?"

"The same reasons you did – money first, uniform second. Except with you the uniform comes first."

Dave suggests that George was looking for status and respect when he left his painter/decorator gig for the police: "From your first day on the beat, you're a somebody." He hints that George sees the job as a chance to get back at those who looked down on him in the past, in the mould of the bullish Dave Litten. Bemoaning the lack of respect on the street, George observes, "We've no status inside the force either. Not even trained properly, just expected to pick it up as we go along. After two years on the beat, you know two things: one, it's the most important job on the force, and two, nobody wants to do it." The intruder turns out to be a notorious ex-pupil who has taken to 'patrolling' the place, believing the caretaker can't do it properly. "Our gaffers aren't keen on self-styled vigilantes," George snaps, getting in his face while Dave stands by looking embarrassed. "You have got a file, intcha? You're scum, and if we don't sort out con artists like you, people won't know who to trust, now will they?" George's anger at heavies and security men who try to usurp the role of the police bubbles up again in his time as Fed Rep, when he has even greater concern for protecting what the job stands for. But, having used the day's events to psychoanalyse him, Dave can see little difference between one overly revved watcher and another. "Strange thing is," he tells his colleague as they take the intruder away, "if it come to the crunch, I'd rather have him on my side than you."

Garfield makes another dubious case for representing the views of the police in *Pride and Prejudice*, which follows up on the discussion of the AIDS crisis in Series 3. A businessman is found setting fire to a sports car, which belongs to a man who has conducted a hate campaign against him, daubing his garage with 'AIDS lives here' and breaking into his house to spray the walls with 'Scum' and 'AIDS Death'. The episode sets out to challenge the tabloid notion that this is solely a 'gay plague'. His daughter reveals he is part of the contaminated blood scandal, the effects of which linger to this day. "He got HIV through Factor VIII sometime in 1984 before screening started" – this refers to a blood clotting medication that passed on the disease in plasma taken from infected donors. "So he joined a pressure group for compensation. They had photos of him, lobbying local MPs and that. They presume he's gay, whoever's spraying. Mum and him divorced years back, so there's no loyal wife standing by. He's been a director at Bendrick's Computers for 12 years: society lunches, rotaries, the lot. Suddenly he's someone who brings the house prices down." The flash loudmouth behind the attacks was sacked from Bendrick's, the implication being that he used the AIDS stigma as an excuse for revenge on his former employer. But, leaning into that stigma, an anxious George tells Cryer that he's never brought in anyone like that before. "Who says? You might have, I might have, anyone might have! These people don't go around with flashing neon signs on their forehead." He asks if there's a "right procedure" and whether he should notify the Chief Medical Officer. He phones the CMO himself and this gets back to a humiliated Conway, who wants an explanation from Cryer. Bob in turn tears a strip off George, telling him he's lost his bottle: "That man, at least in here, has to feel that he is safe from the ignorant kind of prejudice that sprays paint all over his house – but he isn't, is he?" "It's not the same thing," George wheedles, his head down, but Cryer leaves him in no doubt that it's "exactly the same *bloody thing!*" When the man is shown out, Bob accepts his handshake in front of George, who is shamed into offering his own hand at the entrance.

THE HOT WAR

The growing sophistication of *The Bill* is evident in the way that the most dramatic event of this year is seeded in the months beforehand. Barry Appleton had invoked the spectre of terrorism as far back as Episode 2, *A Friend in Need*, only to debunk it in the same episode. When it appeared for real in his subsequent episodes, it was a fleeting background motive for the action on screen. But the show edges towards a deeper look at Britain's most pressing security issue in early 1990, in *Something Special*. A tight-lipped Detective Super from the Fraud Squad, Martins, arrives at Sun Hill to see his old mate Burnside and offer a mystery six-month assignment to one of the CID team. The DI has no choice but to put his men up for selection, only to be told "there are a couple I could dispense with straight off." Learning that he and Roach are off the list, Greig points out the one thing they have in common: they're both Celts. Ted, the very lapsed Catholic, remarks, "I don't have a picture of the Pope on my desk." Greig meanwhile is a Scottish Protestant – "That means hardline, it means Orangemen" – and works out that the job is in Belfast. Dashwood, who was hoping for "sun, sea, sex and surveillance" on the Costa del Sol, is told by a gleeful Carver, "I hear they do a pretty good paella down the Falls Road." But he counters this by pointing out the generous living away expenses. Northern Ireland, the posting everyone from Cabinet level downward wants to avoid, carries with it danger money in the mould of Muswell's bonus payments for getting stuck into the miners five years earlier. This is the incentive needed to fill roles that are both personally and politically risky.

Having spoken to the three DCs, Martins reveals the purpose of the job: to investigate corruption in the Belfast government, namely the willing or unwilling channelling of funds as a result of "sectarian influences." As the RUC are too close to the problem, "an independent team is going over. We'll be interviewing, we'll be collating evidence, and we'll be very unpopular." The episode is a masterful study of the competing dynamics within CID. Jim is dismayed when Burnside takes him out of contention, but is told, "There are enough guys in Northern Ireland with enthusiasm. Look at it this way: who could I most afford to lose round here?" It comes down to Tosh and Mike, with Burnside urging Martins to back the former. The latter gets a broadside about his seeming lack of ambition to progress beyond DC, given his obvious intelligence. Expanding on his languid claim that he "likes to live well", Mike reveals that he hopes to move up the ladder and this could be his big break. "I work quietly, I don't make a fuss, I don't get people's backs up; you'll need those sorts of skills in Belfast." Top of the class in self-delusion, he remains the frontrunner. But Burnside steps in and makes a formal recommendation of Tosh, who duly gets the post. By now the characters are so well drawn that we know why the man who is always overdrawn has got the nod. Tosh thanks the DI for trying to put the extra money in his pocket that he desperately needs. But after calling his family to let them know, he backs out for one simple and overriding reason: "I can't leave them. They need me more than the money; and I need them." "I'll live with it," says a far from unhappy Burnside.

Very soon another mystery man is at Sun Hill holding probing interviews, this time about a person, not a job. In *Citadel* the sinister, clipped Stark, an MI11 officer, installs himself in Conway's office to "deal with the Turnham case." He brings in Richard's low-flying colleagues to question them about their resident seagull: firstly Datta, who has been out for several meals with him lately. Noting that Turnham is a Cambridge graduate, Stark wonders what common ground they had to discuss. "I have been known to read the odd book myself, sir," Norika replies cuttingly. "Without moving my lips." When she is asked why Turnham never made a move after escorting her home, she realises what Stark is getting at: "You think Richard's gay! He's not like the others, he doesn't come into the nick in the morning shouting about getting his leg over the night before." She is dismissed and replaced by Melvin. Here the story follows up intriguingly on the activist beliefs that were goaded out of Ken by a campaigner cum terrorist in *User Friendly* the year before. He is asked about his feelings on the environment and how much Turnham shares these: an issue more pertinent than ever in the present day, when the police are often accused of enabling protest. "So the whistleblowers and protesters have got a point?" Stark tests him. "If some protest group were planning to sabotage a pipeline that put nuclear waste into the sea, Turnham would have sympathy with that?" "If it was against the law, he'd nick 'em for it," insists Ken. Meanwhile, the man himself is being kept out of the way on the vital work of guarding a hole on the high street, pestered by Michael Bilton's hilarious tramp. "Can you smell gas?" "No...!" replies a panicked Turnham. "Me neither; never could... You want to get that filled in." "It's being dealt with, sir." "No it's not."

Stark tackles his next interview in the pub, with Dave Quinnan. "Bow Street – the lad with something in his locker." Dave thinks he has been exonerated but is told the incident is still on his file, and he needs to prove his innocence by co-operating now. "We wouldn't be talking about a certain senior officer's lady wife?" asks Dave, who met her coming down the stairs of his bedsit when he had lent it to Turnham for the evening. Finally, Turnham is brought in and asked about the pub he frequented before he went to Cambridge that "did more than play Irish music. They took up a collection every evening." "For the families of Irish political prisoners." "Oh, you believed that, did you?" Insisting he paid up just to keep the peace, Turnham is asked, "Sign your name under duress as well, did you? 'We, the undersigned, call for the withdrawal of the British Army of Occupation from the six counties of Northern Ireland and for the disbanding of the Ulster Defence Regiment. Signed, Richard Turnham.'" "I had some rather simplistic political views in those days... I was seventeen!" Turnham complains he's being discriminated against because of his background. "You've got a lot going for you," Stark reassures him. "But if you find the process of positive vetting distasteful, you might need to ask yourself whether Special Branch is where you really want to work." It's a rare narrative turnaround: instead of learning of a crime and seeing it investigated, we get the enquiries first and are only told at the end what they have been in aid of. Given the evidence Stark has totted up, if anything Turnham's background is what clinches it for him; the old school tie counts for plenty still. His application granted, he heads for pastures new with a cheery send-off from Quinnan: "Best of British mate, you'll need it. Keep your hands to yourself on ladies' night, know what I mean?"

With 'the Irish question' planted in viewers' minds, it's not long before it resounds tragically in *Trojan Horse*. Once he has given out duties to the relief in their Portacabin, Cryer has a word with the ever-diffident Ken Melvin about satisfying his posh barrister fiancée. "I'm talking about the job! Perhaps she'd like to see some stripes on your arm. I know I'd like you to think about it." Ken is unsure whether to commit to the exams or to the job in general, thinking of taking a university degree. That evening he and Dave are on foot patrol when a Jag comes roaring round the corner and jerks to a halt on a zebra crossing. They establish that the shifty driver has no proof of ownership, and Tony and Reg turn up. Tony is about to take the motor to Barton Street before Ken intervenes, insisting it's his collar. Episodes that hinge on a surprise often lose value when rewatched, but here the benefit of hindsight adds power to the first half: a series of *Sliding Doors* moments that seal Ken's fate. Reg hitches a lift with him to Sun Hill and they idle away a minute of precious time on chitchat. He noses at a picture of Ken's girlfriend Maria before he is summoned to the scaffolding by Cryer. Brownlow leaves for the night, telling Ken to clear the building debris before he moves the vehicle into a corner. Then he returns to his cabin in a huff: "Derek...! You've addressed this to the DAC, it's meant to go to the

Commander." On such fine margins are Chief Supers preserved, with little gratitude in the long term to his sloppy saviour. Things could have gone better, but equally they could have gone far worse. The wheels of destiny put Ken Melvin alone in the yard, heaving planks aside, when the bomb hidden in the car behind him goes off and blasts him to the ground in a heap of rubble.

Several minutes of largely visual storytelling follow, as the officers rush out of the stripped-down building and rescue their comrades. Conway has an injured shoulder, Reg a lacerated back and Brownlow cuts and bruises, but it's Ken who is rushed to intensive care, having taken the full blast. When Supt. Davidson arrives from SO13, the anti-terrorist branch of Scotland Yard, and is told the car's registered owner, he fits the pieces together instantly: "Geoffrey Benson. I always thought he was lucky." Benson is a colonel in the Parachute Regiment, serving in Northern Ireland; the bomb was timed to go off when he arrived at his barracks that evening. Like most of *The Bill*'s major storylines, this idea was plucked not from thin air but from events going on in the real world. It was in early 1990 that the Provisional IRA, having mounted attacks against British military targets on the Continent, switched its focus to the mainland and launched a two-year bombing campaign. *Trojan Horse* was both timely and prophetic; just over two months after its broadcast, the Eastbourne MP Ian Gow, a hardliner on Northern Ireland and close Prime Ministerial ally, was blown up by a car bomb in his driveway, a week after Carol Thatcher had been in the passenger seat.[5] The programme's familiar plot device of overlapping crimes adds an element of chance, and an extra layer of tragedy, to proceedings. When Davidson visits Barton Street to question the unwitting bomber, he opens with the marvellously condescending line, "Right, you steal cars, do you Mr Wilks?" The terrified tealeaf is miles out of his depth; what began as a casual night's nicking has delivered another useful IRA target, albeit a distant second choice, to them on a plate.

Nowhere is the pared down storytelling of the half-hour era used more effectively than in the last few minutes. Consider how many

---

[5] Andrew, Christopher, *The Defence of the Realm: The Authorized History of MI5* (2009), p. 750

times in TV drama a character's relatives are seen sobbing over a saline drip as the end draws near. Instead, meeting Dave in the corridor at Barton Street, Tony asks if there's news on Ken. "Yeah," comes the reply. "He's dead." That line in print captures the bluntness but not the tinge of disbelief Andrew Paul injects into it. SO13 had Benson under surveillance as a known target and saw Wilks scouting his place; the theft could have been avoided if they'd stepped in earlier. Here our expectations of the characters are turned on their head. When Tony and Dave return to Sun Hill, Cryer is his dependable self, reminding them that there's work to be done – but then the news about SO13 is broken to him. He marches up to Davidson in a fury, tearing into him in front of Brownlow and DAC Adamson. "We're working in the interests of national security," Davidson tells him curtly. "What do you want, an advert in the newspaper? Do you think I wanted this, how do you think I feel?" The last three scenes are heartbreaking in their simplicity. After the crumpled photo of Ken and Maria is recovered from the wreckage, Brownlow and Adamson hold a press conference. Asked for details of the PC who died, Brownlow gives a precis of Ken's career, as though reading out his CV. But his voice trails off, and his head bows, once he reaches the nub of things: "He was aged twenty-six, unmarried... and he was a very popular officer." Looking out over the ruined yard, Cryer wipes a tear from his nose.

The show's first *bona fide* death, after the fudging of Ramsey's exit a year earlier, is afforded space that would rarely be seen again. It was another decade before a killed-off regular even got a funeral scene, let alone an entire episode. But it's typical of *The Bill* that his colleagues remember Ken for everything he was: not just an innocent angel taken too soon, or a polite God-botherer, but a one-man disaster area. Having delivered a death notice to the wrong woman, pulled the door handle off a CID car and taken up a stallholder's plea to test the strength of his new gate only to demolish it, he hits a nadir in *Blue Eyed Boy*. Returning from a holiday in Ireland a day later than planned, he has forgotten that he was due in court. After Sgt. Penny warns the "sanctimonious little prefect" that he'd better have a good excuse, he is lectured by Monroe and finally Burnsided: "You divhead, I thought at least you were dead! I don't care whether you were in Rome playing tiddlywinks with the Pope! What are you, a

Section 8? You *cretin!*" Chasing a burglar from a house that day, Ken is confronted by the homeowners, who think he is the intruder. Having dropped his warrant card, he radios in to get his identity confirmed. "Sorry, this is Brick Lane minicab service," comes the cod-Indian voice of 'Dev' Quinnan, "I think you got the wrong number!" Ken is forgiven by Burnside when he meets the lovely Maria in the flesh: "We'll have to get him transferred into CID." The top brass find it less easy to forget his blunder. Writing Ken's eulogy, Brownlow speaks of a "much loved and valued colleague" and the "end of a very promising career", only for the miserly Conway to bring up his no-show in court. "Well, perhaps I should just say 'promising career'," Brownlow concedes.

Rites, in which Sun Hill buries its much-missed colleague, is another masterpiece by a standout writer of this era, Jonathan Rich. For power it not only equals the fireworks of *Trojan Horse* but exceeds them, proving that when enough care and effort is put into characters, we too come to care deeply about them. The return of the regional interlopers Taff and Yorkie, the latter now in flash threads and shades, speaks of changing times. Asked separately to come for a drink after the funeral, they both say half-heartedly, "Maybe," knowing the old days are gone. Penny makes things worse by cracking an unwise joke about life in the private sector being safer for Yorkie. That morning the relief file out of the Barlby Road nick for the last time, past the floral tributes left for Ken. They try to blot out thoughts of the impending ceremony, but it becomes real again when the hearse arrives. The authors of *The Guinness Book of Classic British TV* praise the "poetic beauty" achieved by the episode, "far removed from most viewers' expectations."[6] The shot from the back of the hearse, as the pallbearers shoulder the coffin, quietly marshalled by Cryer, is low-key and discreet. The next few are anything but, the coffin borne into the church as the soundtrack swells to Bach's *Actus Tragicus* – played onscreen on recorders by the choir, but nevertheless a startling flourish, as though this were a conventional drama. To see our heroes among the congregation is an oddity, which we see

---

[6] Cornell, Paul, Day, Martin and Topping, Keith, *The Guiness Book of Classic British TV – 2nd Edition* (1996), p. 261

reflected on their faces as they confront something totally outside their experience. Distance, that most valuable quality in *The Bill*, proves its worth once again. In the same way no-one said goodbye to Ken at his bedside, there are no lines for his mourning family: only a pan across the front row in which a middle-aged man in glasses clutches his forehead, trying to comprehend the loss of his son.

In the opposite pew the pain is especially strong on June's face, when she casts a look at the coffin going past and then sings dutifully through the hymn. She has already turned down a request from Conway for someone to read a psalm, at the behest of Ken's family, as it would be too hurtful for her. In the absence of any volunteers, it's the big lug Tony Stamp who steps forward, to the astonishment of everyone else. "I can read!" he clarifies. Dave tries to coach him through it, only for him to slip up repeatedly. He looks on anxiously as Tony steps into the pulpit, but he delivers a perfect reading, and gets pats on the back afterwards in the pub. Further light is cast on the saintly Ken, when it's noted that Maria had to stand behind the family and his long-time girlfriend Michelle in church. "I feel sorry for all of them," says Peters. "An occasion like this really ought to bring people together." His colleague Penny − who, you might recall, owes his life to the "sanctimonious prefect" he has just said goodbye to − gives Alec some words of wisdom: "Nothing brings people together except lust, terror or hard cash." The WPCs muse on the day's events, perking up a little now they have closure. June tells Cryer blandly that she feels better now, giving him what he wants to hear. Except that for once, he is uninterested in keeping calm and carrying on. "I'm glad someone does, 'cos I don't. I won't feel any better until someone at the top, and I mean way above *Mr* Brownlow, has the decency to admit that they've cocked up. What do you think the chances of that are, eh? We're dispensable, girls − all of us. You'd better remember that." They are left in a sudden gloom as he walks off; while everyone else tries to pick themselves up, Bob alone looks back in anger.

LOOK IN THE MIRROR

We shouldn't be surprised by Tony's successful reading, as it's an example of seeing the actor emerge from behind their role. Graham Cole delivers the lines in his natural register, deeper and more refined than the chirpy Cockney he puts on as Stamp; it's audible in those moments where Tony is glacially offended at being accused of wrongdoing. But whereas he is thoroughly out of his element delivering a Bible lesson, the man playing him would not be. In the 1991 Tony Lynch book on *The Bill*, Cole talks about the importance of making Stamp distinguishable from his real self. When the producers tried to make Tony into a family man (as Cole was in reality) he felt "uneasy about art imitating life quite so closely"[7] and convinced them to keep him unattached. In a long-running series where someone spends more time being a fictional person than not, the blurring of boundaries can be both beneficial and dangerous. Some actors made a conscious effort to distinguish themselves from their part, such as the scar Ralph Brown asked for when playing the villainous Pete Muswell. Others brought a lot of themselves to their role. Tony Scannell's experiences as an RAF serviceman and DJ in Cyprus were salted into the early hour-long episodes; he made an uncredited cameo as the voice of a DJ in Series 1, then in the Series 3 finale *Not Without Cause* we learn that Roach saw military service. "What, selling RAF petrol to the natives in Nicosia?" Dashwood sneers. "Air craftsman, second class?" "Been looking up my record, have you?" As much of a hellraiser as the man he played, Scannell was good for more material, had the writers dared try. Andrew Mackintosh's account of being dragged along to Stringfellows by him one evening[8] makes you yearn for the *Bill* story that got away. One can picture the scene: Alistair, his mind still on that outstanding 'corres', not knowing where to look; Ted, on first name terms with every dancer, ordering Bollinger trebles all round.

When one considers another CID lag who is even more inseparable from the man playing him, things become more complicated. As detailed by his biographies in various books, Kevin Lloyd came from a police household, the son of a sergeant killed en route to a hoax 999 call, and was related to other officers who approved of his work on the show. His trademark 'tache was forced on him purely because 'he

---

[7] Lynch, Tony, *The Bill: The Inside Story of British Television's Most Successful Police Series* (1991), p. 98

[8] *The Bill Podcast* 59: Tony Scannell – A Tribute, 2020

looked too similar to Christopher Ellison without it'[9], yet he had to adopt it 24/7, and with it Tosh's expanding waistline; his large family mirrored Tosh's, some of his actual kids playing his fictional ones; the actress playing his on-screen wife had the same first name as his real wife. Taken together they seem trivial, but not once you add the other defining facet of Lloyd's onscreen life. Of all the gin joints in all the streets in Sun Hill, how many does Tosh wander into on enquiries throughout the decade in which he appears? Even more than the scenes of communal CID boozing, these solo expeditions to pubs now look like the equivalent of injecting poison direct into an addict's arm. This is, however, a judgement from a time in which we are a little more circumspect about the dangers of heavy living. The irony of actors playing at coppers is that the worlds of policing and showbiz naturally intersect in a hard drinking culture. If you straddle that line as Lloyd did, sinking pints in a merry atmosphere on the screen, then doing the same at umpteen cast dos – like his 1992 episode of *This Is Your Life*, where they reportedly became the first people ever to drink the studio bar dry[10] – when are the good times ever associated with anything else? The greatness of his portrayal of Tosh Lines is tinged with the sadness of watching someone being slowly immersed in a corrosive fantasy.

On the subject of difference, the most interesting material in Tony Lynch's book is the biography of Nula Conwell and her observations on the transfer of Viv Martella to CID. She notes that Viv is a conservative dresser whereas she is more casual – to her relief, otherwise she would be "living and breathing this job every single minute of the day."[11] Her say in the character, however, went beyond what she wore. She had to stand her ground about the ways in which Viv would mingle with the men, insisting there would be no affairs, and just as importantly, no recourse to the "old idea" of a woman bursting into tears at the first sign of trouble. She mentions an occasion where Viv had cocked up and was sobbing throughout a

---

[9] Kingsley, Hilary, *The Bill – The First Ten Years (1994)*, p. 62

[10] *The Bill Podcast* 08: Trudie Goodwin, 2017

[11] Lynch, Tony, *The Bill*, pp. 74-75

scene with Burnside, which she was able to get reworked.[12] Hot on the heels of Barbara Thorn's departure, after she was told that Michael Chapman didn't feel *The Bill* "had a place for women"[13], the battles Viv fights as Sun Hill's first female detective are another case of life and art being blurred at the seam. Her first proper CID episode, *One of the Boys*, opens with her sitting behind a typewriter, installed as office dogsbody. Complaining that in the past week she's "only been out for sandwiches and chips", she is given an errand by the sympathetic Tosh, the only one not to treat her as the tea lady. She rehearses her introduction with a warrant card in the mirror, trying to convince herself she belongs; but the 'tom' she is supposed to bring in gives her the slip. Viv's power wardrobe is more than just a makeover for Conwell, it's also a comment on the problems of fitting in. Chasing her suspect over half the manor in a pencil skirt and high heels, she is ill-equipped for the job. At one point she hitches a lift from a young Andy Serkis. In another example of how *The Bill* slips in and out of dark corners in seemingly routine stories, he letches at her ripped skirt and makes her an offer she can refuse. Realising she won't play ball, he stops the car and orders her out: "You shouldn't promise what you can't deliver." Proving that Footwear is a Feminist Issue, she swaps her heels for sneakers and finally collars her woman – only to learn that Tosh doesn't need her anymore.

Seeing Viv's bedraggled appearance, Burnside notes that she "looks like she had a bit of rough over lunchtime." Suddenly she explodes: "Don't you ever talk to me like that again – sir!" "Welcome to the firm, Viv," he replies calmly, and she passes the first of many humiliating hoops. This too, for a girl who really is one of the boys in spirit: packing away food and booze with the best of them, defusing come-ons with her own ready wit. When the plastered Tony tries to sell her the ride of a lifetime at Taff's leaving do – "It'll only take a minute!" – she replies pityingly, "You'd never make a living at this." "When are you gonna come round and look at my ceiling?" comes the relatively subtle approach from Burnside in a later episode. "Why, you got a leak?" But she and we are never allowed to forget that she is

---

[12] Lynch, Tony, *The Bill*, pp. 74-75
[13] *The Bill Podcast* 11: Barbara Thorn, 2017

46

the CID newbie. In *Line Up*, Tony brings in a mugger who he saw fleeing the scene but didn't identify as the culprit. Viv takes on the case with Mike, who barely contains his annoyance at having to babysit her. In the interview room the thug's misogyny gets to her and she loses her temper, leaning in his face. She puts the idea of an ID parade to him, to the dismay of Mike, who insists later that "ID parades are a total waste of time. You'll be public enemy number one round here, and nobody will be doing us favours for the foreseeable future!" Monroe reluctantly agrees and the police cobble together volunteers for the princely sum of £4 each. An angry June says that if Jim or Tosh were running the investigation no-one would mind, but because it's Viv "she's accused of throwing her weight around." The injured woman picks out the right man, but inconclusive forensic means the CPS is unlikely to proceed. Burnside lectures Viv on her conduct in the interview: "I am talking about pursuing your investigation professionally, not pratting about like some masked avenger with a chip on his shoulder!" Unable to keep the cool head he and Roach are renowned for, she sits and learns her lesson, which has hints of that familiar jibe about women letting emotion get the better of them. Christine Frazer was out of touch and unpopular in the ranks, yet a female officer at the sharp end is still somehow in the wrong, needing to learn her place.

Take note, this script is not the work of one of the boys, but the first of forty by Elizabeth-Anne Wheal: *The Bill*'s most prolific female author and one of its all-time greats full stop, who along with J.C. Wilsher remained on the show throughout the Nineties. Wheal's account of how she was signed up is revealing; asked minimal questions in her interview, she was told that the programme wanted to broaden its appeal to a female audience by "developing 'women's stories'", and she made it clear she was only on board if she could tell stories of both sexes.[14] One can understand that desire to remedy things, no matter how reductive, when her debut was the show's third female-authored episode in its first six years. 1990 is more distant from us now than 1960 was then, and at the start of the

---

[14] https://elizabethannewheal.com/whealwrite/talent-is-everywhere/

caring, sharing decade, the progress we assume was there was in fact rather patchy. When the boys' club acquires a female leader at the end of the year, Jim suggests that Viv will be "well in – all the girls together, eh?" and she plays down the idea that it's good news for her: "You can't assume that. A woman that makes it in a job where there's always been men can end up more chauvinistic than they are, there's plenty of examples of that!" In the wake of 'too emotional' comes 'women beware women'. The frosty reception for DCI Kim Reid also had real-life parallels. Carolyn Pickles observed that some people were incapable of separating their fictional resentment at a female boss from real life,[15] proving the point of those cited earlier: a dividing line is a useful thing to have.

WOMEN IN PERIL

If *The Bill* was making slow progress with its female talent on one hand, then it was also commenting effectively on sexism with the other. The show delivers a stinging critique of the boy's club in *One of Those Days*, by Roger Leach – who had by this point resigned from the series to slip past Michael Chapman's diktat that 'actors act, writers write', which had previously scuppered his attempts to write episodes with co-star Larry Dann[16]. Paired with the new and fiery Steve Loxton, June Ackland attends a hit and run where a pregnant woman has been knocked down. As she takes a witness statement, Steve butts in and points her to the ambulance because "it's your job, victim support and all that!" Brownlow returns from a meeting at the Yard where he has been given a dressing down about the lack of female promotion at Sun Hill, and is suddenly exercised about a problem that has always been there. He warns Monroe and Conway of the principle of 'vicarious liability': "It means that the Commissioner can make every supervising officer responsible in law for breaches of the Equal Opportunities Act, right down to the rank of sergeant!" Echoing the way that his deputy dealt with stress the previous year, Brownlow sets up a round of interviews with the WPCs. Monroe distributes questionnaires asking for opinions on working with the opposite sex, Conway advising him to make them anonymous. But

---

[15] *The Bill Podcast* 29: Carolyn Pickles, 2018
[16] Dann, Larry, *Oh, What A Lovely Memoir* (2023), p. 200

they have reckoned without the voice of the shop floor: "It's a Federation matter, sir." Forcing his face into a rictus grin, Monroe steels himself for The Horror. "Equal opportunities has got two sides. If my male members feel that my female members are receiving favourable treatment, they'd be justified in invoking the legislation themselves." Monroe promises to "take it on board" – and as the beaming Reg disappears, Colin Tarrant delivers the best shake of the head ever committed to screen.

June returns from the hospital, having tried to coax a story from a woman in a neck brace sobbing at the death of her baby. In the ladies' she splashes water over her face and her own tears flow. When it's her turn in the hot seat, her agitation is noted. "It's just been one of those days." "We all have those," chuckles the naive Chief Super – and with fire in her eyes, Trudie Goodwin once more unleashes hell. "No we don't, not all of us! Do you know what women are treated like in this job, sir? Oh yeah, a WPC's the station bike when it suits the lads. But when it comes to child molesting, distressed mothers and children, the nasty rape cases, it's always us who have to deal with them. We're needed then, we're respected even! It's always the women who get the 'delicate' jobs – and they are awful, they just tear you apart. And do you know why sir, it's because... emotions aren't respected in this job!" We see this pattern throughout the programme: when people seek 'the female view', they get too little from all the other women, and more from June than they want to know. A chastened Brownlow claims to understand how she feels; "With respect sir, you can't understand."

June's rant echoes beat for beat the diatribe she gave Cryer back in Series 1 about the "dirty, disgusting jobs" dumped on WPCs – but that repetition tells its own story. Pondering why she is still in the police, she learns that the hit and run driver has arrived: a dead-eyed solicitor who rang 999 but "panicked" and drove off. "Bastard, he knew exactly what he was doing! He leaves the scene, sobers up and then comes in to confess later when he knows there's no chance of him being charged with drink driving. There are laws against abortion, but not against killing unborn babies with a car." After he has duly passed his breathalyser test, she updates him: "You might be interested to know that the young woman you knocked down was pregnant. You killed her baby."

From drink driving to domestic violence, June's cynical view of the law as a man is restated in *Near the Knuckle* – an episode seemingly directed in a parallel world to that of *The Bill*'s orthodox and strictly policed house style. The smoky lighting, low angles and close-ups can only have passed muster by design. It may be no coincidence that the boat is pushed out for Dame Dorothy Tutin, playing a battered wife whose husband is not just a GP but a friend of Sun Hill's FME. Unaware that his colleague is responsible for the injuries he is treating, he asks what happened and she claims she was mugged. The violence in 'respectable' households hinted at in the previous year's *Kidding* is explored further here. Having to explain and show her injuries to Datta, a woman half her age, Mrs Curtess-Brown is told "it's nothing to be ashamed of." "You're just a young girl..." she sighs. Then she reveals a bonus use for all those years of scouring *Gray's Anatomy*: "He holds me by the hair and punches me in the body. He knows exactly where it hurts, and the bruises won't show." But like the woman Viv met before she must think of the children; used to putting herself last, she won't press charges. "I can't throw away half my life and start again, I can't!" The man himself is sat on a bench as custody descends into chaos, thinking himself a breed apart from the scum around him. June tells Alec Peters he will probably get away with it: "All they get when they get to court is a fifteen quid fine and a slapped wrist. Some of these judges see nothing wrong with slapping your wife around a bit. They probably go home and do it themselves." Claiming his wife is "hysterical", Curtess-Brown declares as he is released that he will "do what I like with her" and is firmly set straight by Peters. But of all the WPCs, it's Cathy Marshall who is most disgusted at seeing her doctor accused of battery. "It used to be Mrs Hooper, remember?" she jogs his memory. "I'll be finding another GP."

Cathy's own abuser returns to haunt her in *Forget-Me-Not*, which marks a bigger victory for onscreen talent moving behind the lens. Everyone's favourite Sun Hill man PC Banks, aka former child actor Russell Lewis, gets the first writing credit of what would become one of the most accomplished CVs in television, most notably as the creative force behind *Endeavour*. Gordon Wray's old Drug Squad colleague, the polished DS Clive Hooper, arrives to see the station collator and is startled to find her thinning on top and calling herself Ron Smollett. Spotting her former love through a doorway, Cathy shelters in the canteen, where the loudmouthed Quinnan is holding forth on how to handle 'plonks'. "Treat 'em mean and keep 'em keen, is that it?" she snaps. "What's your idea of a really good time eh Dave, knocking them about a bit?" "You know your trouble Cath, you need a good seeing to, sort you out!" June comforts her in private: "They're canteen cowboys, Cath; they're ten a penny, rise above it." But the memories flood back when she deals with a woman in hospital who has stabbed her husband. Disappointed to learn he is still alive, she murmurs, "I couldn't even do that right. Had enough today, couldn't take it again. Rolled in from the pub, just started straight in, no warning, no reason, no nothing – just bang. Something went... I felt it snap." "Makes you wonder whether there's any decent blokes out there at all," Viv muses later. "None in this job," replies Cathy. Viv nominates the charming DS she met that day and, for the second time with Cathy, puts her foot spectacularly in it. Stalking his ex-wife, Hooper catches up at the hospital and tries to win her back; he has a complaint hanging over him and needs to boost his image. When pleading and flowers don't work, he resorts to old faithful and drags Cathy into a laundry room. It's Dave, the gobby knight in shining armour, who comes to her rescue and takes a gut punch to help him turn over a new leaf. But old loyalties count for something; about to radio in, she lets her ex go, so he can bury himself another way.

Proving the ubiquity of violence against women, it's a previous assault case that has spurred Cathy to abandon the collator's room and return to the streets. *Victims/Somebody's Husband*, another standout story from Jonathan Rich, offers further comment on a legal system that doesn't exactly soothe the way for the female victim. Arriving at the station in the midst of the building works, a young woman reaches the improvised front desk, manned by Garfield in "Can I help you, love?" mode. She faints and is carried into the collator's office, where she reveals that she was held down and assaulted on her way home the night before. The sympathetic Tosh lobs her an opening question that elicits a mocking laugh: "You mean, was I wearing a see-through top and a slashed leather miniskirt?" "We've only got to get our man in court, and his defence brief's sure to ask. And all we need is a senile old judge and he'll get off." "I was wearing an old duffel coat, over a dowdy calf-length floral print dress. I looked like a junior schoolteacher." "What do you do for a living?" "I'm a junior schoolteacher." She later reveals that she had a hatpin in her bag but couldn't reach it. "It's probably just as well you couldn't," advises June. "The law states you can do what is reasonably necessary to protect yourself. Offensive weapons are a problem." "*He* had a weapon," she points out, penalised for not having the strength to fight back with her body alone. Tosh realises that the M.O. fits a series of recent attacks confined to one area, all when the police are at peak activity: "It's almost like an inside job." "Well, I don't believe that for a minute!" scoffs Burnside, before nixing the idea of a rolling surveillance: "We've got too many crimes, too few people, and *no money!*" Tosh takes the direct route and phones a story through to the local paper, which challenges Brownlow directly, forcing him to go ahead. His face like thunder, Burnside gives Tosh the same warning he himself got from the Super: "If you ever, *ever* drop me in it like that again... you're out of a job." "No loss to the force, eh guv?" chirps Tosh, before quoting his own recent appraisal back at the DI: "'Fat, unfit, and unambitious.'"

In the second episode, as the team is assigned observation points, the disappointed June is left out of the action. Then she is called to a woman who claims her husband is threatening to kill her, which she later admits is an exaggeration, but she is worried about him. He is out at all hours and never lets her know his whereabouts. The story loses a point for the horror videos and the *Dirty Harry* bedroom poster that prove, in the hoary tradition of crime drama, that the owner hails from Disturbedville; for the record, my brother had a *Dirty Harry* poster on his wall as a teen and has so far as I know never graced the register, though I admit I'm not his keeper. But when the husband appears, a curt figure full of pent-up aggression, we get another take on what Pete Ramsey dismissed as "the nearly people" in 1988's *Witness*. That time, the would-be copper was too nice for the job; this one is anything but. His mantelpiece bursting with trophies, copies of *Police Review* lying around, he reveals he was turned down for being too short. "I could tackle people twice my height, it doesn't matter how tall you are if you're weak. I'm not weak," he assures June. "How is it you get to do the job and I don't, when I could crush you with my little finger?" The police radio scanner he has fitted upstairs is the final piece of the puzzle. June phones in a warning message, then chases him away from another assault. In a cemetery he suddenly leaps on her, and they fall into a vicious, screaming struggle. This fight in two parts tells us everything we need know about June Ackland: first a battle to save herself, then when Tosh sees her and runs to the rescue, a battle to hold onto her attacker and save others. For Trudie Goodwin this scrap was a little too authentic, thanks to the director keeping the actors apart and unchoreographed beforehand; fight scenes, like sex scenes, would seem to be a bad time to deploy The Method.[17] When, after the would-be hardman is caught, June unmasks and slaps him, it really does look like Strasberg's dream come true: no acting required.

This excursion into stranger danger is followed by another two-parter that reminds us that most threats lie closer to home. Working the graveyard shift in *The Night Watch*, Viv and Ted are stirred into action when a call comes through reporting a rape. A young woman alleges that her boyfriend forced himself on her and he is brought in for questioning. Five years on from *With Friends Like That...?* a more detailed apparatus has been installed for rape cases. The victim is taken to an examination suite, the suspect to another nick as before – but now with emphasis on forensics, to prevent claims by the defence of samples being cross-contaminated. The show's adherence to realism is evident in the utter normality of both people: the late Emma Chambers playing the quietly spoken Marie, the young Mark Addy on the wrong side of *The Thin Blue Line* as Matthew, a trainee accountant living with his parents who is gently bemused at the allegation. But there's no rule that would-be rapists have to be loudmouthed machos, and Ted shelves the battering ram approach. All smiles and bonhomie, he claims he has a relative training for accountancy exams, putting his man at ease. "You don't negotiate over a casual bit of sex," argues Matthew. "If a girl like that takes you home and sprawls across the bed... Well, you don't ask her to sign a

---

[17] *The Bill Podcast* 08: Trudie Goodwin, 2017

contract, do you?" Playing on his feelings for Marie, Ted encourages him to confess on the basis that "you can save her from talking about your intimate affairs in court." But his bluff is seen and called. "Oh, he did it all right," Roach tells Viv. "You ought to listen to the tape. One of the longest silences on record as I stare him out. He wanted to cough up, but I think his whole future career flashed in front of him... It's fifty-fifty. A few years ago, what we've got now wouldn't have been enough for a prosecution, but times are changing. Who knows?"

The second episode, *A Case to Answer*, makes clear what we have seen hints of in episode one: that it's the woman who will end up on trial. Marie has to attend a committal hearing at which the defence can pick holes in her testimony, but the prosecution can't do likewise with the accused. We get the first example of what would become a staple, the snide female barrister turning the screws on another woman. Asking Marie about her sexual history, she points out with relish that she is still on the books of an escort agency she joined when she moved to London – which is how she met Matthew. Her credibility destroyed, Marie is grilled about previous examples of clothed intercourse: "You were hardly in the habit of standing upon ceremony." Leaving the courtroom, she rushes off in tears and later says she won't proceed, unable to stomach having her life broadcast in court. Greig's effort to placate Viv – "If it came to trial, the odds are against conviction when there's been an ongoing relationship" – is hardly what she wants to hear: "That's never going to change if rape victims don't get up and fight it!" Ted, committed and on her side throughout, urges her to let it go: "There is a limit. You help the victim, sure. But you don't become the bloody victim! That's a shortcut to a burnout." It raises a question that could be applied to future episodes: should a rape storyline highlight the flaws of real-life cases, or present a better alternative to encourage people to come forward? Bear in mind again the huge reach of *The Bill* in its heyday, comparable only to soaps. They, of course, are continuous sagas with months-long storylines and advice numbers doled out for heavyweight issues – unlike this show's one-and-done approach that brought every story to a definitive conclusion. To the general public watching their main source of info about the police, does realism equal fatalism?

A MAN AND HIS DOG

As the storytelling moves in ever increasing circles, the two-parter above overlaps with this year's biggest storyline besides the new station. The six-episode hunt for the Canley Fields serial killer may be Christopher Russell's greatest achievement on *The Bill*, in a resumé already littered with hits from beginning to end. That fateful location gives its name to the first episode, an apparent wild goose chase on the evening shift. "Any problems?" asks Conway, leaving for a works freebie. "Eh, teatime on a freezing cold Sunday," says a dismissive Cryer. Then a call comes through from two men who claim they saw a blond child being dragged across the road into Canley Fields. Forced to sweep a vast area of parkland, there is some quality bellyaching throughout from the relief. Stamp insists they need way more men to cover the ground: "It's more likely he's already through and gone while Conway's up the road checking with the accountants." Hollis complains about his malfunctioning torch; "Stick it in your gob, perhaps it'll run on gas," advises Garfield. Peters, true to form, echoes Hollis's complaint about having to be out doing anything. Meanwhile Monroe delights in taking gentle pot-shots at a recalled and increasingly harassed Conway, pointing out that the night shift will soon report for duty to find all their vehicles still in use. Learning that one of the men who reported the incident is another wannabe police officer, Roach is convinced they are both hoaxers and wants to charge them. But Conway lets them go, grateful that it turned out to be a false alarm. Only at the very end does he walk into CAD to find Datta taking a phone call from a worried mother: "Graham Butler, aged eight. Blond hair. Left his friend's house at 7.15 – not home yet."

When the story is revived, in *A Fresh Start*, it crawls from under the bustle and optimism of the new station to blight everyone's day. Sun Hill for the twenty-first century is christened in the worst possible fashion when a man bursts in on the mayor's ribbon-cutting, to reveal he has found a body on waste ground. Inside a sack, dumped in a pipe, is the body of another child: this time a girl, strangled to death. Tosh fills in the blanks in a few lines: "There's another one, Ted. Just like the lad we found in Canley Fields a month back... And there was me hoping for a glass of wine and a sausage on a stick." The winos nearby, who "wouldn't see a jumbo jet if it landed in front of them", can only offer wild stories about giant red dogs. CID's family man declares flatly, "Me, I switch off because it's a kid. Just catch the bastard, that's all that matters." Tracing the girl's school jumper, he calls on the headmaster, who notes innocently that Jenny Price seems to be absent. A despondent Tosh moves to the window and waves at his own kids in the playground – but it's Roach who gets to make the house call that nobody wants. Conceding that "we may have a serial murderer on our ground", Conway calls in AMIP, led by the young and ambitious Jack Meadows. Spreading its six episodes over four months, the story makes equally ambitious use of the half-hour format. Instead of the show's usual habit of resolving complex crimes in days, even in the serial stories of the later Nineties, this one takes its time. It comes closer than anything else to the reality of a murder investigation: a slow, painstaking process with endless amounts of graft and growing media pressure to find the culprit. Not only that, it pulls off a feat we see throughout this era: it is equally enjoyable for both the committed and the casual viewer. Though they work in sequence, anyone coming to any of these episodes in isolation could easily pick up both the plot and the themes that underpin it.

In that experimental mould, the next instalment, *Action Book*, takes place the next day but went out several weeks later. Reeling from the loss of their daughter, the Prices are brought in to be questioned and see the efforts in progress. Russell sidesteps the mechanics of a detective story and looks at the internal politics of the enquiry – another victory for *The Bill*'s focus on policing rather than crime. Every tragedy is an opportunity for someone; the death of two children thrusts Roach into the limelight when his boss nominates him as runner of Sun Hill's brand-new incident room and holder of the action book. "Ted Roach can't handle responsibility – show 'em different," Burnside urges him. Tosh and Mike are dispatched to turn over the local stones: "I'd rather screen out pervs than interview the parents," says the latter. As everyone rushes to obey their set tasks and prove themselves, we get a sense that the means are becoming the ends; the investigation is its own little sub-culture, in which being seen to do the right thing leads to a false sense of achievement. But Ted is disabused of his optimism faster than most. Setting the tone for a happy future relationship, and indeed his overall management of CID, Meadows is introduced and looks at him like something he's scraped off his shoe. "Have you ever run an incident room before?" he asks doubtfully – but not without cause. Roach pitches into the role with his usual ham-fisted enthusiasm. Tracing the owner of a car seen in the area, he begins to see visions of an anti-terror raid, eagerly listing ways to surround the man's house. As Jenny's mother is shown into the incident room, a scathing Meadows takes the gold commander to one side: "Do you think you could just cool it a bit, Ted? I think professional calm might make a better impression on Mrs Price than your headless chicken act."

It's only when Burnside interviews the parents that we are reminded what this hive of activity is for – and that it's too late to do any good. "They're working so hard for us. The phones are ringing all the time, people who've heard the appeal. And then it suddenly hit me – you're not looking for Jenny," says the mother despairingly. "You're looking for the man who killed her." Beneath an unfamiliar mask of sensitivity, Burnside has to eliminate a few more possible names. His line of questioning about acquaintances is picked up on by the father at once. "You got half the Met here mate, is this the best you can do?" he rages. "She was all we had, all we wanted, and now she's gone!" When the DI rules out Mr Price, Meadows' disappointment is noted by a sardonic Ted; he may be a trainwreck but he's not a PR fake, voicing platitudes to the media while looking for anyone who will tick a box. Roach later tells Dashwood, "We even hoped the parents did it. You know why? Because we got nothing. Two dog hairs and a fingerprint." He is summoned by Meadows to meet his replacement as co-ordinator of the action book, a DS from outside Sun Hill. "Well, I did tell you you'd only be filling in didn't I?" "No sir, you didn't!" Letting him get back out on the streets, "Where you feel more at home", Meadows thanks Ted for his work with the bland insincerity he later perfected as DCI. Meanwhile, the sex offenders' list has produced no reward. "The two of you, talking to me?" one of the usual suspects sneers at Tosh and Mike. "It doesn't exactly suggest hard evidence elsewhere." "You get seventy-two hours to catch a murderer," Meadows declares at the outset. "After that, you're down to the long hard grind and luck."

The storyline's high point is *Witch Hunt*, not just one of the finest episodes ever made but the best-ever interview episode – and featuring, in Ron Cook, perhaps the show's greatest guest performance. Six weeks on, as newspapers demand, 'Why is this monster still loose?', the enquiry is a poisoned chalice rather than a career ticket. The golden boy Meadows and his team have packed up and left, dumping the case on the new DCI Wray, who asks Tosh, "What kind of man are we looking for?" Bringing up the people Lines screened out, he highlights Peter Angell, the caretaker at Graham Butler's school and formerly a houseparent at a care home. The sceptical Tosh visits for a follow-up chat and learns that Angell recently acquired a dog. He coaches the football team but has no kids himself: "Everybody should think carefully before bringing children into the world. They're too precious to be bred like rabbits... They're alive, fresh, unspoilt. Their eyes shine. How many adults do you know whose eyes shine? Only pity is they have to change – grow up." Twice, in Angell's home and in the interview room, the camera zooms in slowly on Cook's spellbinding portrayal, revealing the torment beneath a quiet exterior. Well aware he's under suspicion because he fits a stereotype, Angell tells Wray, "I'd rather you talk to my face than behind my back." He is reminded of his previous work with social services, who he condemns as "a bunch of mealy-mouthed bastards." After having a go at some kids for coming back late at night with knives, he was accused of touching children: "Of course I touched them – what parent doesn't touch his children?" "But you weren't actually their parent, were you?" "No, I was a bloody sight better than their actual parents! Where were they? Paralytic outside a pub, shooting up in some filthy public bog." Following a long enquiry, he was finally cleared, and "I told them to stuff their caring profession. Care? They don't know what the word means... I've learnt my lesson. Don't touch. Don't even look, because someone with evil in their minds is watching. That's the caring society. Just by not having a child of your own, you're an outcast."

Wray takes his lead firmly from the new playbook: no raised voices, no threats, only gentle probing to relieve a man of his burden. In the same vein as Ramsey and Melvin's garden shed debate on faith in *Community Relations*, Russell proves the interview scene doesn't have to be a series of 'he said, she said' formalities, but can mine philosophical depths. Angell talks of seeing "real" parents, "the ones allowed to care", ignoring their kids at the school gates: "Children are what their parents make them. That's the curse of mankind." "I suppose it could be a point of view that Graham and Jenny were saved in that respect – from being spoiled." In the toilets, Tosh tells Jim, "I'm looking at meself in the face, while I still can." Taking Angell for a break, he asks him "like I'd ask if you'd nicked a packet of crisps. Did you kill those two children?" and tries to wring the truth from him. But his guilt is nothing to that of Angell, who finally admits that Graham called at his house on the night he died. "He's crazy about dogs, but his parents didn't want one. Didn't want him either, come to that." He asked if they could walk the dog on Canley Fields, but "that's the point," Angell declares bitterly. "We didn't go. Me and a young boy, walking in the gloaming, throwing sticks for a dog? Showing affection? I couldn't risk that, could I? I didn't have the guts to give him friendship, so I sent him on his way, and because of that, he's dead. That's the guilt I want to share with you, Mr Wray." His alibi for the Jenny Price murder checks out, and a disappointed Wray lets him go – but the Bad Samaritan has just had his life sentence confirmed. Rarely has there been such a piercing analysis of the harm done by trying to put a sterile fence round 'our most precious resource'. This is what *The Bill*'s stripped back production style was made for: putting words and faces centre stage, letting them speak for themselves. Wray looks at Carver: "Satisfied?" "Yes sir. I love crucifixions."

This confession has its grisly parallel in *What Kind of Man?*, where the breakthrough is finally made by the vigilant David Quinnan. Visiting a burgled school, Dave sees a man giving a talk about animal welfare, accompanied by a mascot: a large, red, stuffed dog. With typical elegance, the throwaway remark that Russell dropped into an earlier episode is the link staring the police in the face. The man, Donald Blake, is a regular visitor to schools including the ones that both children attended. His wife has the quiet, strained air of someone who knows that something is amiss with her husband. Yet she cannot comprehend how he could be a killer: "It's just not possible... He loves children! We've got a grandson of our own, he means the world to Donald... I don't know how you can come here and say those sorts of things." An urgent call is put out for Blake, but Tom Penny finds him by chance at a park, walking his real dog. Far from putting up a fight, he asks, "Is this about Graham and Jenny?" and is grateful to be apprehended. However, he'll speak only to the sergeant who brought him in – and again, internal politics blind people to what really matters. Burnside complains that uniform are "already taking the glory – it's us who've done all the donkey work over the past three months!" Only the newcomer Wray has some perspective: "He kills children. What does it matter who gets him to say it?" "There are limits sir, and Tom Penny is beyond mine!" It's a master stroke to give this role to Penny, the journeyman whose sole interest is thinking of new jibes to aim at prisoners and PCs alike. For a few minutes he gets to be a hero, before he receives his due reward. The eloquence of Angell, the innocent man, is contrasted with the vacant monotony of Blake, a chilling performance from Jim McManus. He wanted to do it again that morning – "Take a child. Oh, I know it's wrong. That's partly the reason why I do it: because it's wrong. Because it's beyond anything normal people do, and I've always been very normal. That's partly what makes it exciting... Even what I feel about myself afterwards: hating myself for having done it. That's exciting too, in a funny sort of way."

Brownlow sets up an open bar in his office to celebrate, much to the disdain of Roach. While the backslapping continues, Blake admits quietly to Penny that "kids of a certain age... do things to me, inside. Exciting things." He met Graham while walking his dog and they spoke: "He wasn't very happy at home. Suddenly he got frightened, he started shouting, calling me names. I started pulling him away... I don't think it was just panic. Deep down, I wanted to be with him in the trees. He got more and more hysterical, and I had to hold onto him tighter and tighter. I've never held a human being that tight before – not even Kath. And the tighter I held him, the harder I squeezed... the better I felt inside. And then he was dead." Now he was hooked, he found Jenny by accident and she and the dog were drawn to each other. Sensing his chance, he trapped her in the car and took her back to his garage, "and it was just as good. Afterwards I felt brave. Strong. Like I could walk through a wall." He reaches out to a disgusted Penny, taking his hand to thank him; it's now "a personal thing between you and me." Both the killer and the story as a whole put another spin on that familiar phrase, the banality of evil. Across the six episodes the usual suspense devices are totally absent: no car chases, no hostage situations, no last-minute rescue of what would have been the next victim. The worst has already happened. In the absence of any reassuring victories for the police, or comforting escapism for us, we are left with nothing but the dull, leaden words of a dull, leaden man – taking, like all mass killers, the easiest route to be a somebody. Brownlow is surprised to learn that Tom is still occupied, "while CID demolish my whisky? That's uncharacteristically noble of him." Penny emerges from his ordeal the same way real officers have come out of a meeting with Brady, West or Huntley, sick to his stomach. While the eager Quinnan takes the credit and the commendation, Penny watches Mrs Blake collect the family dog, clinging to the last vestige of the man she knew.

This seeming finale is followed by a bitter postscript two months later, in *Something to Remember*. While Quinnan attends his commendation ceremony, and is exposed as a two-timing love rat, Stamp and Marshall go to a domestic by the familiar name of Butler. The husband jogs their memory: "Our son Graham was strangled by a lunatic, remember? Course that was months ago, weren't it? You're busy people, intcha? You got shoplifters to nick, and parking on yellow lines... We only lost a kid. We're solved, so that's all right, innit?" he yells, chucking his beer can at the wall. Addressing them by number, he reveals that "number 340 came round with Graham's stuff, in a plastic bag. 'Here you are mate, we've finished with these, happy birthday.' That's Graham as far as you lot are concerned," he declares, chucking the bag in Cathy's lap. They had no further visits and got no updates on the case. "We only found out you caught the slime who done it by reading about it in the paper. Even had to play detective to find out when the court hearing was; and queue up to get in. To see the man. I sat next to his daughter." Knowing that 340 is getting a pat on the back from the DAC at that moment, Cathy points out that he found the killer, but can offer no excuses for the lack of victim support. "You don't go to work, Mr Butler?" asks a glowering Tony, always intolerant of self-pity. "Not since Graham had his neck wrung, no. Sorry, 'property number 2476' to you," he reads off the bag. "You can't help that sort of people," Tony declares outside. "Give 'em the earth and they'd still bleat! If they'd taken better care of the kid, maybe he wouldn't be dead. Mega guilt complex, that's all they're suffering from." Graham Cole then excels as Tony rounds on Cathy, hissing, "I found Graham Butler's body. I trod on it on Canley Fields, and I was the first on scene for Jenny

Price. I found her in a plastic sack. I couldn't sleep for a week, so don't pigeonhole me as a callous bastard!" He does some digging and finds out that Butler has form; "He can't feel grief, he stole a packet of fags when he was eighteen?" "Cath, we've caught the murderer. Justice has been done. We don't owe these people anything!" "It's because they're slag, right? Well, the Prices aren't slag. I've checked – they've split up."

At Sun Hill, Penny complains that Quinnan's "smarmy grin" will be plastered all over the papers when he was the one who caught the killer and got a confession. His mood is lowered further when his paperwork is audited by the joyless Conway, who warns that Quinnan will get a reprimand to go with his award if he doesn't return overdue property. In a tactless class of his own, he motivates the workforce by snapping, "You sergeants have got to screw down on these procedures – nicking people's just not enough!" Once he has gone Penny launches into a vicious rant about Quinnan: "He's up there taking tea with the Queen, I'm here made to look a prat because of his laziness!" The episode highlights the hollowness of the victory beneath Dave's piece of paper. While the loss remains with the parents, the police get back on the treadmill and start from zero, burdened with the same petty bureaucracy. Back at the Butlers', the husband has slashed his wife's arm. "They're locking you up!" "What, so you can have all the blood money?" he yells. She is planning to sell their story to a tabloid, asking, "Why should we live in this dump forever, why should our daughter? What did you ever do for Graham, except give him a slap when he nicked your lager?" He charges at her again and is arrested. "You ignored him half the time, and the other half you were legless!" she screams. "And now you've woken up, well it's *too late! My conscience is clear!*" By examining the effect of murder on the grieving relatives, rather than just the hunt for the murderer, the story anticipates long-form series like *Broadchurch* by more than two decades. The uncaring parents condemned by Peter Angell do not remain faceless but are given their own moment of truth, realising that they didn't appreciate what they had until it was gone. There is no better demonstration of how *The Bill* steps back and allows everyone to have their say than the room it gives to the wife to justify her decision, rather than dismiss her as a callous exploiter. "It ain't blood money," she insists, trying to convince herself as well as Cathy.

"Like the bloke from the paper said, maybe it can do some good – as a warning to people who read it. Graham's dead... You got to take what you can get in this life."

CLASS OF THE NINETIES

In a year of increasingly elaborate, joined-up narratives, there is still room for the twenty-five-minute fantasias of Peter J. Hammond. *Addresses*, an early example of the night shift episode, sees Cryer and Martella stop a woman wandering the streets with a suitcase that, she insists repeatedly, contains "just knickers and shoes." She has a list of addresses of people who used to attend a crisis group where she did odd jobs, and is going round knocking on each door in turn. "These people, they said to me, 'You have helped us, so you come round and see us any time', they said." No-one, however, is pleased to see her, and it transpires that she was a member of the said group. "She's been leaving home with a suitcase since the age of twelve; she always comes back," says the woman who ran it. "She can't hold down a decent job, she can't hold down a decent relationship. There's only two things she's good at, packing a bag and telling lies." Hammond harks back to one of his own scripts for *Z Cars* almost two decades earlier, *Breakage*, in which Fulton Mackay plays a man with a bundle traipsing around in search of his old commanding officer from the war. At the end we realise that he is picking up other people's identities wherever he goes and passing them off as his own, and his service is as made-up as everything else about him. Cryer and Viv are similarly lumbered with an oddity they don't know what to do with; the most real and constant burden of policing is given Hammond's surreal treatment. One of the group, a twitchy old man played by Victor Maddern in one of his last screen appearances, keeps every light blazing in the middle of the night and multiple radios playing non-stop. "I got done about nine or ten years ago," he explains of the improvised defence that has taken over his life since. "It's not what they thieve, is it? It's what they do to you – they do to your home."

Viv gets too close for comfort to another crisis group in *Safe Place*. CID investigate a bank robbery where the manager was ambushed at his home and kidnapped – which happened to him at another branch eight years ago. Refusing to believe this can be coincidence, Roach sends Viv undercover at the psychiatric clinic where he is being treated to find out if his breakdown is genuine: an operation which even then must have violated so many human rights laws that this book would be inadequate to list them. "I've just had another murder thought," a patient announces at a therapy session, picking up a glass and smashing a window behind Viv's head. Roach observes, "It's registered under the Mental Health Act, which means that Brand can be considered incompetent to give evidence. Nice touch – except that in my book, there is no such thing as a safe place. No one's safe: anywhere." But when Jim and Tosh try to reconstruct the kidnap route through his blindfolded descriptions, they tally. Viv, loathing every minute in what she protests is not "a loony bin", triggers off Brand when she starts asking questions. He rants about the damage caused by "people like you", recalling the wife who abandoned him. She thinks he is genuine: "I reckon he's the kind of person that things happen to. All the bad luck: a kind of natural victim. Some people were born to have trouble all their lives, we know that... You only have to look at the man to know what I'm talking about. You kind of feel like you want to do something to him. I mean if I was a mugger, and he was walking through these gardens, I'd have to mug him. I'd consider it my duty." Roach asks Cathy if this sort of person really exists. "Yeah," she replies blithely. "I should know, I was nearly a candidate myself once. For the natural victim nothing seems to change... The same man who's been attacked in three different countries. Or certain women, something about them, some vulnerability – singles them out as targets."

Even more than Julian Jones's blackly comic runarounds, this material would now be beyond the pale. What TV show could allow police officers to freely voice the idea of victimhood as natural selection? But the unhealthy closeness of the police to crimes, and their prurient interest in victims, is part of what Hammond is driving at. Brand, who reveals that both his first and second wife ran off with other people, apologises to Viv for his outburst and asks if they can be friends. But then Ted calls her and winds up the operation; "You sure it's safe to let you out?" Reg asks when he collects her. As Brand watches her leave from a window she is riven with guilt, having helped her sergeant prove that there are no safe places. If one could identify an umbrella pitch for Hammond's episodes, they're about the police disturbing ghosts – but during this year *they* are the ghosts, an unknowable force intruding into people's lives and then vanishing mysteriously. *Answers*, a money-saving episode that bridges the gap between the old station and the new, is even more reminiscent of *An Inspector Calls* than the previous year's *Conscience*. Tosh and Mike visit a suburban house and disturb a morning barbecue in a take that lasts seven and a half minutes, director Christopher Hodson pushing the show's limits even further. They question the owner, celebrating his first wedding anniversary, on his alibi for a series of sexual attacks, and prove it correct – but in the process uncover his infidelity. *Climate*, which gave its name to a Hammond episode the year before, is again an underlying theme. "He thinks there's going to be a storm later on," the pregnant wife says at the outset. "You could be right," Tosh agrees later, "it's getting very muggy out here." Thunder rumbles above the house; and when the couple huddles in the back garden at the end, the trust between them shattered, a downpour begins.

The policeman becomes an avenging ghost in *Scores*, when an old foe of Burnside's, vice kingpin Ralph Trafford, turns up on his patch. Lines and Roach are sent to keep an eye on him and his cronies as they swill champagne and throw money around. In the canteen, the DI meets his fellow divorcee Cathy Marshall, who is amazed at the state it's been left in. "People like us, we're used to living with a bit of chaos," he argues, having still been married – "Just" – in his old division. Told of his target's flash lifestyle, he muses, "I got a mortgage on a one-bedroom box." But Burnside is notably offended when Roach sneers of Trafford's glamorous wife, "Chequebook slags like her, they always land on their backs." Burnside does his own snooping and realises that Trafford is sleeping with one of his allies' wives. When the other man returns home, he comes up to "have a little word." In the pub, Roach gleans from Burnside the fact that he divorced his wife around the time he investigated Trafford, and runs a story past him. J.C. Wilsher has noted that many *Bill* scripts were so tight they were almost elliptical,[18] but there's no scene that requires the viewer to fill in quite as many blanks as this one. "I knew this

---

[18] *The Bill Podcast: Feasting With Panthers*, Patreon Commentary, 2022

copper once when I was working in Colchester. Made a right mug of himself over a bit of tail. He even thought that she was going to give up the good life, run away with him, and live off his income. Of course she didn't. She was with some right bent bastard whom she wouldn't leave." "Takes all sorts," Burnside smiles, saying no more. Roach's parable can be taken as literally as one likes; the vagueness is entirely deliberate. The wronged husband turns up at Trafford's home with a shotgun and both are wounded in a struggle. Burnside takes in the scene at length before he radios in, and Trafford's injuries prove to be fatal. "What happens now?" asks Roach. "That's easy," says his boss. "I can get back to the normal, everyday stresses of life, can't I?" Sun Hill's Angel of Death saunters off down the street, past the grieving widow he has just created.

Both Hammond and Wilsher had an important asset underlying their work that made the show return to them time and again: keeping costs down. Wilsher's station-based episodes were cheap at the price, a vital factor during this year in particular, when the move to Merton swallowed up so much of the budget. *C.A.D.*, confined almost entirely to one room, is another story drawn from his time shadowing his local police and a textbook example of how to transfer the strengths of radio drama to TV. Having chipped in to Reg Hollis's blood drive, Viv is taking it easy when she is ordered out on the streets by an irritated Peters. "They want your blood *and* your body in this job," she notes. Sent to investigate a robbery, she is heard chasing the suspects before contact is lost. As the minutes tick by the increasingly anxious Peters throws officers into the area to find her, a job then taken over by Conway. Ben Roberts always played the part with the air of a man working on a permanent ulcer, but his mounting concern here as the responsibility weighs on him is especially effective. This simple set-up gives a role to half the PCs as disembodied voices searching the ground. The unspoken dread in the room reaches a climax when PC Able radios in to announce, "I'm sorry, it's bad news." Stamp and Datta freeze in horror. "Come on son, spit it out, you're a police officer," says Peters quietly. Able passes on the awful truth – he swerved to avoid a dog and hit an ice cream van. "When you've got a police accident you say, 'I've got a POLACC', you do not prat around like a big fairy!" Finally, a familiar voice crackles over the radio: Viv had been trapped in an underground garage by youths and could not signal through a dead zone. Having spent half the episode in a fit of pique, the other half worried out of his mind, Peters issues a final order that is delivered tenderly by Larry Dann: "Viv? Come home."

During his fourteen-episode haul this year, Wilsher delivers on one of *The Bill*'s USPs: the crimeless crime drama. By reasoned guess, it's *Workers in Uniform* that the author heard two crewmembers in front of him on set deem only the *second* dullest episode they had ever made, much to his relief.[19] The intricacies of a brilliant slice of station politics may have been lost on them after ten hours holding a boom mike or peering at a monitor. When a community festival thought to have been cancelled is suddenly reinstated, Brownlow must find the troops to police it. He plans to call in the relief on a Sunday they were supposed to have off, with only a day in lieu as recompense. "When my manpower and my budget don't add up to what is going on out there on the streets," a harassed Chief Super tells Monroe, "I have to find a way round it. I'm going to have Hollis up here soon, trying to break my heart with the grievances of the toiling masses!" Sure enough, after an exchange of pleasantries Reg sets out the battle lines, pointing out that with less than twenty-nine days' notice the relief should get time and a half, not time off. Brownlow is unimpressed by the "sob stories" he is hearing: "They're just bargaining counters, aren't they? Yet again I'm being held at gunpoint by overtime bandits." As he would do many times, Wilsher finds the interest in the bumf: the policies and procedures of public sector bureaucracy, and the horse trading that springs from them. The Super points out that officers can have leave cancelled at any time under 'exigencies of the service' – only for Reg to produce a dictionary to debate the meaning of 'exigency'. "I'm not playing Scrabble with you, Hollis!" Reminded that the police have no right to withdraw their labour, Reg concedes, "Absolutely not – but they have been known to feel poorly."

However, the solidarity of his much-cited members is built on shaky ground. Stamp is mouthing off about standing up to the guvnors when he is taken to one side by Peters, who urges him to watch his Arthur Scargill routine. The TSG training he wants to go on can

---

[19] Wilsher, J.C., *Paper Work: On Being a Writer in Broadcast Drama* (2022), p. 76

always be withdrawn if he's deemed a troublemaker. "You're not the only one. There's people after promotions, transfers, courses – all sorts. The job giveth, and the job taketh away." Suddenly Reg's comrades begin to lose the spirit of '26, just when he needs a united front. As ever, the most telling picture of apathy comes from Tom Penny: "You've got to make a good show of it... When push comes to shove, orders is orders. We have to put up a fight, have a good grouse, but we're a disciplined force of men, not a shower of skivers." Deep down, Reg's membership believes that the Fed Rep post is about token resistance and nothing more, just enough to preserve a status quo. But this time he stands his ground, telling Tony, "If I'm going to tell Brownlow to stick his orders where the monkey puts his nuts, I want your fingerprints on the scene as well as mine." Brownlow meets the relief in the rec room to explain his decision, but Reg squeezes Tony's true feelings out of him and the resulting chorus of discontent forces the Super to back down. Rather than accept a counteroffer of overtime payments, he pulls officers from other reliefs and desk staff to plug the gap. Cathy Marshall gets a call in the collator's room: "Well it was on the understanding that this job was nine to five, Monday to Friday... Exigencies of duty, of course sir. Doesn't really matter if I like it or not, does it?"

Wilsher returns to the training ground in *Effective Persuaders*, another budget-saver where crime is surplus to requirements. CID and uniformed officers are sent on a course in interview technique – the kind that the real police and *The Bill*'s personnel were learning lessons from at the time. "I think it could be really useful. I don't mind admitting I've still got a lot to learn." "I don't mind admitting you've still got a lot to learn, Alistair," says a generous Burnside, hacked off by Wray sending him back to school. Much as *The Office*'s team-building episode remains its best, this story strikes an instant chord because we have all been there: most recognisably, the domino effect when the keen as mustard Greig starts taking notes and the others reluctantly follow. The instructors gather a list of buy-signs, the verbal and visual clues that a suspect is willing to talk. Then the officers are split into groups to practice interviews about supposed crimes. Burnside is sure he can get into the role of a villain, a confidence doubtless shared by his colleagues; a robber of days past once told him, "'Frank, you'd have made a brilliant armed blagger.'" In a sign of the times, he has to settle for playing a roving knicker thief. After he coughs, he tells the camera that he'd "like 375 other offences taken into consideration – black frilly ones!" Then, as Viv is about to open up in her interview, he ruins the mood by going in hard. But the real saboteur is Quinnan, one foot still in scumbag territory. He uses his role to bait a frazzled Carver, late for the course because he is going through a bust up with his other half Sonia. "I was visiting a girlfriend," smirks Dave. "We stopped seeing each other. I found out she was a bit of a slag... Sonia. Not surprising I left prints; probably left some on her and all." Jim loses it and tips Dave's chair onto the floor, resulting in a scuffle that has to be broken up. "For a moment there I thought they'd brought the Muppets back," says Burnside.

The DI is asked what would happen if that was a real interview, and a prisoner complained. "In the real world, the co-interviewer would swear it away, no problem! It happens, it gets squared – you know it, I know it." He is told there are pilot projects in the Met to videotape interviews: "Then what we've just seen would be evidence. Do you want to stand in the box while that's shown to a jury?" A glaring Burnside watches his hinterland die in front of him, as the series predicts a daring step that is now a standard – and necessary – part of policing. "I've seen some very good, professional work from Sun Hill officers here today," the lead instructor concludes. "But some of us have got to think seriously about our ideas and our behaviour – before it's too late." The arrangement of characters in the final shot on a moral slide, from Greig and Ackland at one end to Burnside and a slouching Quinnan at the other, is a brilliant touch by director Nicholas Laughland – just one of the subtleties that added value to the show. The police's attempts to overhaul their dinosaur breed gave Wilsher plenty of useful material, but he does more than observe changing practices; he also interrogates them, asking if effort is being applied in the right places. Like Christopher Russell did five years earlier, he highlights who is pulling the strings, and why. "Is it your opinion that we can shrug off the crack epidemic, despite what we've been told?" Brownlow asks Derek Downer in *Middleman*, ahead of Burnside's raid on a supplier. "Not at all, sir," he replies, before pointing out what is blindingly obvious to anyone on the front line: "If you look at our figures, you can say we average about seventy-odd arrests per week. Sixty of those are related to alcohol. I haven't seen any Members of Parliament dancing up and down about the booze epidemic, but then an interest in the latest dope fashions ensures more free trips to the United States."

The show as a whole begins to turn down the pathways Wilsher is interested in; other writers come to prominence who would go on to write for his BBC creation, *Between the Lines*. Russell Lewis's second *Bill* episode, *Blue Murder*, hinges on an idea he would develop further in his script *Out of the Game* for the later series. When word comes through of an armed robbery, authorised firearms officers are deployed from Sun Hill. "Pink card time," Cryer tells Stamp, and they end up in the firing line as the bandit car is cornered. Bob challenges the lead robber, walking towards him with a shotgun, to drop his weapon: then lets him have it. He is soon a goner, and the dazed Cryer must surrender his gun, ammo and holster in evidence bags. It turns out that the shotgun cartridges are spent: "So chummy here couldn't have fired even if he'd wanted to. He'd already shot his wad, so to speak." The mordant humour laced through Lewis's episodes comes to the fore. "There they go, Burke and Hare," notes Phil Young as the undertakers zip up the body bag. "Dying trade, mate," Dave Quinnan chips in. Cryer returns to a red-carpet treatment from the anxious kids he normally mothers, no-one knowing how to tread around him. With very little dialogue, Eric Richard's subdued performance here speaks volumes. At the end, Cryer walks numbly past the canteen window and the sound fades to silence before the drums kick in. When he returns from leave, Brownlow is keen to dissuade him from taking his firearms refresher course, one eye on the bad publicity. "Marvellous, isn't it?" says Monroe. "We give him a gun, tell him kill if you have to, the ultimate decision. And when he does, lawfully, we say, 'Well that's your problem. Get on with it kid, you're on your own.'" "It seems to me," Cryer later tells the Chief Super, "that people are beginning to dance around me like I've got the plague... I've got to live with what I've done for the rest of my life." He hands Brownlow his application form for the course: "I've got at least another five years to do, sir; a long time if I've lost my nerve."

Another future *Between the Lines* author, Steve Trafford, delivers a similarly biting story in a different context, in *Beggars and Choosers*. The divide of the title is made clear in seconds, as June and Tony discover the beginnings of a new Cardboard City beneath a flyover. Barton Street have pushed their vagrants onto Sun Hill's turf, a game of pass the parcel that is played with beggars and prostitutes throughout the show's run. Tony remains the model of sensitivity: "There's more slag kicking about here than a coal board tip." One man heads to his work on a building site, sleeping rough in order to send his wages back to his family; the homeless are not automatically the jobless, but the margins are too tight to avoid both. A northern lad who catches June's eye is later arrested for begging, stuck in a vicious circle: "Can't get a job without an address, can't get an address without cash, can't get cash without a job." June gets him to call home, but his mother makes it clear they've no interest in having him back. This Ken Loach-esque tale of deprivation is contrasted with Brownlow's visit to a Rotary Club lunch, to discuss policing in the Nineties. Conway gives him a helpful primer for his speech: "You can tell 'em from me, policing the Eighties was a joke, the Nineties is going to be a nightmare!" When he arrives, the Super is sat next to a silver-haired bigwig who opines the need for greater discipline, and greater police powers such as the use of CS gas and rubber bullets, to combat the rising tide of disorder: "Your hands are tied by namby-pamby liberal opinion." "As you can see," a retired headteacher tells Brownlow, "Some of my friends have firm opinions." "I believe in people speaking freely." "Oh yes, so do I – but it always profoundly depresses me when they do."

Brownlow keeps his counsel until he delivers his speech, which turns into one of the show's longest and most excoriating. Observing that the good old days of looking up to the police are long gone, he describes the reality of policing the inner cities today: "On the streets, my officers daily encounter disrespect, abuse and downright bloody-mindedness. Respect for the law among all sections of the community, both high and low, from yobbos to yuppies, is in short supply... But there are no simplistic solutions – and if you were to ask me what I want most of all from you, the public, it's this: a realisation that you cannot go on looking to the police to hold the lid down, and to paper over the cracks, of a society that is in fundamental moral and material decline. The root problems are unemployment, poverty and an increasingly desperate housing situation... We have a younger generation, many with no proper jobs, no homes, and little prospect of ever being able to afford one. I make no party-political point here; governments of all persuasions have failed to tackle the problem. What then is the answer? A tougher approach? Saturation policing, harsher punishments? I spoke to a young man arrested for throwing petrol bombs at a recent riot. He said to me: 'I've had no proper education, no job and no home. I've been nicked for thieving, I've done borstal and I've been in prison. What else can you do to me?' What else indeed? Bringing back the birch will make little impression on such young men as these." Stressing that these are his personal opinions, he declares, "We must stir ourselves from our own comfort and complacency and deal with the problems of inner-city deprivation. Police officers may not be able, or willing, to act as the front-line troops for a society at war with itself." The hesitant applause he earns is not as telling as the response of a hitherto silent Home Office mandarin nearby. "Thank you for your speech, Mr Brownlow," he says as he exits. "I'm glad you enjoyed it." "Oh, I didn't say I enjoyed it."

It's rare for the show's standard left-liberal viewpoint to become outright polemic; Brownlow's insistence that he "makes no party-political point" rather finesses the reality of what could easily be a Labour Party broadcast. But, as well as being illustrative of the reforming ambitions that Peter Ellis found in real Chief Supers during his research for the role, it also marks a resurgence of the blunt political comment from the early years that had been expressed in more roundabout ways in the half-hours. The show observes that inequality is so ingrained it has become a grotesque tourist attraction. Several times during the course of 1988, the police encounter "cultural slumming": privileged youth roughing it for the novelty, a straitened version of the 18th century Grand Tour. First come the squatters in *Home Sweet Home* – "Bail forms covered with addresses in Hampstead" – then the overdosed junkie whose partner tries to extort money from her wealthy dad to save her in *Personal Imports*. Finally, there are the Bullingdon-style antics of *The Assassins*, obnoxious aristos and diplomats' kids who trash restaurants and use their titles or their immunity to bail themselves out. But in *Beggars and Choosers*, the other half fights back with a vengeance when the police try to break up Cardboard City. Giving a cue to some of today's van drivers, Monroe orders a carrier to plough into the crowd to disperse it. "Cut the backchat and move it!" Stamp yells at a vagrant who's giving him lip. At the end, the homeless youth hangs around the steps of the Rotary Club, scrounging change off the members. He heads off down the same street as the briefcase-clutching Brownlow, the two ends of society rubbing shoulders. In the first of many examples through the Nineties where *The Bill* was eerily in sync with real life, this episode went out two days before the poll tax riots in central London that signalled the beginning of the end for the Thatcher government. Were it not on the commercial channel, the show might have been accused of sedition.

UNEASY BEDFELLOWS

The subplot in *Beggars and Choosers* of Tony Stamp's struggle to get on the property ladder highlights how the police themselves can't all be grouped as 'the establishment'. Realising from a call to his bank that a mortgage is way beyond his means, he wonders if he will spend the rest of his life in the section house. It's not hard to see why Stamp became emblematic of the ordinary copper and the show's best recruiting tool for the real police; he's a trier, and Lord knows he can be very trying. Throughout this year, his blunderbuss approach gets him into trouble. When a man is found nursing a broken arm in a bus queue, it turns out that the woman who administered it – "I only touched her on the shoulder!" – had an excellent tutor: "The man's a policeman from this station." Tony is called in from one of his self-defence classes to account for himself and gives a perfect demonstration of his people skills. The instant the woman reveals that her assailant also put a hand up her skirt, Tony gives her his own, delighted pat on the shoulder and rushes off to check the perv's record. "If you don't want your extra-curricular activities to be used against you, I suggest you clear them with the Chief Inspector," warns Cryer. Hollis gets the woman to demonstrate on him the move she used, just as Burnside is driving past. Double-taking to his right, he sees Sun Hill's finest staggering in the arms of a lady and, like Monroe, shakes his head; there are no words. The same figure stalks Tony through all his misdeeds. When he prangs the area car in a chase – for the first time on screen, but the fourth overall – he fears this POLACC may be the final one. "Who's reporting the accident?" asks an innocent Marshall. "Who can you think of you would least want to do it?" With perfect timing, the hair-gelled one makes his entrance: "Hello Tone, you've come up against it this time, intcha?"

But Stamp's heavy-handedness is a source of more than jolly japes. *Body Language* continues the ongoing goalless draw between the police and the black community; a gang of youths flee at the sight of him and Stringer and are chased on the assumption they are up to mischief. Tony corners one in a warehouse and nabs him in a struggle, leaving the youth with facial injuries, but when he brings him in, he discovers that no crime has been reported. The youth in question is a polytechnic student called Nigel – "Do you think somebody who looks like me ought to be called Leroy, or Winston, or Wayne?" – whose lawyer sits on a local police accountability committee. "We're sick and tired of being stopped and searched just because we're black, listen! You guys, all you have to do is see us picking our noses to have us up against the wall on sus of sniffing coke, that's why we don't stop any more when you tell us to!" A defiant Tony tells Monroe, "If you think I've broken the rules then fine, chuck the book at me. But nothing I've done is against PACE, not as far as I see it anyway." "Yes, well whatever the circumstances, you've given them all the ammunition they need." Having opened a crime prevention caravan on the high street that morning with a glowing speech, Brownlow is returned sharply to the real world when he attends a town hall meeting of the police committee. In scenes reminiscent of the early Christopher Russell episodes, councillors from opposing parties snipe at each other about the responsibility for cutbacks, before protesters take over the public gallery and begin chanting, "No collaboration with the racist police!" As the officers leave to a round of slow handclapping, Datta gets the standard punishment for being their face of the future: "You're in the wrong lot, darling... How can you go against your own people?" When one heckler tells her to go back where she came from, she snaps, "What, to Uxbridge?"

Back at Sun Hill, Norika asks Barry how she's supposed to defend herself from accusations like, "'My honky colleagues go around knocking the living daylights out of anyone they fancy.'" The Chief Super gives Tony a further lecture about how he has set back community relations: "There is the world of difference between an 'anti-police organisation' and the police accountability group!" But the latter is unconvinced, suggesting the day's events fit a standard tactic by black youths to provoke the police and claim harassment later. Norika runs into Tony and demands to know the truth, leading to an argument that spills from the male to the female locker rooms. "I heard you got a rough ride and I'm sorry," he says bluntly, "but that's the price you pay for being Sun Hill's token black. If you can't handle that sort of garbage, pack it in, quit the lodge, here and now!" "I can imagine what happened this afternoon, and I hope to God it's not true," she snaps, pushing him out of the door. Tony's parting shot is illuminating: "I'm an ethnic minority as well, we all are – the day we join the job. So *get off my back!*" Like Conway's joke about getting rid of the moderates in *Community Relations*, it demonstrates the police's view of themselves as a breed apart, absorbing hostility from all sides and growing a siege mentality as a result. Tony is ordered to meet Norika at the crime prevention unit, but it becomes academic when she turns up to find that the caravan has been stolen: "Lock, stock and burglar alarm." The final shot of her standing amid the downed bunting, a forlorn 'Come and Meet the Met' sign behind her, sums up the equivocal stance of a show that could never be accused of peddling comfort food for the law.

The relief's 'token black' faces a familiar cocktail of prejudice, bearing insults from the public with quiet dignity, less so ignorance from her colleagues. In *C.A.D.* Reg praises her for giving blood that could be useful "if one of your ethnics turns up." "I've got the same blood as you, moron, when I cut myself it's not mango chutney that comes out!" The circumstances that made Norika Datta are revealed in *Enemies*, the only contribution to *The Bill* by the late, great Philip Martin. His groundbreaking series *Gangsters*, a show that defies description as it grows from an offbeat thriller into a bizarre fourth-wall breaking fantasy, gave watershed roles to many black and Asian actors in its exploration of the ethnic communities in Birmingham. But, having depicted a rainbow nation of crime, here Martin shows how the efforts of officialdom to promote 'the correct' idea of race relations can do the reverse. Sent to a domestic involving the Gopal family, as "our resident expert in ethnic matters", Norika reminds Tom Penny of her exotic roots: "I was born in Uxbridge!" "Nobody's perfect." The father is angry at the wayward attitude of his daughter

Sonora, who has "changed" and no longer obeys him. Sporting a bruise on her cheek, she wants him arrested. Meanwhile, rising hate crime figures have prompted area to send in their own expert on community affairs: Superintendent Jarvey, an old foe of Derek Conway's. Alec Peters brings in an Asian youth he saw stealing from a till and Jarvey is horrified: "That is Jamir Gadwani – eldest son of Aslam Gadwani, chairman of this area's community relations committee. You've made a mistake. He was frightened by you running towards him, so he panicked – understandable, to anyone who had any ethnic sensitivity." He tells Cryer to drop the charges and is reminded politely that he cannot override the custody officer's say-so. "You could be igniting a powder keg. Have you forgotten about Brixton, and Broadwater Farm?" "I was at Broadwater," Cryer responds curtly. "I didn't see you, sir." When Jarvey has gone, Cryer's cool vanishes. "Where do we get these dead-legs from?" he snarls at Peters. "From the knacker's yard. Useless at anything else, so they're promoted to where they can do the most harm."

Since Peters is the only witness and Jamir has no prior record, Cryer lets him go. When Datta brings in the Gopal family, Peters tells her she's wasting her time: "Only nicking whites today." Sonora was brought up in Bombay by her aunt and got used to her freedom, but on coming to London she has stepped back in time: "Do this, don't go out." "My dad was like that," Norika smiles understandingly, "until I trained him." "You are cleverer than I; I can only fight." But the father is pouring out his feelings of disgrace to Jarvey, who assures him he will "sort it" and marches into the interview room to instruct Sonora to drop the charges. "You're upset at the moment, but when you've calmed down, you'll realise: you don't want the shame of going to court over a family disagreement. He is your father: your family, the head. You know your place. He has his." "Do I have to talk to this person?" she demands. "Do you not employ somebody who understands the modern Asian community?" The two women take refuge in the front interview room. Working out from her high and mighty attitude that Sonora has servants at home, Norika reveals that, "My parents had servants in Uganda, before they were expelled." When he found out she wanted a career in the police, "my father had forty fits. But I proved I was serious. Did the training... And my dad – well, we went up to this wedding in Huddersfield and everyone knew me as being 'that very fine policewoman from London'. He'd been boasting... Our parents need time, that's all." She persuades Sonora to drop the matter, and to use the stubbornness she shares with her father to convince him the world is changing. Datta's work in domestic violence would often pit her against her own people; her argument here *not* to involve the law is in stark contrast to later episodes, where she is often trying to persuade an abused wife to take her husband to court. The futility of Jarvey's role is proved when Jamir is caught thieving again and is proud of it, confirming to his mates that he is not one of the drab do-gooders.

Datta finds herself in an uncomfortable spot in *Small Hours*, when Carver borrows her to help bring in a witness. When they get no answer at the door, they settle down to wait in his car, and he asks how she is finding the job. "Of course, it's important to have something else in life. I don't expect that's easy with your... culture. No arranged marriage?" he enquires, still cycling through the Asian stereotypes. But if his knowledge hasn't broadened since Series 3's *Sun Hill Karma*, his tastes have. The intent behind his 'woe is me' routine becomes clear: "I'm not seeing anybody just now. As a matter of fact..." "My boyfriend's a teacher," Norika cuts in benignly; if Viv's defence mechanism is the smart mouth, and June's the angry one, then sweetness and charm are her way out of a tough position. "I don't think I could stick that, could you?" His attempt torpedoed, Jim drives them back to base. But once her shift is over, he offers Norika a lift home and she is forced to spell it out: "Listen. I've tried it nicely. Get the message – not interested, all right? Sierra Oscar, out." Watch Jim's reaction when his 'witness' fails to show and it's obvious she was only a pretext to get Norika on her own: even the choirboy has his calculating side.

It's not as though it's a passing fancy, either. The extent of Jim's feelings is revealed in *Just for a Moment*, when he turns his back on a disturbed youth in custody and the latter grabs a knife from Peters' desk, holding it to Norika's throat. This time she is grateful for the blunt approach of Tony Stamp, the inside man hiding in the cells. Playing John McClane, he uses his tied-together shoes to jolt the kid and body slams him to the floor. The devastated Jim takes Norika's hands: "If anything had happened to you then I..." As the shock kicks in she rushes off to throw up, and Jim's hopes too are down the toilet. Little does she know that his advances are only the dress rehearsal for another suitor the following year, who really won't take no for an answer.

The course of true love never runs smooth for Jim Carver. In the final episode of the year, *Friends and Neighbours*, we learn that Sonia has slung him out and he is "shacked up with Tony Stamp – not in the Biblical sense," Roach clarifies to a startled Burnside. The DI reminds Jim of the rent allowance rules that he himself supposedly bent for Tosh and consigns him to the section house. Meeting its gruff sergeant Wally Redfearn, Jim is sent back to boys' school: "Higher-ups out of bounds, female officers only. Some houses mix the sexes – we don't. No one in your room after ten o'clock, no dirty pictures on the walls as it upsets the cleaners. You like your shower hot, don't even try between seven and eight in the morning." Gazing on the four walls he has been reduced to, Jim knows his situation can't get any worse – and then a beaming face materialises behind him: "Hullo, neighbour. Welcome aboard!" Drowning his sorrows with Roach, he ponders, not for the last time, what has gone wrong. "I'm nearly thirty years of age, where have I got to? A cell, in the Met equivalent of Strangeways. The section house is my true home – washing my smalls with Reg Hollis." Reg visits Burnside to assure him he will take the newcomer Jim "under my wing", and this time induces a full-on Clint Eastwood *Gran Torino* shudder in the DI. In the pub, a plastered Ted sounds off about his own career failings, Tony Scannell slurring his way through one of the best drunk performances ever seen on TV. "I'm going to go round *Mr* Burnside... or through him," he vows. Jim helps his paralytic skipper back to the section house, carrying him up to his room. "Hell's bells Jim, you're desperate," grins Garfield as he wanders by in a towel, not exactly Cary Grant himself. Ted passes out on Jim's bed – only to spring awake just before six a.m. the next day, rushing them both to an arrest that he got the info on. He discovers that Burnside has already claimed the credit, shafting him yet again; this is the life of a seasoned detective, to which a struggling Jim can only aspire.

Jim makes a passable sleeping partner for Ted, now that he has lost his only real confidante. Kevin Clarke brings the story of Roach and his transvestite informant Roxanne to a close, for now, in *Information Received*. But this is no longer a party for two – a third player is introduced, of a surprising kind. The trial of crime boss Mickey Owen collapses because the witnesses have been frightened into silence. Following two of Owen's thugs on their extortion rounds, Roach is lured into a trap. The top man makes an appearance: a sinister performance by Michael Feast, whose lean hawk-like features always suggest the reverse. "You lost fair and square in a court of law," Owen reminds Ted. "Far as I'm concerned, it's over – yet all evening, you're carrying out your own little stewards' enquiry." He runs down his shabby lifestyle, including his flat, "all those takeaways... Where is it now, second floor, 109? By rights I owe you a good hiding for tonight. I'll leave it to you. Stay away, or you're a dead Ted." When the heavies have gone, their place is taken by officers from the Flying Squad who have been tailing Roach. Owen is going up in the world, branching out into armed robbery. Ted is shocked to learn that he has used the Cockatoo Club as his alibi. "Didn't you know?" asks the down to earth, unglamorous DI Kellner, whom Ted must call Ma'am. "Mickey don't like girls. But it gets better. The story is, he's in a private room with someone who just happens to be one of your snouts. Calls himself..." "...Roxanne. I don't use him anymore." Roach makes it clear he is no longer chasing promotion: "The one advantage that brings is that I don't get pushed into anything I don't want to do anymore!" Burnside finds Roach and tells him, "You'll have to get Mickey before he gets you", urging him to overcome his guilt at putting Roxanne in hospital a year ago.

Ted learns that Roxanne is Mickey's live-in girlfriend and arranges a rendezvous in a local knocking shop. "We always meet in the most romantic places," she muses on his doorstep. She reminds him of the catalogue of injuries she was left with last time, and that she had to move home. Ted shows her a photo of a man done over by Owen and points out that she can demolish his alibi. "If you're going to put dangerous people away – people who hurt other people and take their property – *this* is what it costs!" There are no brownie points on offer for him: "I failed the board again; they'll never promote me now, this is it – sergeant for life. You should have seen me when I first joined the force. Keen? – phew!" "Welcome to the grown-up world, where you don't get what you want, where you *never* get what you deserve."

Ted observes that his life is in danger too – and it's this that sways Roxanne. At Sun Hill, "Mr McCarthy" gives DI Kellner the info she wants but fears the consequences. She scoffs at the idea of returning home to keep a low profile: "All the fellers dress as women in Birkenhead." A reluctant Ted tells Roxanne that she will have to stay Mr McCarthy for her court appearance, in front of "respectable people." "Can you imagine what it took to go out like this in the first place? No, of course you can't!" Given the debates attached to pronouns these days, it's notable that Ted refers to Roxanne as "he" at first; but at the end, speaking to Kellner, clarifies "he's a she." "Whatever," says the dismissive DI. In an industry where leading men guard their image carefully, insecure about how they're photographed, how many lines their co-stars get and whether their character is outshined, this storyline illustrates how fearless Tony Scannell was. If the idea was an interesting one, he was all behind it. Agreeing to Ted's terms, Roxanne looks up at him: "You know why I'm doing this, don't you?" The moment passes between them, unspoken, and she breaks down in tears. When this curious love triangle returns a decade later, neither Paul O'Grady nor writer Kevin Clarke would attend the party.

ROGER AND OUT

If Roxanne and Ted's is the love that dare not speak its name, then June Ackland and Gordon Wray's is the romp that never gets its kit off. *The Bill*'s first office romance since June's dust-up with Dave Litten in Series 1, when the show wasn't sure exactly what it wanted to be, is further proof of how flexible the supposed golden rule about personal lives really was. What is avoided at all costs is the dreaded, "You don't care about us anymore", over a dinner table thick with red wine and rancour; very little else is off limits. Ted's girlfriend and Taff's bride-to-be both show up in the early years, but they are blue-off-blue pairings. By contrast, the lopsided gender balance of those years made it very difficult to match up regulars. Six years on, it's still Trudie Goodwin, one of the two female members of the original cast, who is given a relationship to explore. But with the number of women in the 1990 line-up approaching half a dozen, the feminine mystique is not what it once was. That place of intrigue for most of the relief, the WPCs' locker room, is now one of the show's regular haunts. Closing the door on her Richard Gere poster, Suzanne Ford, a walk-on role from the early series that was steadily expanded for Vikki

Gee-Dare, points out the drawbacks of dating in the police. "No way round if you think about it, get a bloke with a normal job and he's not going to put up with you being on shifts. Find one who's on shifts himself and you might never meet!" June observes, "Oh, so you want a bloke who does absolutely nothing." "I'm spoilt for choice." Where else could such gems originate but from the pen of J.C. Wilsher, who had Siobhan Redmond observe in *Between the Lines*, "Men are like dog turds: the older they get, the easier they are to pick up."

It's Wilsher who starts and ends the liaison between Ackland and Wray, giving Clive Wood an exit route from the show. Taking a shine to June through her work on a burglary initiative, Wray invites her to dinner – and when they separately cry off a night with the lads, Roach, the biggest gossip in the nick, instantly puts it together. Burnside is impressed: "The one thing that's always gutted me about Wray is he's such a bleeding boy scout! I mean he's clean, in thought, word and deed. You can't hold a sensible conversation on that basis. But a man who's going over the side? Now that's a man I can do business with. And if he's cracked it with June Ackland, well he's a better man than me – and that's saying something." Roach raises an eyebrow, but his suspicions are soon confirmed. Wray takes June to an upmarket restaurant for lunch, unaware that CID have traced a drug deal to the same place; Viv and Ted arrive hot on their heels. The dynamic between the lovers is a clever inversion of the norm. June notes uncomfortably of their plush surroundings, "This is the sort of place bosses bring their secretaries to play footsie under the table." Gordon, the Nineties New Man, chastises her backward thinking: "A man in a restaurant with a woman doesn't have to be a boss seducing his workforce. They could be two businesspeople, having a working lunch." That is seemingly how he tries to downplay, and rationalise, the affair – but the desk photo of his wife seen earlier confirms it is just that. Viv walks into the ladies' and sees June, who rolls her eyes skywards. Wray has clocked the woman that CID's target is lunching with, a courier he encountered in his Drug Squad days. The cops are never off duty, a fact of life that comes crashing home to June. "Oh, what a tangled web we weave," Roach grins from ear to ear. When June returns to the locker room, Norika asks teasingly, "Did you have a good day?" The picture of gloom, she realises what has been let loose.

The real purpose of the most chaste affair of all time – no steamy bedroom bouts, no clinches in cars, no racial incident figures swept off desks – is to show how it affects everyone around the couple, who take it to be more than it really is. June is despondent because she knows who will get the blame. Tosh learns she is unable to attend his birthday party as she's got "things to do." "Yeah," he growls, "mucking up some guy's marriage." "Oh, come on, she's hardly a vamp," says Mike Dashwood - who, as we see whenever he is paired up with June, gives her the respect he affords no-one else. "He must have made all the running. How come you've never gone over the side, Tosh?" "Who'd have me? I need a block and tackle at home as it is... In me last nick I was the only guy in CID who was still on his first wife. Made me feel a bit like a virgin." The affair is brought to a sudden end in *Out of the Blue*, just after Wray has had an upbeat meeting with his one acolyte in CID. "In my view, we're moving in a very positive direction," enthuses Alistair Greig. "We all still talk as if our snouts and our street cred are all that matters, but we're actually paying attention to the paperwork these days!" "And it's the paperwork that makes a good result stand up in court." "Absolutely." Wray has high hopes of moving into a specialist team, and hints that Greig could be his first choice to join him. But then he is summoned to Brownlow's office, to be told he is being transferred to a CID training post. He rages at the lack of gratitude for turning "a bunch of cowboys" into a proper department. "Sadly, that's not the only consideration," Brownlow observes, before spelling it out for him. Asking what disciplinary offence he has committed, Wray is told, "You're being transferred, not punished." "It takes me out of line operationally, which means I'm off the promotion ladder!" "It's been settled from above, there's nothing I can do about it." Having resisted a previous attempt by the Super to inculcate him into the Masons, on the basis that "I spend most of my working day with men", Wray asks venomously at the door, "Is it too late to take up your kind offer and learn the funny handshake?"

In CID, Greig is assembling a Venn diagram to illustrate a complex fraud case. Burnside is unable to find any coloured pens for him: "Nor have we got any plasticine or jigsaw puzzles, neither." Hearing Wray's door slam, he exclaims, "Alistair! You didn't forget to warm the bog seat for him this morning?" On learning the truth, he rubs salt in: "What a choker. Bit gutty for you Alistair – all that time you've put in on your knees." "Actually, I think it's very bad news for this nick. Oh well... back to the Stone Age, eh guv?" says an unusually lippy Greig, taking his DI by surprise. June is dismayed to learn that Gordon is taking a fall for something that's "practically over... You're not prepared to be a bastard to your wife and children, I'm not asking you to be! When you've had your candyfloss all you're left with is the stick, I found that out years ago." Her occasional martyr complex gives way to a more familiar pose when she realises someone has ratted on them. Having endured a chat with Monroe about any "problems of a personal nature" she might have, she is sure she's found the source. "He tried to give me the old Dutch uncle routine this morning. It's like watching a gorilla doing brain surgery." Marching into his office, she unloads a rant for the ages: "Since you took over this relief, you've established yourself as a petty-minded, rule-bound little Hitler with all the warmth and humour of a rusted-up Dalek! We can live with that. But what you don't do is grass on us. That way you'll be giving the orders, and nobody will be listening." The terrified Monroe insists that this is the first he's heard about Wray getting canned, and rumour got back to him about the affair, hence his little talk; but she doesn't believe him. "Like I said, you've done a lot to make yourself unpopular on this relief. But you did have respect. We never took you for a liar."

On a riverside walk, Wray is enlightened by Conway: "You weren't blown out from inside the nick, Gordon." The instruction came from the new DAC, who happens to sit on the same social affairs committee as Wray's wife. "She doesn't know!" "She knows more than you think, mate." He urges Wray to keep his head down and do his time, and his career may not suffer in the long term. Losing his zeal to fight his corner, Gordon incurs the fury of June, who points out that she's had to put up with the gossip and hurtful remarks. Closer to home the damage has been done, and a snide comment from Tony about loyalty escalates into a campaign against Monroe. He has a pile of manure dumped in his driveway, and the relief start working to rule, assembling for parade at two o'clock and not a moment sooner. June becomes less and less enchanted with the vendetta being waged on her behalf: "If I'd have wanted to put on a uniform and mess people about, I'd have got a job on the railways."

Reg has made it into a labour dispute, citing a "range of regrettable supervisory attitudes", but she can sense he is on an ego trip. She and Monroe end up at the hospital, dealing with a woman who is clearly not the mother of the baby in her care. He proves he can still roll his sleeves up by changing its nappy himself: "I hate watching simple jobs done badly." June relents, accepting he did not grass on her, and the campaign is "suspended." Meanwhile Wray tries to ask Greig about his fraud case before he leaves, but to his chagrin learns that Alistair would rather discuss it with the incoming DCI Reid. In the space of six months, tomorrow's man has become yesterday's.

But Wray is not the only man to find himself suddenly in the cold at the end of this year. Bob Cryer lays it on the line for his fellow sergeant, Tom Penny, when he explains why he gave Dave Quinnan the nod for a commendation, not him: "For quick thinking and initiative. When did you last use any initiative, eh? Apart from digging yourself out of the mire or putting someone else in it! You're right Tom, they do not give commendations for nitpicking, for bloody-mindedness, or for being a twenty-four-carat pain in the arse!" Refusing the peace offering of a drink, Penny concludes, "I don't fit in here anymore. Not with you or anyone else; I'm out of step. So, I'll drink where I like. You can go and be mates with the lads." If only he had stuck to his vow – but his reluctant decision to attend Cryer's bash to mark twenty years in the force, in *One for the Road*, turns into the worst of his life. Lured to the pub by an unusually sneaky Monroe, Cryer is ambushed by the relief in heart-warming scenes. Jim Carver turns up on behalf of CID, announcing that "Sgt Cryer taught me everything I knew! It's true – thanks mate." He hands him the most fitting of gifts, a model policeman. As Cryer gives a speech, the camera pans slowly round each character until it alights on a pensive Penny, who looks on knowing he will never generate such warmth. When he leaves, his car is tailed by officers from Barton Street who have been staking out the pub. They pull him over and enact a familiar routine, warning him of a defective brake light and querying the alcohol on his breath. Penny demands to know their game, confident he is not over the limit, but his world is shattered when a positive breathalyser test is flashed in his face. Taken to Barton Street, the man who persecuted Tosh to the letter of the law tries to get his own trifling offence dropped. "They were waiting for me; I've been set up!"

The threads woven earlier in the year, by multiple authors across different episodes, converge perfectly as Penny's chickens come home to roost. The two PCs who collared him recite the rulebook in monotone fashion. The custody sergeant takes him into the office to provide another sample, talking him through the same procedure he has himself delivered countless times. Penny's indignant stance dissolves into fear as a cold, hard possibility approaches. "Anything over fifty..." "...And I lose my job, right?" Having worked out what this is all in aid of, he pleads his innocence: "Listen – I tried my hardest... You know I was quite happy to let it go, Terry's a good sergeant." "Was, was a good sergeant." "I didn't want to see Coles get done. You were there, I tried to cover for him! It was Peters who pushed me into a corner!" Unmoved, the sergeant orders him to blow into the machine – which produces a reading of fifty-two. Penny diminishes before our eyes. It's not without reason that Brownlow called it "every officer's nightmare"; this is the weak spot for policemen, where they are most likely to overlap with their clientele. It was in *A Clean Division* that Jim Carver, up on his own charge of drink driving, had to share a bench with two hooligans for a few hours and contemplate the thought that he may be one of them now. Led back into custody, a traumatised Penny leans on a pillar as two vandals are brought in kicking and screaming; unlike Jim, he has crossed over. You know he's out of luck when his last resort is the utterly unmoveable Inspector Twist, the black and white BBB we would come to know and not love. "All I know is the facts: fifty-two on the old clapometer and didn't he do well! What you don't want to understand, Tom, is that it doesn't matter whether you were set up or not. What does matter is that you've been caught."

Penny prepares for his court appearance in *Start With the Whistle*. He dismisses his GP's opinion that he has never recovered from the trauma of his shooting and has a solid case for retirement on medical grounds. "That'd put me in the waste bin with no embarrassment for the job, won't it?" Suddenly he's never been more popular, receiving a string of visitors: first Hollis offering Federation advice ("If you need my help..." "I'll jump in front of a Tube train!"), then Conway asking tactfully if he's willing to fall on his sword. "If people could see the speed and enthusiasm with which police officers wash their hands, they'd never call us pigs," Penny observes in disgust. Finally, Cryer turns up to talk sense into him. The last appearance of Tom's demure wife Wendy demonstrates how *The Bill*'s light continuity is exactly on point when it needs to be, even if by accident. When Bob asks, "Can you cope with this?", her simple reply – "Who else is going to?" – not only illustrates the hidden burden that falls on women but evokes her two past revelations; that she had an affair with Bob, and that her husband takes out his frustrations violently on her. With twenty-five years in, Penny is entitled to full pension but refuses to stick to the script, planning to go down fighting. "Driving over the limit isn't like other crimes," Cryer impresses on him. "It's not about your state of mind, what your intentions were, there's no room for blowing smoke. Guilt is a fact of biochemistry." Moreover, resignation is better than dismissal, which may deny him a pension and references for other jobs. "What other job? I've spent my adult life as a copper, what else can I do?" The mention of security work incenses him: "That bloody shower? I've spent my career locking up the kind of scum who get jobs with security firms! God almighty Bob," Tom asks plaintively, "where's the justice?" From one veteran to another comes the score: "You're a bit old to believe in Father Christmas, ain't ya?"

When his moment comes in the dock, Penny pleads guilty but is then asked if he has anything to say. He unfolds a piece of paper, ready to outline the criminal conspiracy against him – and after a glance at the CIB officers in court, instead delivers just what is expected of him, soft-soaping the magistrates about the stress he has been under. It's another expression of the awkward reality that *The Bill* was always so good at depicting: that people don't make the perfect or the heroic choice but settle for less because they have to. The expected penalties follow: a fine, a year-long ban and notice of disciplinary proceedings. Penny returns to Sun Hill to see Brownlow. Thanked for his long service, a last hint of defiance wells up in him and subsides, as he realises he can't fight the inevitable. His eyes glistening, he submits his request for retirement on medical grounds. Brownlow promises him he will leave with excellent references. Penny makes a feeble promise to Cryer about coming over for dinner, but it's clear he is heading into oblivion. The stores officer assures him he will never shake off the job: "I see it all the time. Nobody really leaves, you know. In years to come you'll keep in touch, you'll know what all your mates are doing, who's been promoted, who's got transferred. You'll sit at home thinking about them all getting on with the job. In my experience, blokes invariably 'lose' their helmet, stick and whistle," he adds coyly. "Souvenirs, you understand? Mementos of your police service." Pushing these across the counter, Penny sums up a quarter-century of duty in two words: "Stuff 'em. Make it easy on yourself – start with the whistle and work upwards!"

That the other man's prediction is entirely borne out by Tom Penny's return as a guest the following year only adds to the poignancy of his exit. Penny is one of the finest cases of how *The Bill* never needed to make cartoon villains out of anybody to make them compelling. Neither old and wise nor young and keen, he inhabits a shadow ground. If Cryer is the copper we'd all want to be, Penny is who most of us actually would be; selfish, blinkered, hypocritical, but not without sympathy. Tony Stamp, who had his own memorable run-in with him, notes on the day of his hearing, "I feel sorry for the miserable git." In some respects, he is like the parents of Graham Butler, taking something for granted and only recognising its value when it is snatched away from him. But Penny, lest we forget, was given a lifeline and a second chance in the job three years earlier. Perhaps his storyline is a prolonged comment on how, in the long run, people never really change; how they get worn down by routine and their own narrow expectations. But a long-running part in a hit TV show also confers immortality. The lugubrious features and Ausso-Cockney drawl of Roger Leach who, as Oliver Crocker has observed, played vulnerability so well[20], are preserved forever even though the man himself never got to tell his story in detail: a man who lived to only fifty-three, but who inspired all the affection in his teammates that his alter ego never could.

---

[20] *The Bill Podcast* 08: Trudie Goodwin, 2017

Verdict: The increasing difficulty in this era of listing a dozen standout episodes for each year is a good problem to have. Everything that made *The Bill* special is present in dense layers: the breadth of stories, the tightness of the scripting, one-liners too many and telling to capture in their entirety here, and an exceptional cast bringing them to life with panache. By introducing a stronger note of continuity, the programme starts to feel like one huge novel telling a sweeping story, individual volumes of which can be taken out and enjoyed on their own too. The downfall of Tom Penny is a perfect example of setup and payoff over time, and there is more to come in this vein. The number of small, indoor-bound episodes that produce some of the show's greatest drama illustrate how writing restrictions can be more of a help than a hindrance. Perhaps it's because, not in spite of, the problems faced behind the scenes in the move to Merton that the conveyor belt rolls along better than ever. It's a daunting task to create an all-year programme in which there is virtually no filler, and most episodes have something to recommend them. But, back at the helm, Michael Chapman achieves this and guides the show firmly into a new decade.

REVIEWING THE BILL: 1991
First Broadcast 1 January – 31 December 1991
Script Editors: Zanna Beswick, Gina Cronk, Peter Eyers-Hill, Tim Vaughan, Nicola Venning. Producers: Brenda Ennis, Richard Handford, Tony Virgo, Peter Wolfes. Executive Producer: Michael Chapman.

Key Exhibits:

1. *Fear or Favour*
Written by Christopher Russell. Directed by Mike Dormer.

2. *Cold Turkey: Parts 1 and 2*
Written by J.C. Wilsher. Directed by Gordon Flemyng.

3. *Cry Havoc*
Written by Russell Lewis. Directed by Stuart Urban.

4. *Without Consent*
Written by Julian Jones. Directed by Derek Lister.

5. *The Best You Can Buy*
Written by Christopher Russell. Directed by Moira Armstrong.

6. *They Also Serve*
Written by Russell Lewis. Directed by David Hayman.

7. *Lest We Forget*
Written by Victoria Taylor. Directed by Bill Pryde.

8. *Losing It*
Written by Russell Lewis. Directed by Jim Goddard.

9. *Shots*
Written by J.C. Wilsher. Directed by Chris Lovett.

10. *The Square Peg*
Written by Christopher Russell. Directed by Jim Goddard.

11. *Thicker Than Water*
Written by Matthew Wingett. Directed by Sarah Pia Anderson.

12. *Vital Statistics*
Written by Christopher Russell. Directed by Jeremy Summers.

OLD FRIENDS

Now installed in its all singing, all dancing station, *The Bill* gets a chance to spread its wings and stop crisis-managing. The first year since the show's debut not to see some kind of disruption behind the scenes, be that a change of producer, place or format, also has very little turnover in its cast. With two new faces added to the mix, two old ones bookend the year, making return visits in civvies for different reasons. The final appearance of Yorkie Smith, sporting a stuck-on moustache that Robert Hudson had to endure otherwise people 'wouldn't know it was him', gives the show's first New Year's Eve special an extra boost. Back in the police and a member of Sheffield CID, Yorkie arrives at his old nick to take back a prisoner. He and Jim end up on a northbound train, knocking back lager as they ponder the ways they had hoped to see in the New Year. If this low-key story feels like a sad way to bid farewell to someone who was so beloved at Sun Hill, there is greater sadness in the return visit from one of its least loved members. The musings of Roy Galloway, attack dog and sometime prophet, are loud in everyone's head when a bad Penny once again turns up, just as the DI predicted at the end of Series 3. The man who dismissed the security industry as "that bloody shower" before his forced retirement has rapidly seen the light, now head of it at a local engineering company. He bowls up to the front desk expecting to be let in automatically to his appointment with Roach – as though he is still 'one of us'. The first lesson that he is not comes from the man whose help he so politely spurned before his court appearance. "Hello, Tom!" chirps Reg Hollis. "He used to be a skipper here," he tells the civilian lady manning the front desk, giving her the OK to let him through. If Penny thought he was due the deference of his old rank, the voice of the union has other ideas.

We see the painful spectacle of somebody who is no longer one of the cool kids trying to hang out with them. Penny chunters on about the huge thieving operation in his new workplace, while Peters and Roach try desperately to get rid of him. Quickly making tracks, Monroe remarks to Cryer, "Security bloke now, isn't he? There but for the grace of God..." Even Bob is reluctant to accept Penny's offer of a drink, knowing that no-one else will. "Tell him if he gets any more hunches, take them to Barton Street – he owes them a favour," snipes Peters, showing he has neither forgotten nor forgiven Penny's actions the year before. Roach is given a guided tour of Penny's workplace, but Tom's new boss is strangely reluctant to have his firm turned over as a hotbed of crime: "You are not a policeman anymore, you're a security officer, now just remember that!" In the private sector Penny's duty is to uphold the business, not the law. Roach, better than anyone, sees the irony of Sun Hill's biggest PACE jobsworth turning keen sleuth, now he is alive to what his old job really meant. He gives his former foe some home truths: "You don't get it, do you? He didn't hire you to do a job; he hired you to cut his overheads. Having a chief security officer with police background cuts his insurance premium by thousands – more than he's paying you, and that includes your medical insurance, and your private pension, and the minicabs you have to have to visit the other factory because you're a disqualified driver. He knows what's going missing, and it doesn't worry him. And, to be honest, if there's no victim it doesn't worry me either." "And you call yourself a policeman?" "Yeah, I do – but maybe you shouldn't call yourself one any longer." More than how he is addressed, Tom's loss of standing is brutally clear in the apartheid of the closing credits. As per convention, all the regulars are billed first, with their ranks, followed by a man now known simply as 'Penny'.

That episode, *Start to Finish*, is a wider discussion on the changing fortunes of policemen. Brownlow attends an interview at the Yard for a senior command course; already running late, he is further delayed when he and Stamp come across an RTA, and his quick work ends up saving the victim's life. He is dismayed to learn that the board includes DAC Hicks, the plummy-voiced bureaucrat who handed out Quinnan's commendation, elevated to a semi-regular role this year. What the show does so well, in examining the lives of the top brass, is to place each of them in context in a wider rat race. Hicks will be to Brownlow as Brownlow is to Conway, the immovable obstacle to progress who remembers every one of his faults and brings them back to haunt him. Echoing the failed board of the other man Brownlow keeps forever under his thumb, Ted Roach, the Chief Super gives the same hollow PR responses as he falters under pressure. When he brings up the recent success of cracking the Donald Blake murders, Hicks is instantly on his case: "Do you think the party you gave the day Blake was arrested did very much for your close community relationship? I understand it was quite a knees-up, and yet the man downstairs hadn't actually been charged." "I don't make any apology for what happened, it was a good clean result and everybody knows it!" Brownlow insists. "Now if I choose to congratulate my people, if I choose to open a couple of bottles at the end of a shift, then so be it." This sharp piece of continuity reminds us that even the high-ups are under constant scrutiny, their victories not all they might seem. On his return, Brownlow suggests to Conway that these boards are used "to have a pop at you and your division" and is more to the point when he calls his wife: "Well, I survived." We can guess the result, and the whole story serves to enhance the Chief Super as a sympathetic figure. It's not that he is a hypocrite, simply a middling figure in a dog-eat-dog world: pushing down on those below him as he is pushed down from above.

Brownlow has older sins that return to haunt him this year, his status as one of the longest-serving officers in the Met put to good use. Hicks observes that many people, like Blake, confess and then retract or are released on appeal: "I'm sure I don't have to remind you of several such cases recently." The show does just that, however, as it draws on a climate of increasing doubt over police infallibility that had been there since its first series and had reached a head of steam at the turn of the Nineties. This was the period in which one high-profile conviction after another was overturned thanks to the exposure of malpractice. In March 1991 the Birmingham Six were released after sixteen years behind bars for the IRA pub bombings of 1974, their confessions obtained via threats, beatings and flimsy forensic evidence. This came hot on the heels of the release of the Guildford Four two years earlier. All this was grist to the mill for one 'Victoria Taylor' – better known as former script editor Tim Vaughan, who throws Brownlow into an engrossing two-hander in *Lest We Forget*. Early in the year, with CID under suspicion of leaking info, Conway muses, "I thought we'd put all that behind us, sir. The years of anarchy – 'the firm within the firm.'" "I still don't believe there's hardcore corruption on anything like the scale of fifteen years ago," Brownlow cuts in. But his own part in that era is later critiqued by DCC Fuller, investigating a seventeen year old case of his that may go to appeal. He was a DC "stationed at Hillingdon – a position you held for just over two years. What made you go back to uniform?" The defensive Brownlow claims he was "temperamentally better suited" to it; "I don't doubt the wisdom of the move," replies Fuller tellingly. Two brothers accused of murder in a botched burglary were convicted in October 1974 and are serving life sentences. The question marks about the man who led the case, DI Mowbray, won't affect him as he is now dead and "beyond worry" – which Brownlow disputes, suggesting he can still be smeared beyond the grave. Once the suspects were charged, "I had a couple of drinks, but I left early; I'd just got engaged to be married." "It had nothing to do with the fact that the Wilson brothers were crying 'fit-up'?"

Fuller notes that the younger brother had schizophrenia and was educationally backward, yet signed a confession even though he "could hardly write his own name!" Electro-static detection has been used on the confessions: "He never knew about the trick with the piece of Formica, Mowbray, did he? Under the sheet of paper? If you're going to add to the confession after it's been signed, it pays not to leave a calling card. Of course, nobody knew that in 1974, the test hadn't been developed then." He shows Brownlow a lab report which proves that pages were written later and inserted into the original: the ESDA test having been used during the late Eighties to expose false confessions drafted by the West Midlands Serious Crime Squad, which handled the Birmingham Six case. However, the window in which this occurred rules out Mowbray. Brownlow is quizzed about his relationships with the DI and his subordinates, Henderson and Davis – the latter was Mowbray's protégé and has now risen to Assistant Chief Constable. Brownlow had invited them all to his engagement party in Suffolk; except Davis backed out at the last moment, saying he had "things to finish off. It would explain everything, it's the work of a novice. It would also explain why there was an unholy row when we got back." Davis is still a close friend of Brownlow's and invited him over recently – now he knows why. "Davis is one of the finest police officers in the country, he could even make Commissioner," observes a glum Fuller. "This won't do much for force credibility." "I thought it was the truth you wanted," says Brownlow, realising that under his apparent zeal Fuller hoped to pour water on the fire. The Super accepts he may have to give evidence in court, but feels no sense of triumph at outlasting Davis. CID did not figure in his particular career race: "To be honest with you, I didn't really fit in. I didn't have the confidence, or at least that's what people used to say." No sooner is Fuller gone than word comes through: "Mr Davis on the line", wanting to speak about weekend plans.

Innocence, a follow-up episode that Vaughan wasn't keen to write,[21] becomes a good stepping stone towards his work on *Between the Lines* the following year: particularly the audition piece it gives to the great Tony Doyle, who could play slime like no-one else and would prove it as the dastardly John Deakin. At a swish riverside restaurant Brownlow relives old times, and new charges, with his former DS, now squarely in the frame. Davis produces his trump card: while they were all in Suffolk, he was with Mowbray's wife. "I was seeing her, Charles – or seeing to her, if you want it in the vernacular... He found my watch on his bedside table. I stood up to him in that row we had, faced him out. I suppose he had to take it out on somebody, so he fitted up the Wilson brothers." "You make it sound like a fit of pique," says a disgusted Brownlow. "You were right to get back into uniform," notes Davis. "They really were the bad old days of CID." Brownlow realises that his remarkable deductions are not recent. "You knew, didn't you? You knew at the time, and you never said a word." "I was a DC, who was going to listen to me? I wouldn't have lasted five minutes, a corruption allegation in those days?" "What were you thinking of, your career prospects?" "It was 1974, people like Peter Mowbray were getting away with murder! I will say whatever I have to, to get those men released." "But you'll wait till the call comes?" sighs Brownlow, who has tried hard to work out which of his peers he misjudged so badly – only to realise it was both of them. "Stay in touch, Charles," Davis urges him, for the same reason he always has; but when the Super walks away this time, he turns his back for good on a world he had too many scruples to stay part of.

NEW FOES

Gordon Wray's replacement as DCI is designed to head off any possibility of another embarrassing office tryst. "Not a Mason?" Conway enquires. "Not a man," Brownlow informs him. "Kim Reid, from the Fraud Squad. Very able officer." There was nothing of course, save the expectations of her sex that meant Reid couldn't have indulged in the same distractions as her predecessor: especially

---

[21] *The Bill Podcast: Lest We Forget* Patreon Commentary, 2021

surrounded by all that male talent in CID. But, playing Sun Hill's highest ever ranked female officer, Carolyn Pickles ruffles feathers in other ways. On her way into work on day one, Reid gives a blaring lorry driver the finger and makes an arrest, all in the course of obtaining her morning sandwich. Continuing the managerial ethos espoused by Wray, she applies it with the brisk, businesslike air of someone who doesn't have to go through the lad-bonding routine first. When Greig tries to explain the details of his complex fraud case, she quickly pinpoints an angle he has overlooked, using her squad background. "I should have thought of the VAT..." "Yes, you should," she agrees sharply. Forewarned and forearmed by his struggles with Wray, Burnside tries to head off more of the same by talking the talk: "If we're going to adopt a proactive approach to innovation and change, then training is the key element." But when Reid tries to impress the notion of career development on the DI's partner in crime, she gets a prickly response. Told that he will be sent on the next interview course, which he couldn't attend due to "pressure of work", a tight-lipped Roach gets to his feet. "I look forward to working with you," she announces. "Likewise, I'm sure," he flannels back. Reid's face falls slightly as she realises she is in for a battle, every inch of the way.

This battle works its way up through the ranks, as the new broom takes a fresh look at people who have become set in their ways. First into the psychiatrist's chair is a man long overdue analysis, in the year's opening episode, *Grief*. Still taking contrary routes to victory, Dashwood escorts the elderly victim of a purse theft onto her day centre bus, then gets it to stop by the courtroom where the alleged thief is due to emerge. This shaky attempt at corroborative ID is blown out of the water when a CPS official reveals that the case has been postponed: "All parties were informed of the application for a month's adjournment." In full on prima donna mode, Mike heads for the Crime Support Unit to demand an explanation. The secretary there explains she's "not used to these new word processors" and gets a broadside in return. After a complaint is made about his behaviour, Reid calls him in for a chat that turns into an expose of his failings, including his ID stunt. "Three years ago, you could have got away with it. But you knew he was going to be there! It would stink to high heaven as a set-up job, it wouldn't even get beyond CPS! No Mike, it's like car conversations, they don't – no, can't – happen anymore."

When she tries to get under his skin, asking if he has problems at home or work, he denies it. "There's something niggling at the back of my mind about you," she persists. "All right, so you're always immaculate and your pocketbook is spotless, but if you were giving it one hundred per cent you wouldn't really have the time. Tell me, what are your ambitions?" "I don't want to talk about it." "Which confirms my feelings about you. You have an attitude problem. I believe in saying it as I see it, and in my view, you are a loner, and somewhat on the defensive." Mike is taken to his desk and asked if he's looked at his in-tray. "I've been stitched here," he protests, grudgingly reading out a memo about the case adjournment. "And what date was that signed?" "Yesterday." "Now I want you to take stock − I don't know where your mind is, but it's certainly not on work. And you can resist me all you like, but I intend to find out."

Reid homes in on another DC in *Now We're Motoring*, a beautiful character study of "the last one on my little list... Whenever I fix up a heart to heart with Tosh Lines, something always seems to come up." "Well Tosh likes to put himself about a bit − you and I might see him as a bit of an old-style DC." "Alistair, we're talking about a man who's pushing forty. We've got kids who could do the legwork. Frankly, I'd expect a man of his commitments to be setting his sights a bit higher; looking for advancement?" "Not everybody's leadership material." "No, but being a detective on my firm is going to be a bit like riding a bike: you've got to keep moving or you'll fall on your head." If she and Greig are pushing for success, "Where's Lines going?" Tosh is adamant he's "not competing for brownie points. I get the job done, that should be enough." Leaving his rust-bucket at a local garage, he tells a mechanic wistfully of his early days as an amateur racing driver, and the ambitions he had. "We were going to go places. But you need sponsorship, money to burn − you get married, start a family, they burn your money for you. I've done hard graft now for twenty, what − twenty more years? Never taken a penny off the dole or the S.S., and what have I got to show for it, nothing! Nothing but debts!" If he got a flash car like the one he sees in a photo, "I'd floor the gas pedal and go for it. I wouldn't come back." "What about the wife and the kids, and the mortgage, and the MOT?" "Life is not a dress rehearsal, Billy. You get a chance and you go for it. It might not come again." Impressed, Billy arranges a meeting with a business contact who offers Tosh the chance to drive a stolen car all the way to Spain that evening. "It can't be too soon for me, mate."

Inspecting Tosh's case file, Reid fishes out an empty peanut wrapper and passes it to the apologetic Greig. "Looks as if he hasn't got around to writing up his notes yet." "Looks to me as if he hasn't got off his bum – where is he?" She tracks him to a cafe and enters to confront him, moments before his new business partners return. Vamping, Tosh reassures them the deal is still on, but she is part of it: "Kim and me, we're going to Spain – together. We don't have any secrets, do we?" he asks, taking her hand; her smile turns into a covert scowl. "We're doing a runner, we can't turn back! I'm ditching a wife and five kids!" "Alfie said this was our big chance together," she continues, picking up the baton and gilding it with her expertise. "I work for a building society. I've been transferring money into a fake account. We're going to use plastic to rip it off in slices at every service till between here and... the Spanish frontier." Her hangdog expression falters when Tosh asks if they can get a double cabin on the ferry. "Sure," replies the boss. "I'll ask 'em to lay on a bottle of champagne and a Janet Reger nightie, how about that?" "There'd better be a result out of this, or I'll have your guts for garters!" she hisses at Tosh. But they keep up the act while they collect the motor. On the open road, Reid makes it clear she wants to be kept in the loop on secret jobs like this from now on. Tosh is supposed to deliver the car to Spain for shipping to Morocco, in exchange for cannabis. He suggests hopefully that they play their parts to the end: "Keep on going, through France, over the border, front up the real barons." Reid tells him someone may, but it's a job for an agency way above their heads, and directs him to take the next left. "Yeah, I know ma'am," he replies in resignation. "It brings us back to Sun Hill." The Willy Loman of CID was only part-faking his tale of crushed dreams; if he had the chance, he would ditch the overdraft and run for the hills.

But Reid is more than a supervisory busybody. We see what she is made of in *Just Deserts* (that's what it says on the opening caption, so who am I to argue? Not a camel in sight, however), a story of a man pushed to his death at a building site. Reid has Dashwood drop her at the scene; a passing workman asks, "Want a piggyback, love?" and gets the instant riposte, "Are you licensed?" Burnside accuses Mike of trying to impress "Madam" and Tosh zeroes in on his hang-up: "He doesn't have your problem with women in the job." "I do not have a problem with women governors." "Neither do I – but I'm married to mine." Reminded by Reid that hard hats are a site rule, Burnside picks up his and chucks it in his car. Told to liaise with SOCO and the factory inspector, he protests, "With all due respect ma'am, I'm not very good at liaising." "No? Well, I'm not very good at driving a desk," she replies affably, leaving him to it. Her playful humour, and ability to cut people down to size, are apparent when she and Mike question a slobbish builder whose alibi for the murder is a woman. "I think I can say it was pretty memorable for her," he boasts, swilling a can of beer. Reid points out he could be in trouble if the lady denies all knowledge of their exploits: "Which is likely – I mean, toms are about as reliable as the building trade when it comes to remembering." While they get the deceased's criminal record from CAD, Burnside radios in irritably, asking for the whereabouts of his boss. Reid shakes her head at Peters and makes a quick exit, preferring to keep her DI guessing! "If Reid feels the need to go glory-hunting, that's her problem," the selfless Burnside tells Dashwood. "I must say, I'm not too happy about the way you've suddenly changed sides, though." "We don't have sides in CID," Mike replies coyly. "We're a team."

The extent of that piss-take is revealed two episodes later in *The Better Part of Valour* by Arthur McKenzie, a superbly packed story that shows how much detail could be crammed into a twenty five minute *Bill* script. Opening with an impressive aerial shot of the wreckage left by a bullion hijack, it follows the hunt for the robbers, but its real focus is on those doing the hunting. The knives are out for Reid, whose responsibility to recover a haul of six hundred grand is looked on with keen interest. "First division job, this," Roach observes as he and Burnside make their way to the burnt-out van. "It'll certainly test Madam." When Reid asks if someone is with the security guard in hospital, Ted shrugs insolently, "I don't know!" and is told to find out. "Attitudes like that have to be jumped on, Frank," she declares once he is gone. "At times like these I'm pleased to be a woolly," says Monroe, knowing the media is about to descend on the case. Reid becomes the face of the enquiry, her image plastered over the front pages. The publicity doesn't faze her: "This report is basically correct.... as far as the photograph is concerned, it's definitely not my best side." But she finds it less easy to keep a rein on the toxic pit of ambition beneath her. Still putting the 'me' in team, Roach has a lead that he wants to pursue on his own. "You've got two pips, I haven't," he reminds Burnside. "A job like this could put them there." Suspecting an inside job, he visits the security firm that hired the guards to see their head of personnel, his former colleague Chris Harkness. "Same old Ted Roach," the latter grins, "kicking verbals to the front, brains and strategy down the pan."

When Harkness refuses to hand over confidential files, Roach suddenly, and unpleasantly, switches tack. "Let's stuff the turkey a different way then, shall we? Does your boss know the real reason why you decided to leave the force?" Harkness's good cheer vanishes. "You slug... I was cleared of that." "Never went to court, my old son. Lack of corroboration, if my memory serves me right. And if they'd asked me, I would have been able to supply it." "So, this is blackmail?" "Persuasion – and unlawful sex with a fourteen-year-old does carry with it a stench... I would be a foolish man not to play my hand." "You really do leave a trail on the ground, don't you?" "One for one, Chris. You get me the details; I develop amnesia." Unearthing a likely suspect, Roach wants Harkness to sign a statement to make it official. "You're a user, Roach." Ted looks at him blankly, playing dumb as he always does when it suits his interests. "I've always wanted to know what people meant by that. There's only two words that mean anything to me: winners, and losers." Roach slips the info to Burnside under a cubicle door in the gents', pleading that he keep it between them for the time being, and Burnside agrees to "bat her off for a while." Reid, however, sees through his blithe assurance that a lead will turn up. "You're keeping something from me, Frank. Like why you haven't mentioned the fact that Roach has been making enquiries there. This is a public investigation, and I'll tell you this: Roach has not only alienated the whole company against us, but he may well be receiving a complaint for harassment." Unimpressed by Burnside's defence of him, she warns that "we work as a family. You and your pal Roach had better learn that, and learn it fast."

The varying patience levels of Burnside and Reid are exposed when they tackle a crime of savagery that is truly without parallel in Kevin Clarke's *Skeletons*. When a man reports noises coming from a supposedly deserted flat, Cathy Marshall sends in "the experts", in the form of Sun Hill's Watson and Holmes, Stamp and Hollis. They find it crammed with skeletons, all tagged and labelled. Some of the bones have been jumbled up, male and female remains merged into one. "We are about to go down in history, Tony," Reg enthuses at his less than delighted partner. Burnside puts into words what he has expressed with looks alone: "There's something very unhealthy about you, Hollis. I don't know what it is. You sounded like a dog with two wotsits on the PR." The maniac behind it all shows up and makes a run for it, but is soon cornered. "We've got Dennis Nilsen the Second here!" Burnside tells Tosh. Sadly, he must narrow his ambitions when he and his boss speak to the nonplussed killer – Ken Campbell at his nasal, droning best. "Elvis," he declares when asked for his name. "It's OK," Reid pacifies a hostile Burnside, indulging the King just as her predecessor soothed suspects the year before. "I know everything about Elvis... You see, I get the girls to call me Elvis and then I, uh, *do the songs for them*," he growls seductively while a baffled Reid stares at him, deadpan, in what must have been Carolyn Pickles' hardest acting challenge. He is in fact a lab technician who imported a job lot of skeletons on the cheap from the Philippines, hoping to flog them to medical students in need of practice. But "some of them got broken on the way over, so I needed somewhere to put them back together..." He shows Reid and Burnside a crate in his garage filled with "the rest of them", then hands over the (legit) paperwork, asking if they could overlook all this. "I mean it's not as if I've done anything wrong, is it?" he concludes, as they turn on him in disbelief.

Reid's most overt enemies may be in CID, but they are by no means her only ones. Easily triggered by anything new, her opposite number fears her high-level connections will eclipse him. Criticised for a rare use of initiative, Conway snaps, "Ever since Kim Reid came to this nick, I've had to take a back seat. Well fine, but I've kept this leaky ship afloat for a long time!" "There is nothing wrong with your career prospects," Brownlow assures him. "It would be nice to be told that now and then," he says, failing to realise it will sound more and more hollow with each passing year. "The vibes aren't exactly warm and inviting, Derek," Reid quips nervously when he later gives her the brush-off. "I'm not after a padded shoulder to cry on, Kim." After an unwitting Reg helps a car thief tow away a motor, Conway hauls him in for an earbashing. "I have bad dreams about you, Hollis. But even in my worst nightmares, you don't pull strokes like this... It's bad enough that we can't stop thousands of cars being nicked all over London every year. But the public, disillusioned and cynical though they may be about our performance, still don't expect us to function as accessories to acts of larceny!" When Conway learns from Ron Smollett that no info on hook-up thefts had been passed to uniform by CID, he spots a chance to put the boot in. In Reid's office he gives a prize performance, insisting "you could have knocked me down with a feather. I said, 'That's not the way Kim Reid's running CID, she's got that mob by the short and curlies'... One way or the other, the DAC's gonna hear about it; which is particularly unfortunate, given that he's been such a strong supporter of yours."

BENCHED

Given Carolyn Pickles' background as the daughter of a high-profile judge, James Pickles, it's ironic that her character is one of the few not to be eyeballing a beak this year. The sudden abundance of court stories is another sign of the need to economise, following the expensive move to Merton. The show's new courtroom set sees so much action throughout 1991 that we realise how absent they were up till now. Save for a brief scene of Galloway collecting an arrest warrant from a magistrate in Series 1's *The Drugs Raid*, we are kept out of court until the early half-hour episode *Witness*, where Taff gives evidence – unsuccessfully, natch – at a trial. It's no great surprise that the show had kept away from court proceedings, the same way it avoided undercover work. This territory had been well-traversed by other police dramas, and by the daytime show *Crown Court* for over a decade. *The Bill*'s M.O. was to get out into the real world, on the shoulders of the officers, following multiple plot strands at once. By its very nature, courtroom drama is static, defined by a rigid verbal and visual framework. At this point too, we are some way off the change in emphasis that would put regular characters in the dock as well as their customers. There, the drama derives from the gradual turning of the screws on someone we know is a thoroughly decent sort, like Tony Stamp; or Sally Johnson; or John Boulton; or Eddie Santini...

Hmm, maybe that's not the appeal after all. But in the early Nineties, the show puts the police on trial in every other way besides literally forcing them into the box. It's the criminal classes who are being tried – and usually being acquitted. This is the unwritten bind of courtroom stories; a 'twist' is only really possible through a failure, meaning it's the police's errors that are held up and picked apart when someone gets off scot free.

But the devil is in the detail, and this is what *The Bill* was made for. Mike's rant at the CSU in *Grief* highlights the importance and the conflict in paperwork, which the show latched onto as it recognised the increasing 'professionalisation' of the police and maintained for a commendably long time. Rather than stick to courtroom battles, it looks at the ground on which they lie: digging below the surface of the justice system to ask why the same assumptions, and mistakes, are continually made. This is the ground covered so well by serialised twenty-first century shows like *The Wire* and *Spiral*, which over ten episodes take in the view of the police and the courts and how the two overlap and influence one another. In spite of a completely different format of self-contained episodes, *The Bill* was equally well placed to take this 'big picture' view, each story highlighting a connected aspect of the same problem. Every good result we see is stage one in a long haul; a case weighed and measured before it is submitted for prosecution has to be weighed again by the lawyers to meet the threshold for success. And once it reaches court, the issues are only beginning. In Peter J. Hammond's *Machines*, the efforts of Roach to put away a fraudster are hampered by his defence team's claim of a medical condition, peritonitis of the kidneys, which has kept him away from the committal hearing. "It's my bet they'll try for a further remand," says the prosecuting counsel, "with bail again." "That can go *on and on* until it no longer looks like a triable offence!" Roach explodes. "Which means we can't take it to a higher court, because some clever bastard will start saying that a long remand is sentence enough! And why was this case switched to a bench? Because a stipendiary wouldn't have put up with this, he'd have seen right through the bull!" "You'll have to thank Price's solicitor for that one... Let's say she know her courts, and when to keep her clients away from the stipes. It's just a matter of ducking and diving at the right times, we all do it." "Do we?" asks an acid Ted.

It turns out that the magistrate chairing that day's bench is none other than a member of the General Medical Council, and therefore inclined to look sympathetically on a medical ailment. Despite the prosecutor's request that he be committed to trial at a higher court straight away, the magistrate insists that Price is given the chance to present his case in person first, and bail is duly granted. Sneering that he "plugs himself in and out of the mains whenever it suits him", Roach sets out to prove that Price is faking his illness and stakes out his home. "I bet he's in there now with his feet up, a glass of Scotch in his hand, laughing at us and toasting to British justice... To think I paid my national insurance contributions all these years to support toerags like him. Haven't got a pair of pliers, have you?" he asks Jim hopefully. "You could get up on the roof and disconnect his electricity supply." They seek the advice of an ex-DS from Sun Hill who was invalided out of the job after a brutal assault that left him needing dialysis four times a day. But the ties of a life-changing condition are nothing to those of the cloth; he recommends they "make him sweat", talk to neighbours and locals without hiding it, to panic him into error. It seems to work when a woman runs into Price's home and they leave together, driving away at top speed. Roach and Carver give pursuit until the car crashes; its hysterical driver rages at them, desperate to get her father to hospital because his dialysis machine has failed. But with Hammond at the helm, there is no pat ending in which we learn the importance of not jumping to conclusions. "What about the warrant?" Jim asks as Price is wheeled off to a hospital ward. "What's the point? He's just bought himself another six months' freedom," observes Ted – and sure enough, Price is well enough to give them an airy wave goodbye from his trolley.

Each time the courtroom beckons, the use of a defendant's name is misleading: a better title would be 'The Metropolitan Police vs The Crown Prosecution Service'. The real battlefield is outside court, a tribal war more bitter than that of uniform and CID. The two sides have their own culture and rules that they guard jealously. When prosecution lawyers explain the latest tactics of the defence it's couched in admiration for the skill of their opposite number; the police, who only face one way rather than two, are unimpressed by this professional detachment. One writer in particular, Carolyn Sally Jones, specialises in the clash between the police and 'the experts'. *In*

Chambers sees DS Greig visit the CPS office to discuss an upcoming arson case. "You know your CPS onions Alistair, there's no denying that," says Tosh. "Yeah, you don't get files back marked 'try harder'," Viv adds bitterly. But the only CID officer, save Mike Dashwood, who could socialise with the legal fraternity without being asked to top up their glasses is still well out of his element. Told he can't park in the space reserved for the head of chambers, Greig meets the foppish barrister assigned to the case, his first priority to tot up the expenses on his last job. "Must be odd making the switch from defending to prosecuting, sir." "Oh, it's all play-acting, isn't it?" he drawls, to a stony look from Alistair. The arsonist now admits that he started the fire but claims not to be of sound mind. A psychiatrist arrives, is introduced to DS "Alan" Greig, and comments on the weaknesses of British law: "There's no doubt he's suffering from a serious psychiatric disorder." "So, you'd side with the defence psychiatrist?" "That's the trouble with an adversarial system, experts are supposed to take 'sides.' I'm just here to give you my unbiased opinion." Greig realises the plea of diminished responsibility could work. "You must look like miracle workers, doctor, to devious bastards like that," he remarks venomously. The embarrassed CPS man beside him realises that Alistair is a copper at heart.

The sense of people enacting a ritual continues in Jones' next episode, *Jobs for the Boys*, which focuses on the front line of the legal profession and the legacy of Tom Penny's 'that'll do' approach. Stamp and Datta bring in a conman suspected of breaking into an antiques shop and Tony calls in Ray Baker to act as his brief. "He never gives us any aggro, does he? Sgt. Penny used him a lot. Good as gold, is Ray. I mean there's some briefs that like dragging things out – it's a bit of an ego boost, and a waste of taxpayers' money." When Baker arrives, he is all smiles with the PCs, handing out gum and laughing with them about old cases. This is brought to a halt by the new deputy in town: John Maitland, the young, ultra-orthodox sergeant who even Monroe wishes would lighten up a bit. Baker immediately advises his client to put his hands up, as per usual, so he can move on in search of his next fee. Maitland declares he is not happy and wants further investigations: "I don't like tame briefs." It transpires that this conman 'swapped' jobs with an accomplice, committing a much bigger robbery and using the smaller one as an alibi. Baker returns, asking why time is being wasted on a guilty plea, only to learn he nearly perverted the course of justice. Realising that Tony wants to distance himself from him, Baker reveals that he saw an illegal pocket search in custody earlier. "Now I could have kicked up a fuss over that, but no – I keep my mouth shut, like I always do. Only it's not appreciated any more, is it? Even if you don't make trouble, certain people treat you like you're some kind of bad smell, now why is that?" "Maybe because you're *supposed* to make trouble," Tony replies tellingly. The adversarial system extends to police stations as well as the courts.

The police's animus towards the Criminal Protection Society comes to a head in *With Intent*. Jim Carver and Tosh Lines, working on an aggravated burglary, learn that the original solicitor is ill and have to deal with his replacement, Mr Meed, who sees "problems" with their two main suspects. "Would you believe it, they've done it to us again," snarls Jim. "Sent us a two-bob lawyer who doesn't give a toss what happens!" The suspects are willing to plead guilty, but only to criminal damage and ABH. Jim can't believe it when he is told there isn't enough for more substantial charges. Nor is the photocopied medical report he submitted admissible as evidence; he was sent a request for the original, but like Dashwood before him, never got it. On his return to Sun Hill, he continues to rant about being saddled with "some pillock from the agency." "It's impossible to use in-house lawyers every time though, Jim," Greig points out. "Look at the courts they have to cover." After another unhappy visit to the Crime Support Group, where he finds the mislaid correspondence, Jim suggests that "stuff gets sent over by carrier pigeon next time, it seems we haven't quite got the hang of the fax!" With perfect timing, he is sent to a seminar where the hapless assistant branch prosecutor, Robert Hayward, has been given the unenviable task of explaining, and defending, CPS procedure to a room of sceptical officers. "I hope this isn't going to end up in a lot of personal axe-grinding," a worried Reid tells Conway beforehand. "I don't blame them for wanting to let off steam, do you?" he replies. Hayward declines Brownlow's offer of a drink, saying he needs his wits about him: "I've got my flak jacket ready. They make it regulation wear on occasions like this."

Hayward opens with a history lesson on the origins of the Crown Prosecution Service – the reform that hit the police at the same time as PACE, in 1986, providing Series 3 of *The Bill* with two gift-wrapped topics from which to make hay. Its primary goal was to relieve the pressure on overworked police departments and their legal teams. "Because you were trying to be two hundred people at once, too many weak cases reached court. Nobody knew which legal criteria to apply; officers wrote statements on the back of cigarette packets. Well, you'll notice that doesn't happen any more. Nowadays we send you hundreds of forms... It must seem like a never-ending pain in the neck. Am I right?" Roach challenges the idea that police knowledge of a suspect's form is prejudicial to a new offence. "Isn't there something to be said for that old adage, 'Let the courts decide'?" "It's a very old adage, indeed; it encourages a certain laxness in officers. Why weigh up all the evidence when you can just have a slanging match in court?" His frustration boiling over, Carver starts to heckle Hayward: "You only back odds-on favourites. You cover your backs, don't you?" "It's a fallacy, this belief that we only back winners. If you look at the code, you'll see that all we ask for is a realistic prospect of a conviction." "Well maybe we should turn back the clock, to a time when we did our own prosecuting. Because one way or another, we're getting a second-rate service; the CSG doesn't know its arse from its elbow half the time, there's no communication, there's no backup!" His discontent spreads to other officers, and an annoyed Reid tells him in private to listen to the answers. Conway sits on the fence, agreeing that the CPS do good work but pining for the days of his own prosecuting. "Of course, if it was a complicated case, we'd call in our own legal aid service to give a bit of advice – and I must say, we had a pride in the reports we sent in to them. They were works of art!" "And occasionally, if you'll forgive me Chief Inspector, they were works of fiction. Only nobody mentioned it because in those days, when a police officer said 'jump', the lawyer said, 'how high?'"

Back on the offensive, Jim argues that isolated instances of cases falling through are in fact the norm. "Like this morning, getting some second-rate lawyer who bottles it out, lets the defence get away with every dirty trick in the book. I start wondering whose side you're on!" His tirade is only curbed when the "second-rate" Meed shows up and turns out to be another senior crown prosecutor. "When did you get your law degree, Jim?" Reid asks scathingly afterwards. "Night school was it, or was it some kind of correspondence course?" Taking him into her office, she announces an immediate ban on overtime: "I've been there Jim, I've done it, seen it, got the T-shirt. Live this job every waking hour and you're in the funny farm." The legacy of an era in which the police had unrestrained control of the legal side, resulting in the miscarriages of justice exposed at this time, is a system split into two branches, with all the issues of communication and clashing perspectives that this brings. The episode stops short of endorsing Jim's view that things are now skewed in favour of the criminal – but it does observe that the two wings of the law have very different priorities. Getting 'personally involved' is not that mythical danger of cop show cliché, but an unavoidable result of the police's dealings with crime and its devastating effect. This meshes awkwardly with the clinical view of prosecutors, examining facts months after the event; objectivity, always a prized quality, has its downside too. Hayward's observation of the difficulty, in law, of establishing criminal intent shows how the most traumatic experience in one sphere of life becomes a theoretical exercise in another.

MORAL MINORITY

Carver's outburst at the CPS is interrupted by that of a woman whose grievance makes his look like the pettiest of quibbles. When June Ackland tells Hayward that the system has failed her, she has every reason. In the wake of his serial killer storyline from the previous year, Christopher Russell strings together another masterpiece, this time on one woman's fight for justice. He also provides arguably the show's most in-depth look at a perennial problem. The first instalment, *Fear or Favour*, opens with those two likeable stalwarts of the Nineties, Tony Stamp and Dave Quinnan, subject to a racial harassment complaint by Everton Warwick, a community representative of the notorious Jasmine Allen estate. It's only in this year that Russell's creation really becomes the bugbear to Sun Hill that it would be through most of the show's life. At parade, Monroe instructs the relief to ensure they handle themselves with courtesy and tact when policing the estate. Once they are gone, Cryer protests at the implication that "this relief is suddenly full of racists... It's like football. Active players, the ones that get stuck in, well they're going to get a booking now and then, it's inevitable. And it's the same with active policemen." "So, it's all right for Stamp and Quinnan to push the likes of Everton Warwick around and call them bastard spades?" Monroe challenges him. "Allegedly call them." "Allegedly, of course – the classic defence of the crafty copper. Sit tight, say nothing, and they can't touch you." "Well, it works for the criminals, why shouldn't we have the same rights?"

The issue is given added perspective by the newest member of the relief, the motormouthed Delia French. The former head of the civilian typing pool, who terrorised CID with her blistering rants on their sloppy paperwork in 1989's *Don't Like Mondays*, passes through training at Hendon and returns as a fully-fledged WPC in 1990. To paraphrase Russell's title, Delia is a woman without fear or filter. When she backchats both Ackland and her supervisor Alec Peters on her first day, she is warned she is no longer a big fish in a small pond but part of a disciplined service and must follow orders. She is, however, free with her views on the history of ethnic recruitment when she reveals that a relative was turned down by the Met: "There were only certain jobs immigrants were allowed to do, even though he'd done ten years on the beat back in Kingston. Can't help wondering, you know: would race be such a problem now if they'd recruited black bobbies way back in the Fifties?" "It's not an easy job," Brownlow cautions her, "especially for somebody with a black skin. We have to accept that." "I have no problems with my skin," Delia declares with the beaming sincerity Natasha Williams brings to her role. "If other people have, that's down to them; I intend to give this job one hundred per cent." But other people's problems have a habit of becoming yours. Cautiously, Delia asks her brother officers what the complaint is about. They explain they were called to a car theft on the estate and were questioning a suspect when Warwick suddenly popped up to harangue them. "He must have radar," says Tony. "Any arrest within a mile radius and Warwick or his mates are there discussing your parentage." "So, we discussed his," Dave adds bluntly.

The management is trying to build bridges, as part of the Met's real life Plus Programme of reforms, launched the previous year. Brownlow, Conway and Reid meet Warwick, his friend Rice and a local councillor, Lawrence Joseph. The youths are unimpressed by this charm offensive, shaking Reid's hand limply. Joseph is straight on the attack: "What is Everton to think of his chances of getting justice when your own statistics are against you? More than three hundred cases of racial harassment in the last three years and only one per cent of officers involved get disciplined. *One* per cent? Does this mean that ninety-nine per cent of black people are liars?" "To your people on the streets we're still crap and that's how you'll go on treating us!" Warwick declares, which ignites Conway's temper. "That does cut both ways – our officers are a constant target!" Brownlow drags them back to the wider issues of policing Jasmine Allen, but faces more criticism for heavy-handed tactics and sudden TSG raids. "If pushed too hard," Joseph warns, "members of our community may also start acting without consultation." Brownlow later describes Conway's input as "not the most constructive I've seen you make", pointing out that two years ago the likes of Warwick and Joseph would not have set foot willingly in a police station. Conway is having none of it. "We both know crime is flourishing on Jasmine Allen – not big crime, admittedly. Crime we turn a blind eye to. And when the crime gets a little bit too big, and we act, what do we get? Co-operation? Community understanding? No! We get a bollocking from Councillor Joseph, and a threat! He's virtually telling us to keep out. Policing is a very simple thing. You screw the ones who deserve it, and you help the ones who don't, and you do that on the Jasmine Allen estate just as anywhere else – without fear or favour!"

Tony and Delia have drawn the short straw; "I hate this place," the former tells the latter as they set off on foot patrol of the JA. With the misanthropy that only years in the police can formulate, he observes, "I don't mind the architecture. I suspect it looked quite impressive as a model. It's just a pity they had to move people in and spoil it." On a walkway, he measures the progress of the last two years in slightly different terms: "Two years ago they would have dropped a telly on your head if you walked under these. They don't drop tellies any more; they've all got new ones." They pay a visit to a sympathiser, a middle-aged black man called Monty who is happy to "make tea for Babylon now and again" because of his concerns over the growing drug problem. When Tony spots a deal in progress, he convinces the doubtful Delia they can make a quick, low-profile arrest, which turns into a full-on disaster. Chasing the dealer through the estate, Tony sees him run into a club guarded by Rice and his mates, insisting they won't allow anyone in. Delia begs Tony to pull out, but he insists he's not leaving without a body. "You got a body, Babylon," Warwick purrs menacingly as he appears from nowhere. "Keep it." When back-up arrives, Tony and Delia are being chased by a raging mob.

In the darkness of the garages, a scuffle breaks out in which Ackland is punched in the stomach and face by Warwick. She is bundled into the car with Delia and the troops are hastily extracted from the 'Nam. The full scale of the problem becomes apparent at the nick, when Peters is charging Warwick and learns there are two witnesses to the attack: PCs Stamp and Quinnan. "So, this is policing without fear or favour, is it?" Brownlow asks Conway. "Acting on your personal instructions, was he? Stamp. He couldn't have made a better hash of it if he had been."

Delia too has taken the first knock to her confidence. In floods of tears, she admits she lost the bag of drugs that was their only evidence. "I was so hyped up to do well this week, then I was no bloody good when all the trouble started, I know that! They could have done anything... anything, and I couldn't have stopped them... I was like an observer, you know? Pathetic..." "You're not pathetic, you've got plenty of bottle," Cryer reassures her. "What happened today is different. It takes a lot of getting used to. Pure hate, it shakes you up." When he asks if Tony was "doing his Lone Ranger bit", she gamely insists he did nothing wrong; she, of course, must work harder than most to prove whose side she is on. The injured Ackland, told, "It's lucky that you weren't pregnant", is sent to hospital by the FME, who doubts that a charge of GBH will stick. "The injuries are worth an ABH, no question. Are your witnesses, that's the point?" Brownlow wants Peters to bail Warwick as soon as he is charged, worried at the damaging picture of him being the police's sole arrest. A scene of angry exchanges that had a long life, shots of Brownlow and Cryer reused in the opening titles for years, is stolen by Larry Dann as Alec throws a 'Can you believe this?' look at his fellow skipper. "Aren't we forgetting something?" Bob demands. "June Ackland has been assaulted! She was punched in the face, whacked in the stomach. She may be permanently damaged for all we know. And all I've heard since then is, 'Ah, are we sure, can we prove it, why have we arrested him, what about his friends?' I don't give a *toss* about his friends. A police officer has been hurt!" "Of course I'm concerned about June Ackland," Brownlow hits back. "I'm also concerned for the welfare of life and property in this borough. And I do not need you to teach me my responsibilities, thank you sergeant."

Meanwhile, Conway gets straight to the point: "Are you a racist, Stamp? Only whenever there's a point of friction with the black community, you're the piece of grit they're rubbing up against. Would you like a transfer to Aberystwyth?" "No thank you, sir. I hate the Welsh." "You are a racist then." "Only against the Welsh. Otherwise, the only people I hate are slag – black, white, pink, green, the colour's immaterial." Brownlow suggests that he escort June to hospital, "As it was effectively you who put her there." But Tony only realises the wider cost of what has happened when he drops June off at casualty and sees his ally, Monty, being stretchered in by paramedics. "I fell down the stairs," he insists. The "political implications" that Brownlow hints at begin to unfold in subsequent episodes. When he learns from Reid that the case papers have been returned by the CPS, "discontinued in the public interest", he opines that this is probably for the best. "I'm not sure that's how Ackland will see it, sir." At an Area meeting with DAC Hicks, he reassures him that everything is quiet on the estate at present, only to be told there is a whisper of "something being orchestrated London-wide, on certain estates – and one of those estates is Jasmine Allen. The community initiative on Jasmine Allen means a lot to us at Area. It would be a pity to see it go up in flames: metaphorically or literally." Learning that the officer concerned will probably want to take the issue further, Hicks asks, "Why, does she have a querulous nature? Perhaps your 'very sound' officer could be encouraged to take the wider view. We are here to preserve the social and physical fabric of the capital. We do that through team spirit: by shrugging our shoulders, not by developing chips on them."

But June is unwilling to accept the big picture, even when told she could set off the "tinderbox" that is Jasmine Allen. "You have to ask yourself which is the more important, the possible loss of life and property or you pursuing your pound of flesh?" "It's not a pound of flesh sir, you're being totally unfair! I don't see how denying someone the right to justice can possibly be for the greater good, not in the long term!" Warwick is facing two months suspended at worst if found guilty: "How can that *possibly* be an excuse for mayhem? It's blackmail, on you and on me, and it's dishonest to pretend otherwise! Whose public interest are we talking about anyway? The ones who might get in the way of the petrol bombs; or senior officers at Area, who do sod all for community relations except write papers about it?"

"Disappointed" at her attitude, Brownlow acknowledges her negative feelings about the job in the wake of Gordon Wray; and June proceeds to show him what a querulous nature looks like. If, as argued in Volume 1, Trudie Goodwin in full flight is the best the show has to offer, one shouldn't overlook that characteristic touch of Peter Ellis – the head bowed in defeat that signals, *Oh God, she's off on one*. "Actually sir, I do have 'negative feelings' about the job at the moment – and they have nothing to do with my sex life! They have to do with questions like, 'What the hell are we doing, and why the hell are we doing it?' And it seems to me that all we're doing is screwing up other people's lives! And if we're not doing that, we're letting other people screw ours up, by assaulting us! It seems to me, as a humble foot-soldier, that *nineteen thousand* assaults a year on plods and plonks is a good few thousand too many. And as far as I'm concerned, if the CPS won't prosecute, then I will. I shall take out a private summons against Mr Warwick – and if Area don't like it, they can write a paper on it. And you know what they can do with their paper!" As a chastened Brownlow informs Hicks by phone: "I'm afraid you rather overestimated my powers of persuasion."

The next chapter, *Saints and Martyrs*, highlights the thankless task June has taken on by pursuing her claim. With a further appeal to the CPS rejected, her only option is a private prosecution, at her own cost. She asks Reg if the Federation can contribute and is told "they should be able to come up with something in a defence situation", but not in other circumstances. Unsurprisingly he wants to turn it into a political issue, emphasising the lack of support from management, and is keen to check that she isn't backing out. "You've got a wider responsibility here, you know." "My only responsibility is to myself," she corrects him sharply. She is then sounded out by Cryer, who points out that she had little hope of keeping her private summons private: "Consult Reg Hollis, consult the world!" Bob asks if she's thought it through. "If you want to throw away five hundred quid on a barrister that's up to you. What exactly do you think you're going to win?" The woman who isn't trying to be a moral exemplar ends up speaking for every officer in the force when she declares, "The right not to be used as a punchbag!" "Your card will be marked. You will be the WPC that put two fingers up to the system. If you've got any ambition left in the job, think about it – carefully." Hurt by the attitude of someone she thought would be an ally, June insists she will take her chances. Later, Cryer suggests to Reg that June has never got the support she needed, hence her now being out on a limb. "She ain't out on a limb! You ask anyone in this station, we're right behind her, one hundred per cent!" "Right behind her?" Cryer scoffs. "Canteen cowboys, egging her on from a safe distance?"

Brownlow attends a further Area meeting about Jasmine Allen, where a press officer puts the cold, calculating bottom line: "If Warwick went down, riots, either spontaneous or manufactured, would be on the cards. But if that was as a result of the full and fair process of the law, the PR damage would be sustainable. Certainly more sustainable than what might result from the alternative. If you keep putting the squeeze on this stroppy WPC to pull out, who's to say she won't squeal? There's plenty of newspapers, quality and tabloid, not entirely in love with us. They'll have a field day. Whatever the truth of the matter, you're talking another big dent in the image of the Met. She's likely to lose the damn case anyway, why don't you just let her go ahead?" Finally, the Chief Super summons his missing backbone: "No sir, I don't think she should be allowed to go ahead. I think she should be positively encouraged to. She is not 'stroppy'; she is an efficient, conscientious and loyal officer. She feels badly let down, not by the CPS, but by senior management. It seems to me that we expect an awful lot from our foot-soldiers. We control their lives whether they like it or not, both on and off duty, we never let them forget that they're police officers. June Ackland accepts the high standards we set, and she lives by them; it seems to me she's entitled to expect loyalty and support in return. If we're going to put image and damage limitation first, and police officers second, then morale in this force is going to reach the rock bottom that we deserve." Cryer is surprised at Brownlow's return, thinking he would have stayed for lunch. "No, I might have got ground glass in my soup," he mutters darkly. He calls June into his office and this time promises that he will support her "to the hilt, in any way that I can. Now that may not amount to very much, but at least I can assure you there'll be no repercussions career-wise. Not while I'm your chief superintendent." Gobsmacked, June thanks him and the episode ends in a rare moment of happiness for her, grinning from ear to ear.

With *The Bill*'s usual prescience, a story about the sacrifice of individuals to "the wider view" was quickly mirrored in real life. *The Public Interest*, in which Hicks raises the spectre of mass riots on the Jasmine Allen, was transmitted four days after the beating of Rodney King by Los Angeles police officers, captured by a witness on a camcorder. The chain of events in L.A. over the next four years echoes all the beats, predicted and real, of this storyline: rioting followed by a high-profile court case in which the police's actions, not the accused's, were decisive. When Stamp arrives to support June at the magistrate's court in *The Best You Can Buy*, she has to remind him that "this isn't us and them – it's me against Warwick." He proves her point by assuming the black barrister he sees is Warwick's brief, when she is June's. On the stand he declares his confidence that Warwick's complaint against him will be dismissed. Quinnan backs up Stamp and is sure afterwards that they are winning. "Pity you couldn't have done it without smiling all the time," notes a disapproving Monroe. The defence's tactic is to malign both witnesses, arguing that in the dim light June made a mistaken ID that they reinforced because of their prejudice. The prosecutor does her best to smear Warwick in return, pointing out his three previous convictions in the last three years. "And on each of these occasions, you pleaded not guilty: is that correct, Mr Warwick?" Reminded of a previous complaint of racial harassment, he admits, "Yes, it was dismissed – they were all dismissed. What chance have we got against Babylon?" he proclaims, playing to the gallery that has cheered him into the witness box. Even June is briefly convinced by his barrister's theory that "she glimpsed a face – and that her colleagues' certainty became her certainty." "You sit there listening to the defence and half the time you wonder whether you imagined it all," she muses.

The relief file into court hoping for a victory that instead becomes a wake. Having prefigured the OJ Simpson case, the story echoes the scenes of a divided America after that not guilty verdict: every white face dismayed, every black face jubilant, save those linked to the police. "Can we move?" Tony snaps as they watch Warwick's team celebrate. "It's a travesty, whole system's on their side," he rants in the corridor. "I'll have him next time. I'll do a really professional job." Ackland is straight on his case: "You mean you will fit him up?" "June, he's given you a hiding and walked away from it!" "Yeah, why?"

114

"Because what is laughingly called 'the criminal justice system' has got naff all to do with justice. It's all about poncy briefs playing word games!" "No, it's all about juries listening to people like you and thinking: I bet he can tell porkies if he has to. If you want a jury to believe you, then tell the truth – *every* time, even when it hurts!" The use of those legends, Dave 'n Tone, as the weakness that drags down the police is significant. For a start, at this early stage in their history they are not 'the mainstream' they later became. But more to the point, it doesn't have to be the extremist Mark Fuhrmans of the police that end up tainting its image in public eyes. June Ackland, the punchbag turned political football, follows up the purest ever expression of her standards with a heartbreaking attempt to downplay them. "No, there's nothing to drown," she assures Cryer, declining a visit to the pub. "I gave it a go; that's it. You did warn me." On the steps she runs into Warwick, in a huddle with his mates. He steps aside for her in the tiniest acknowledgement of his guilt. But there are no verbals, and no promises to get even; June must abide by her own principles. Offering a terse "Thanks", she walks away as the party begins. The moral high ground is a lonely and unrewarding place, as the show so often demonstrates – and at the summit, June is lonelier than most.

Trudie Goodwin did not enjoy the half-hour episodes as much as the hours[22] – and if one looks at the first eighteen months of half-hours it could be argued, in a supreme irony, that the only two characters who are slightly underserved are June *et* Jim. But as the action shifts to Merton, she gets a heftier role in proceedings, and in the Chinese calendar 1991 is the Year of the Perm: twelve months that open with June assaulted and denied justice, and end with her being held hostage by an escaped con and his deranged lover, also fit in an armed siege where she plays a central role. J.C. Wilsher's two-parter *Cold Turkey* differs from those that have gone before in that the action follows on continuously, giving it the feel of an hour-long episode sawn in half. The detective work is confined mainly to Part 1, in which a series of crimes are connected to an addict suffering from barbiturate withdrawal who takes refuge in the flat of his partner and her child. Tony thinks he is dealing with a domestic as he calls through the letterbox. "If there's one thing that really gets on my box,

---

[22] *Crocker, Oliver, Witness Statements: Making The Bill 1988* (2022), p. 104

it's dumb insolence; slag just ignoring you," he whinges, and almost has his face taken off when a knife is thrust out at him. With Conway taking charge on the ground, June is asked to deploy her training as the relief's fallback negotiator. She is installed in the flat next door with the ultimate siege-breaker, Reg Hollis: "Just you and me, and the hotline." "Do you think Conway'd agree to swapping me for the hostage?" The addict, Barry Cutler, is getting increasingly wound up by the activity outside. "While we're talking, nothing bad's going to happen," June promises him over the phone. Trying to build empathy, she asks him about his past life, and he reveals that, "People have been telling me not to worry since I was a kid. I'm the sort of bloke, I walk down the street and old dears say to me, 'Cheer up love, it may never happen.'" "They say that to me sometimes," June observes. "It comes of taking things on board too much. You start feeling you're responsible for everybody else's problems."

The police try to rush Cutler but only enrage him further. Conway radios Brownlow, saying he wants PT-17 to take Cutler out, and the Chief Super backs him up: "Yes, Derek. Shoot him." "You heard it," Conway tells Tony in the area car. "You log it." Reg passes a note to June that expands the role of negotiator to that of game beater. Hearing the child crying of thirst, she says hollowly, "You must be thirsty too, Barry. Why don't you get yourself a drink? You go to the bathroom, you get a drink for yourself and Micky and come back and talk, that's what matters." We see the marksman's POV as Cutler sets the child down. The moment he moves to the window, a shot rings out. TSG break into the flat and the boy and mother are removed safely. Conway finds June with her eyes screwed up, holding the hand of Reg, the station joke, for comfort. The boss offers his hand, and she snatches hers away, rushing out in fury. Cryer, having been in her shoes lately, urges her to see the bigger picture: "It was a damn sight better result than we had any right to expect. Thank God we pulled the plug when we did." "Who's we?" demands June. "I did it to him! I've never touched firearms, I've never wanted to, I'd jack this job in if we went armed!" "Now look: stop wallowing in your own grief and think of other people," she is reproved; somehow, caring too much ends up looking like selfishness. "From the moment the DAC sanctioned firearms, he was responsible for a death. Mr Brownlow didn't have to turn up, but he put his fingerprints on it. Then there's

116

the boy who pulled the trigger." "So, there's a whole load of people with bad dreams stored up, is that supposed to make me feel better?" Wilsher looks at the reforms to the use of firearms in more detail later in the year. Does the transfer of power away from the frontline officer just spread the guilt among others? Ironically, the boy who did pull the trigger may be sleeping the easiest of everyone that night.

If Tom Penny proved what could be achieved from looking at the amoral middle, then June Ackland is exhibit number one of what the goodies are worth, when examined in depth. Trudie Goodwin never phones in a performance, never misses a beat of truth in the role. She brings to life the fascinating paradox that runs through June: the hardness and cynicism of someone who is really anything but a cynic, who has a bigger heart and hopes than anyone else. She is ready to believe the best of people and situations until they disappoint her. And, we see again and again, she gets no reward for highlighting what is wrong; this isn't a 'woman in a man's world' who gets to bamboozle the boys with a few quips. Still deemed a misery by most around her, she fights the same battles repeatedly, which is a truer reflection of the graft for many women in the workplace. But there is no other option for someone with POLICE stamped through her – as Barry Appleton, who fleshed out the character in her early days, observes in *Kids Don't Cry Anymore*. Finding a child's lunchbox with a notebook recording drug deals – "and my mum used to think the Rolling Stones were a threat" – June goes to the local school to identify the boy. His teacher is emphatic that she cannot disclose names. June spots a drawing of a racing car that matches one in the notebook, and feigns an interest in the kids' artwork. "You know it's funny, when I was a kid I always used to draw these quaint little cottages – you know, blue sky, smoke billowing out of the chimney. I suppose it was the kind of nice little home I wanted when I grew up. Now *that* kid knows what he wants." "Oh yes, Louis Boosey, he wants to be a racing driver." Realising she has been conned, the teacher observes that June made the right career move. "Well, I forgot to mention – that little house I used to draw when I was a kid. Used to have a little blue and white police car parked in the driveway."

OUT OF SIGHT

While *The Bill* continues to push the boundaries of its 8pm timeslot during 1991, one type of story arguably proves that it works better in that family slot, where things can only be told, not shown. The show is unstinting in its exploration of sexual crime, the nasty details rarely compromised by its PG rating. This is where *The Bill*'s police-only perspective comes up trumps. By following the officers after the crime has occurred, the truth is uncovered in words rather than images: a slow, creeping revelation of the unpleasant, not a graphic depiction of it. In Arthur McKenzie's *The Girl Can't Help It*, Ackland and Quinnan learn of a missing fourteen-year-old girl, Veronique, who has been gone five days without her parents reporting it – not for the first time. "She's always come back," her mother assures them. Confined to a wheelchair, the embittered father tells Dave she "does what she bloody well likes, and what can I do in this thing?" Dave finds a diary hidden in her room, between the movie posters and childhood toys, and passes it to Monroe with the warning that "it's not the sort of thing you want to leave lying around for anyone to read. It's obvious she's on the game... Some things get through sometimes, don't they?" In the canteen, cryptic details emerge about why this case has struck a chord with him. "I got sisters, June. When my old man screwed off, I saw what happened to them. The youngest, especially the youngest, I saw what happened to her. I won't forget having to chase her halfway round the country. She won't get over it. He destroyed her. And that bastard destroyed the whole family, and I'll never forgive him for that, *never!*" Up till now McKenzie has presented Quinnan as a fairly unlovable rogue; without being explicit, he suggests that Dave's affable, blokey persona is partly a shell to cover up a traumatic past.

Dave tries to break the news to Veronique's father, only for him to admit he has known for some time. "I've seen them drop her off... Have you any idea what that does to you? Blokes in *suits!?*" It is Burnside who finds her by accident, courtesy of his infatuation with Brownlow's secretary Marion, an odd thread that runs through McKenzie's scripts. They are having lunch in a restaurant when he spots a teenage girl, dolled up to the nines, with a man thirty years her senior. When uniform arrive, her prospective buyer is dismayed to learn that she is only fourteen but was clearly in no hurry to ask. Begging not to be involved, he tells Cryer he's a married man. "Aren't we all?" comes the loaded reply as he is led past the other diners. At the station the unrepentant Veronique claims she knows what she is doing. "You're too young to understand. You need us," her father insists. The family's newest breadwinner gives a chilling reply: "No – you need me." Adamant that she won't go into care, she triggers a scathing lecture from June: "Well you'd better do some pretty serious thinking hadn't you, because that's where you're going to end up if you can't be controlled! Don't think you've got it all sussed, my girl, because you haven't. I've seen dozens of little girls like you, and I've seen where they end up. Believe me, it's not very nice. You heard of AIDS? Do you know what can happen to prostitutes? Well don't look like that, that's what you are! You're a little prostitute – and they end up in the gutter, with heroin habits and beaten-up faces. They won't be taking you to West End parties, they'll be taking you to the casualty department at the hospital, if you're lucky." Suddenly acting her age, Veronique whines "Dad!", seeking protection from the nasty grownup. Then she falls back on a more recently learned reflex, smiling at Quinnan – who replies flatly, "Don't do that."

It's not long, however, before the show adopts a different, and daring, perspective on underage sex. While June fights for justice in *The Public Interest* she investigates another wayward teenage girl, a fifteen-year-old living with someone three times her age. The predator turns out to be an innocuous man in a golf jumper, who insists they are aware of the age of consent and decided together that it didn't matter. "I'm not sure that's your decision to make, Mr Townsend," PC Stringer comments. The girl, Becky, makes it plain she is there of her own free will and does not want a medical exam or the input of her despised mother. This time it's parent, not child, who is the hardened professional. Dragged away from a "customer", she sits coolly in front of Inspector Monroe, declaring she has no control over her daughter and no idea where the father is. "She's always had boyfriends," Becky explains to Ackland. "Well, she calls them boyfriends, but she's on the game more often than not. They used to give me the eye and all. And a bit more if they got the chance." Her mother gives her assent to the exam out of pure spite. Once it is over, Becky declares, "I feel like I've been raped. Gerry's never raped me. You know what the best thing in the world is? It's when we snuggle down in bed at night, and I'm lying there in the warm and the dark, listening. There's a pub at the end of the road and you hear them at chucking-out time. You hear them going past, shouting and swearing, fighting sometimes. Men and women. And I'm lying there with Gerry and I think: poor bastards."

119

With home not an option, the child protection team can only go for a place of safety order. "Look, she has care with Townsend," June insists. "She has genuine affection and security. We won't be stopping abuse by taking her away from him, we'll be causing it!" What could be condemned on one level as dangerous vindication for paedophiles is simply a comment that one size does not fit all; adamant there must be a victim, the system ends up creating one. "Letter of the law equals public interest in Mr Monroe's book; all very simple," notes June. "Still," she adds bitterly, "Becky Curtis has nothing to complain about. We've got her a social worker and a bed in a children's home. What more could she want?"

The use of the care system as the Sword of Damocles in the above episodes is no coincidence; it was in a Christopher Russell story two years earlier, *The Key of the Door*, that a worried mother pointed out the local children's home was nicknamed "the rent office." A related concern is examined in *Too Many Chiefs*, the debut of one of the early Nineties' best writers, Tony Etchells. Returning an absconder to "home sweet home" – only to see her run straight past them as they leave – PCs Marshall and Quinnan are called to a suicide on an upstairs floor. The overdosed girl, Caroline, had made an allegation of sexual abuse against her father, then against a worker in another home, and as a result was moved to a place for young offenders awaiting trial. Monroe speaks to the assistant director of social services, Mrs Randle, who fits the mould of the harassed middle-aged woman we see on front pages after a major abuse scandal. The young and dashing home manager, Paul Walsh, is about to resign from overwork. "Wouldn't this normally be handled by Mr Walsh's principal officer, rather than yourself?" "Shortage of staff. He finds it rather difficult to be in six places at once." She complains to Brownlow about the media feeding frenzy the police have set off. "The multi-agency approach is supposed to be us working together. Do you know how much mileage the opposition group will make out of this? If they get elected, they will just use it as an excuse to make more cuts, and then you can forget about the multi-agency approach, because we simply won't exist!" Quinnan finds explicit photos and another revealing diary, this time about Caroline's trips away with a man called Mike. But they turn out to be pure fantasy – an escape from the latest man in her life, who was none other than Walsh, a spotter of easy pickings and a budding photographer on the side. "She didn't mind the head and shoulders. Then when I suggested the others, she was too far in to say no." Monroe takes a long soak in the washbasin afterwards to try and expunge the dirt.

Water cleanses another victim of other people's deeds in *Profit and Loss*, an even more hard-hitting story from Etchells later in the year. The body of a woman lying in a bathtub is found by bailiffs who broke in to recover a debt and are impatient to get on with their next job. The use of women as slab-bound cadavers in crime dramas has been increasingly questioned of late; here Dolores Edwards does at least earn a credit for the indignity of lying in a puddle, coated liberally in stage vomit, while her shirt is yanked up for a gaggle of blokes to inspect her bruised torso. The signs of a struggle result in AMIP being called in. They find a passport for Latifa Dogan, a Turkish woman whose visa had long run out, but who worked as a cleaner for a 'franchise operator', Michael Dace. Checking out his business addresses, Carver finds a cellar crammed with trafficked immigrants. "Whoever organised this wants shooting," he tells Monroe. The police discover that Latifa was sold for sex, including to her fellow employee, a decrepit sleazebag named Kellet; well, we tend to view the one-t Kellets as an entirely different strain, no accounting for them. When the weaselly Dace is tracked down, he runs from what he thinks are loan sharks, hanging off a chain and calling frantically for the police. "We *are* the police," says a dry Ted. Dace insists he tried to save her life; finding the "stupid cow" had taken an overdose, he ran a bath to put her in, not realising she would choke. "Why'd she want to go and kill herself? She wasn't even getting any work. She was half-dead at the best of times... Did Kellet tell you he asked for his money back?" By his own words is he condemned, but we get the condemnation of Jack Meadows on top, giving it the full self-righteous act. More effective is the quiet probing of Roach, who asks repeatedly, "Why didn't you call an ambulance?" "I don't know," comes the feeble response. Bleating that he has lost a friend, Dace is set straight by Ted: "You haven't lost a friend, Mr Dace. You've lost plant and machinery. Get him out of here."

Before crowning Ted Roach as a champion of abused women, however, we should consider the most outspoken and contentious of all the sex crime episodes from this year. Julian Jones adopts the same fearless approach to a tough subject that he always does in *Without Consent*, when a well-known local tom, Linda, walks into Sun Hill with bruises on her high-heeled feet to report a rape. Lounging at the front desk is sex worker advocate and good egg Steve Loxton, who declares, "Sorry love, we class that as non-payment for goods," and sends her on her way. Ackland tracks Linda down and they argue about the details at full volume as she follows her through an Underground station. Linda is finally convinced to make a statement, but the nearest CID to hand are Burnside and Roach, taking the case largely for the giggles. Their interview reflects the infamous questioning of a rape victim in the Roger Graef *Police* documentary a decade earlier, which caused widespread outrage. "Some bloke jumped me as I came off this job last night," Linda reveals. "He put a sack over me head." "Can't say I blame him," Roach mutters, loud enough for her to hear. She reveals that after she got free, she came across a couple in a car who drove off rather than help her, which didn't encourage her to go to the police. "You believe her?" Roach asks Burnside in private. "Well, she's had a few drinks. But who'd want to rape her anyway?" The DI then asks her what she is expecting to get out of this. "Let me put it crudely. What you do, basically, for a job, is get raped for money." "You don't go with these men because you want to," adds Roach. "You've made things very difficult for forensic; you've been with four or five different blokes." "Now look, don't get upset," says Burnside, "I'm trying to be straight with you. A lot of people aren't going to be sympathetic. Now if we're going to do anything, you gotta help us." "You haven't been exactly 'honest' with us in the past, have you?" notes Ted.

The story points out what is seen in the examples above, and in most forms of crime: they involve people at the margins, already lacking credibility because they are seen as damaged goods. The past mental illness of the woman interrogated in the *Police* documentary was used to suggest that she was crying wolf. Prostitutes are another special case, a familiar presence and hassle for the police. In a way, Jones questions the show's own reliance on them as a source of material, implying that that very familiarity breeds contempt. "He doesn't know how to deal with it, so he doesn't want to know," Ackland rants at Cryer. "All Mr Burnside wants to do is nick villains; spin round to chummy's house and get a body. That's not what this is about!" The DI tells Linda the files show no recent assaults on prostitutes; "Nobody reports it," she replies simply. Cryer has a word upstairs and Reid gets involved. "The thing is, we know Linda," Roach tells her. "It's not like her to come to us; she's an old pro, she's virtually bulletproof." "There's a statement of intent on your office wall: to meet the victim's needs. I don't care who she is, do you understand?" Reid and Ackland take over the enquiry, but it seems increasingly pointless to Linda, who has internalised all the negative attitudes towards her. "These things happen, I'm a prostitute. It's what I'm paid for: to make sure that men don't go out and rape 'ordinary' women. If he'd have paid me, I'd have put the sack over me head!" She is reassured that they can isolate the different DNA traces on her body, and is sent to be examined. "Why do women allow themselves to be treated like that anyway?" Burnside asks Reid. "Something you don't suffer from, Frank – low self-esteem." A story so critical of police attitudes did not pass unnoticed. No less than the Met Commissioner himself labelled it "a 'disservice' both to the police and to rape victims who might be dissuaded from reporting their cases."[23] One starts to notice, in the early Nineties, the increasing number of stories that cover issues or advice the police wanted to highlight. After the top brass's criticism of *The Bill* in its early days, this episode may be the point where they realised they had to live with it; and that it was better to use its reach to advance their own messages.

BACKWARDS, FORWARDS

The strength of this era lies firmly in *The Bill*'s 'authored' approach. The show is still the property of a fairly small number of writers, and most of the all-time greats are at the height of their powers, from the newest to the oldest. The episodes from Barry Appleton tail off in the Nineties as he moves to another long-running cop show, *Taggart*, to supply it with award winning scripts. The immense input of the man who almost single-handedly defined *The Bill*'s storytelling slowly winds down. He maintains the thread to the turbulent CID of the old days: including the thwarted ambitions of the surviving 'originals', Roach and Dashwood, which are exhumed in *Kids Don't Cry Anymore*. Harry

---

[23] Kingsley, Hilary, *The Bill – The First Ten Years* (1994), p. 30

Hopwood, the ex-Murder Squad chief reunited with Ted Roach in *Conscience* two years earlier, returns in a story that illustrates how Ted is standing still while his peers move onwards and upwards. "Why is it that retired coppers always go in for the security?" ponders Burnside. "You'd think after twenty-five years they'd have had enough." Hopwood is setting up a firm with a Mayfair address, to "attract the right clientele", and wants Roach seconded to him to investigate missing stock from a major communications group. "Get stuffed!" Ted erupts at his boss, and is hauled into his office for a dressing-down. "Don't you ever speak to me like that again!" "I object to that man's presence in the nick." "I don't give a monkey's what you object to – Harry Hopwood is well respected in and out of the force, a reputation that will outlast yours, unless you know something different." Dashwood asks Hopwood what their feud is about, and his response is telling: "The job is full of people who think they've been hard done by, and Roach is no exception." Ted spends his lunch break in the local boozer, nursing his grievance. "There are two kinds of copper I detest. Those who spend all their time studying to pass exams, and those who keep you under their thumb because it suits their careers. Hopwood's the worst kind – guilty of both." "You know, I've seen 'em come and I've seen 'em go," the landlord declares, "but without a doubt, you are the most bitter and twisted Old Bill I've ever come across." "It takes practice; and I've had plenty."

Forced to comply with Hopwood, Ted works out why he is in demand. "A job that you can't afford to go wrong, and if it does, you'll blame me. You never change, I can read you like a book." Hopwood has plans to expand internationally, opening offices staffed by ex-coppers, of which Ted could be one. "So, you want to put me in your pocket? You just flash a credit card and it's all there, even a clear conscience." Roach again brings up the murder case they handled in the Seventies, which resulted in the conviction and suicide of the wrong man. "You know the trouble with you, Roach?" retorts Hopwood. "You're a fatuous idealist. The hardest job I had with you was getting your head out of the clouds. You should learn something: people who spend their lives tilting at windmills end up by losing out." "Maybe they do, but they still sleep at night." When the lorry they are tailing makes an unscheduled stop, Roach ignores Hopwood's plea to call for back-up and snoops around on foot. He is almost done over before he is saved by reinforcements Hopwood has whistled up. "If he hadn't phoned for assistance, you'd be a candidate for intensive care," Dashwood reminds him. "You owe the man a lot." But Roach maintains that he was only looking out for his own interests. "You're an ungrateful bastard," says Burnside. When the hero of the hour turns up with a bottle, Ted supplies the glasses from his permanent stock – but that's as far as he will go. "Aren't you having one?" "I'm particular who I drink with." What Appleton never forgets about Roach the idealist is the selfishness under that high and mighty act; while more than skin deep, his convictions are never as firm as June Ackland's. His latest disastrous effort to fly solo and grab all the glory fits a pattern he adheres to stubbornly, because it has worked for others and therefore should for him. The real reason for his dislike of Hopwood is clear: not for playing the game, but for playing it better than he can.

Roach's younger colleague threatens to join him on the long road to bitterness. Burnside calls Dashwood into his office and tells him that his transfer request to the Fraud Squad has been rejected. Turning fact into fiction with typical cleverness, the show suggests that the designer lifestyle practised by Mike, and criticised by real life officers, has become a hindrance to him for that very reason. "You made all the right noises, said all the right things... you want me to tell you why? When a certain Chief Superintendent is sitting on a selection board wearing a Burton's suit, and his subordinate is standing there in a Giorgio Armani number, flashing a moody Cartier timepiece, he starts to think! I mean, if I didn't know you, I'd start to get the wrong messages, know what I mean?" "I'm not a bent copper, you know that." "It's not what the man knows, it's what he thinks. He's not interested in how many commendations you've got; doesn't give a damn about all the good work you've done." "I think I'll jack it in," says Mike in a fit of petulance. "Don't be stupid! You've got a great future ahead of you. Do you want some advice? At home, I've got an old grey suit, stinks of mothballs. I hate it, everybody hates it – my old mum tried to give it away to Oxfam twice. Now I keep that suit, and do you know what for? Purely for selection boards and funerals, nothing else. That suit makes a statement about me." "That you have no taste?" "Do yourself a favour – if you want a transfer that bad, sit for promotion. Follow the system. Show 'em what you're made of." Hopwood tries to court Mike, offering his card; he's helped "young officers who've become... disenchanted with the job." Ambitious as he is, Mike does not accept what could have been a very long spoon.

The wake-up call Mike badly needs is delivered in *Furthers*. About to bring more charges against James Bailey, a con nearing the end of a three-year sentence, he learns Bailey has escaped from jail. Doing the rounds of Bailey's former associates, Mike is told he has acquired a shotgun; one barrel is his for his old business partner, "and the other's for you." "If Bailey manages to shoot you," asks a hopeful Tosh, "can I have your suit?" Those two equally harrowing images do nothing to dent Mike's bravado; nor does the news that one of the men he spoke to has been gunned down in broad daylight. AMIP arrives and Meadows is keen to know why Bailey has in it for Mike. "Because I do my job." "That's a clever answer Mike, I don't want clever answers." Meadows asks if, during his recent prison visit, Mike told Bailey he was going to send him down again. "It must have come up...." He went "to clarify a few points of evidence. I knew I had a case." Bailey also knows his girlfriend Trish is now seeing his former accomplice, who helped put him away. "It's a pity that somebody told him... you didn't happen to mention it?" His composure cracking, Mike insists that "he was asking for it – his attitude." "Oh, you just wanted to knock him down a bit? How did you feel? You were pleased. You enjoyed it: inflicting pain. We all know Bailey's unstable, but he wouldn't want you dead without good reason." Dashwood is still hung up on the idea that the job is all about needle; the thought that one of the villains could hit back doesn't compute. Spurning the DI's offer of the section house, he heads home just as news breaks that Trish has been abducted. Putting on the dulcet strains of Eric Clapton's *Wonderful Tonight*, Mike takes out a pizza and is ambushed by the gun-toting Bailey: a brilliantly intense performance by the steel-haired, steel-faced Nigel Terry. Moving to the radio, Mike is told, "I shouldn't bother, I'll just plug you back. Wouldn't want to waste that anyway, would you?" Bailey nods at his dinner. "A man should enjoy his last meal."

Bailey takes Mike to the bedroom, where, looking not so wonderful, the result of his verbals stares up at him with blank eyes; all those cheap shots have led to an expensive one. "I've done her a favour, really," muses Bailey. "No more crap." If only that were true – but the young Felicity Montagu has decades of it waiting for her, as PA to one Partridge, A. Word reaches CID of a shotgun blast at Mike's place. "Weren't you brought up to finish your plate?" demands Bailey as the condemned man tries numbly to eat his pizza. "Some little chap died for that, the least you could do is chew it." They hear the sound of sirens. As Bailey moves to the window, he eulogises his former love with the black humour for which *The Bill* is never credited: "She'd have liked it, great big fuss. Horrible bang it made, sending her off. I could have strangled her with piano wire, but, uh, I don't have a piano and even if I did, I wouldn't know how to play it... Looks like you'll have to miss pudding." Forced to his feet, Mike is taken to the roof and his head thrust into the guttering. "Go on Mike, there's your pudding. Eat what you feed everyone else!" Bailey makes him wave to the police below, then announce how scared he is. Besides his immediate worries, Mike should be concerned that a slag can pinpoint the flaw even Reid couldn't: "Are you scared, or scared to say you're scared?" Unlike the men around them, Bailey is no marksman: "I like to get up close. I can't afford to miss, I've only got the one shot. This is for my life... what a waste," he declares, moments before that last shot is fired. When armed police hurry onto the roof, they find his dead body and Mike sitting against the railing. "You scared the life out of me," Burnside tells him quietly. "Mind you, you didn't half look a prat, up here waving." "Well he got what he came for, then," concedes a humbled Dashwood.

While the old guard struggles, the new wave and its efforts to modernise CID are explored by another of the show's greats, J.C. Wilsher. *Initiative* kicks off a story arc that tackles a growing problem. Reid has done some number-crunching at area and informs Brownlow of the results: statistics show a rising trend in street robberies. "Look at what the customers want – all the survey evidence shows that street robbery is the public's number one priority. It generates an exaggerated fear of crime and makes the public think the police can't do anything for them. With burglary and auto crime at least we can tell people to do something for themselves: lock doors, fit alarms. What can we say about robbery, stay indoors?" Her proposal to run a project targeting the Bannister Estate is met with hostility by the Chief Super, who has bitter experience of the drawbacks. "I don't know where you were in the early Eighties. We tried to deal with muggings then with saturation policing and swamp operations. I was sending in uniformed officers against petrol bombs, I was having local politicians sharpening their knives to stab us in the back, and I am not going to put myself in that situation again!" Reid argues they should stop acting as if they're above politics: "We've always been in the political game, but up till now we've pretended to be the referee and been treated like the football." Brownlow tries to kick her ideas into touch by suggesting she draft a paper, only to learn she already has. "I've got plans for this place," she tells Burnside on a tour of the estate. "I thought fighting our way in here through burning rubber tyres was the worst experience you could have," he muses. "Then I thought about living here." Running through the recent catalogue of burglaries, arson attacks and muggings, he asks what those plans are and gets a simple but emphatic reply: "I want it recaptured."

Reid's planned multi-agency approach doesn't enthral Burnside, but she reassures him there is another angle: intelligence gathering, targeting and surveillance. "Yeah, but that's treating teenage toerags like armed blaggers!" "They're more of a problem than armed blaggers," she points out, echoing Galloway's argument with Brownlow in *This Little Pig* back in Series 2. The glamorous Division One crimes that merit both overtime and TV time are a distraction from what concerns most people. Wilsher uses the greater scope offered by *The Bill* to maximum effect: not just on an overlooked area of policing, or one that takes an authentic amount of time to yield results, but which *does* yield them in the end. These streaks of positivity are vital to the show's balanced look at its subject. Brownlow attends an Area meeting and learns that street robbery is now DAC Hicks's main focus, prompted by concerns from the Commissioner. Suddenly changing his tune, he reels off Reid's figures as though they're his own. Hicks wants a proposal from each Chief Super for tackling the issue, and Brownlow is able to offer him a ready-made scheme. "Changed your name?" a cheerful colleague asks as they leave. "Charlie Brownnose is it, these days? Oh don't get me wrong, Charles. Swimming's my sport. I admire a good crawl." When Brownlow catches up with Reid, he observes how remarkable it is that she and the DAC were thinking in the same terms. "Well sometimes an idea's in the air, isn't it sir?" He gives the green light to her proposal, but warns it will have to be presented as that of the Sun Hill management team. "That's what I'd assumed," she smiles benignly, knowing how to play the system: stroke the egos of the men in power, get on with the job herself, and try to earn her credit in the long term. When she and Burnside learn that a prolific robber, turned murderer, was missed because of poor information sharing with uniform, they are united at last by a common drive. "You and me together, we could turbo-charge this nick," the DI suggests to his boss. "Darling," he calls the barmaid, "there is a woman dying of thirst over here!"

In *Targets*, a youth arrested for carrying a knife claims it is protection against two teenage muggers. Seeing possibles for the street robbery scheme, Carver puts it to the DI, but his recommendation is only the starting point. Lines produces a costing breakdown of the men, vehicles and hours involved. Like Galloway before him, Burnside can't stay a maverick forever; he becomes an accountant not through gritted teeth, but as part of a mindset that is now second nature. "I have to be satisfied on various points before I apply the resource, right?" he notes as he studies their figures. "These are currently active street robbers; you've also come up with a feasible action plan, so the final question is: is your budget offering value for money? You do need the numbers; that's why you're only going to get half the hours, and I'm going to have to go cap in hand to find that." "So if they haven't offended by six pm...?" "You've blown it." This is the man who was found 'blending in' to criminal gangs in his early days; now he can only break them up from a distance, with the aid of a calculator. "The essence of crime management is the precise application of limited resources," Brownlow declares. "We speak of little else in CID," Burnside assures him, and the joke is that there isn't one. Reid's plan includes discussions with the council, courts and probation services, the show acknowledging that this is where criminals return to the start of a vicious circle. Covering all the bases, when a reporter takes a shine to Dashwood the DCI notes, "We need good informal channels to the media, so... get stuck in! Do you think you could slip a few column inches to young what's her name on the *Gazette*?" "I'm hopeful ma'am," he replies smugly, seeing no downside in being pimped out by his guvnor. But, first into the fray to arrest the muggers, he gets a smack in the mouth that renders him less than photogenic. "Not the image you want to present to young Julie, is it?"

says Reid sadly. "Especially when he's trying to give her a controlled leak," adds Burnside, forcing the DCI to hide her smirk.

One of the arrested muggers started nicking at the age of twelve, under pressure from an older boy. The way in which the young are groomed and coerced into a criminal lifestyle is explored by Wilsher in his next episode, *Joey*. June Ackland helps out with an anti-bullying initiative in schools, focusing on an unhappy kid whose teacher suggests he is getting good practice for the adult world. "He's quite low down in the pecking order, but then somebody's got to be. Come on, there always *is* a pecking order, wherever you go in life. There's certainly one in this staff room. I bet there's one in your station." When the kid reveals that an older boy is stealing his pocket money, the headmaster's strategy is one of containment: "He'll be warned off in no uncertain terms. He's not exactly one of our academic prospects. He'll be out of our hands fairly soon." "Yeah, and straight into ours, I shouldn't wonder," says June. Steve Loxton brings in another youth for stealing a piece of jewellery, so terrified that Steve is thought to have intimidated him. He reveals the full story in one long unbroken take that zooms in slowly on his face. A boy who used to take his money left school but then saw him again in the street and accused him of slagging off his mum. To prove he hadn't, he had to go out that evening with him and his mates. "We went up the graveyard. They said, we're going in here... There was this new grave; like it had just been dug. It was empty, with all the dirt piled up. They pushed me in... they said I had to do what they said, or they'd push me in again, and put all the dirt on top." This led to a gradual path of thieving and robbery, taking bigger risks as the pressure increased. "You were what they call his 'Joey'?" asks Monroe. "He said if I got caught, I'd get off with it 'cos I'm only a kid." The story illustrates deftly how different layers of crime are connected, victims becoming perpetrators; the seemingly run-of-the-mill offence has its own dark underbelly. Mirroring real life, problem youth was one of *The Bill*'s most constant themes. Here Wilsher gives it an edge it lacked in later years, when sheer repetition rendered it mundane.

However many victories she scores, Reid is still viewed with suspicion for belonging to "the brains department." After Dashwood is cleared of an allegation made by a disgruntled snout, the DCI plays it down at a senior meeting: "It's no big deal, I mean malicious complaints are an occupational hazard, we all get them." "I've never had one," Monroe replies pointedly. His low opinion of CID is validated by the shady company they end up keeping. Reid's brief tenure is overshadowed by the sheer number of guest appearances by her eventual successor, Jack Meadows; it feels as if Simon Rouse was being courted for the DCI role well in advance. The then-Detective Superintendent is keen that people know it every time he is called in, even when not on AMIP business but to conduct an audit of paperwork. "It's all right son, it's not a kit inspection," he drawls at a slovenly, shaking Carver, before criticising Reid for her "ropy" crime management system. "Pompous little prat!" snaps Roach when he has left. "Ted, he's your senior officer." "He's still a pompous little prat!" Though bang on the money, his descriptor applies even better to Meadows' factotum DS Chris Lovell, a constant source of irritation. "Sir! Could you make sure in future you attend the morning briefing sessions?" he lectures the DI during an enquiry. "A message from the guvnor – do you have a difficulty with that?" "No; I have a difficulty with you, Lovell." With Greig, the safe pair of hands, now installed as incident room manager, Roach is made exhibits officer and gets more criticism from Lovell about his handling of them. It's little wonder that when the two dinosaurs get the jump on a major source of info, they are stingy with it. "You want me in on this?" Lovell asks feebly as they take a woman into the interview room. Burnside is happy to oblige: "Yeah – go and fetch us two teas."

"You mustn't let Burnside wind you up," Meadows later advises his deputy. "He's all wind and water. Put it down to the generation gap, Chris – you're the future." The same episode proves him devastatingly wrong; a year of internal suspicion and finger-pointing turns out to be an extended practical joke on the viewer and on Meadows in particular. In *On the Take*, a no-show from a team of armed robbers suggests that info is being leaked. Roach looks into a garage used by the robbers, on the pretext of checking its MOT certificates, and discovers one belonging to a C. Lovell; the Lovell he knows used to be on the Robbery Squad and still drinks with them, so is up to date with all the gossip. Reid hands Burnside the job of telling Lovell's boss. "That's, um... an extremely serious allegation, Frank," says the head-scratching Detective Super. Rouse, up till now the image of confidence, gives the first hint of the fumbling regret we would see so often from Meadows. "I just thought you should be put in the picture." "Oh, you're just giving me the gypsy's warning? Don't patronise me, Frank! Chris Lovell rubs you and Roach up the wrong way, he always has!" "There is nothing personal about this, guv." "Well there is to me! Do you think I could have a bagman for three years and not know him inside out?" In the tradition of Brownlow, patsies persist even in less innocent times. The garage owner is pulled in and names Lovell; Meadows listens to the tape and is forced to call in MS-15. Like the unmasking of H in *Line of Duty*, the Big Bad turns out to be an innocuous little weed hidden in plain sight the whole time. Grilled over his lack of supervision, Meadows learns that his own car was taken into the garage by Lovell to be MOTed. "I trusted you!" he yells at his former subordinate as they meet in the corridor. "They're going to throw the book at me on this one," he tells Burnside − and a punishment of two decades awaits him...

At the end of the year the pieces are aligned for the next handover of power, with 'Victoria Taylor' supplying the bridging material. Reid's closeness to the higher echelons provides a useful pretext for moving her on. Leaving a meeting on European inter-agency co-operation, Assistant Commissioner Renshaw asks cautiously if everything is OK at the nick he parachuted her into. "Personalities − nothing that can't be sorted out," she assures him. Carver is sucked into her ongoing feud with Burnside, the latter dragging him off on enquiries when he is supposed to finish a report for her. As he settles down to a long night at the typewriter, he gets a warning from Mike: "When two worlds collide, if I were you I'd try not to get stuck in the middle." Then in *A Woman Scorned*, Reid suggests Burnside should be encouraged towards a new role that suits his "obvious leadership qualities." Renshaw sees through her bluff: "Your predecessor at Sun Hill, Gordon Wray, tried to get him moved on. He may have been a bit more honest about his feelings. He said he couldn't get on with him: found him belligerent and obstructive. Turned any disagreement over policy into a personal battle. But I've never believed in solving a problem by shunting it somewhere else," he declares − an attitude not shared by the series, as it is about to prove. "If this is your way of telling me you can't cope with him, it's something I'd rather not be hearing; at least, not in any official capacity." Reid returns to Sun Hill to find that the DI has authorised overtime for Carver without consulting her, and tries to contain her anger. "You're mucking me about, Frank," she announces, ordering him in for 8am the next day. "We've got a lot to discuss." In the ladies' she meets Viv Martella, who sympathises with the woman she has just arrested for murder, after taking months of abuse. "Taking a spanner to the back of a man's head?" "Well, haven't you ever felt like that?" "You want to know how often? Every day of the working week," declares Reid, in a line that may have resonated more with Carolyn Pickles than was intended. "But there are more subtle weapons."

AS GOOD AS A REST

The infighting in CID is harder to pull off in a uniform branch seemingly set in its ways, the stories focused on one relief and whatever problems the next shift brings. Another of the show's long-standing authors, Julian Jones, broadens our horizons over the course of this year. 'Our' relief is part of a wider Sun Hill world that gets overdue recognition. *Dead Man's Boots* sees speculation over who will replace the deceased duty sergeant. Alec Peters is being courted, to the disbelief of Roach: "No way, duty sergeant? Most powerful job in the station?" "Brownlow's gonna need someone he can talk to," suggests Burnside. "Bob can be a bit 'moral' at times." "Alec's a nice guy, but it's no use talking to him unless you're talking about runner beans." Roach opens a book on the winner, Quinnan insisting that Peters has no chance. "He couldn't organise a brothel in Bangkok," he remarks as the man himself comes up behind him. Of the former incumbent, who has dropped dead at forty-nine, Cryer observes that "he was a nice man, but what I didn't like about him was that when it came to going on courses, or people needing overtime, he always favoured his old relief." He claims to be uninterested in a nine to five job, "sitting up there like the Olympic flame – you never go out"; which, long-term viewers may recall, was precisely his role in the early days. Conway suggests to Brownlow that moving the ever-popular Cryer from his relief to a desk job could give them greater sway over him. "How very Machiavellian of you, Derek." Peters is favoured but wants time to discuss it with his wife. "I'm a relief man, I'm happy where I am," he tells Cryer, insisting that Bob deserves it more. He later reveals to Burnside that he has turned down the job. "Don't screw yourself Alec, this is your chance to move up! You'd be upstairs!" "I dunno. Maybe I'd get vertigo." Given the chance at something new, Alec ties himself in knots, and soon pays the price for remaining at a literal sharp end. By contrast, when Bob is offered the role there is no dithering; he says simply, "OK."

Bob Cryer's new job effectively rubberstamps what he has been from the beginning; the show's most powerful figure. Now his control of the relief extends to the whole station, there are fears that those dead man's boots have become too small for him. Like June and Gordon's brief encounter the year before, Bob's stint as duty sergeant is really a look at those around him, who project a change onto the man himself that isn't there. Reg is surprised to find him in the normal washroom rather than the executive one, and is set straight: "Contrary to rumours being circulated, I am not Mr Brownlow's minder, nor am I his snout; I'm the duty sergeant, that's all." "I ain't heard no rumours." "No, well you wouldn't, would you? You start them all." Hollis brings up the sick cards that Cryer passes to Brownlow each morning: "If that ain't snouting, I don't know what is." "I have shown him the sick cards of officers injured on duty, so he can phone them up and ask them how they are. I'm trying to educate him into showing a little concern." Cryer's legendary thoroughness starts to work against him. In Philip Palmer's *Empire Building*, a crackdown on fine defaulters leads to a stream of prisoners clogging custody, which the harassed Peters must control. Cryer wanders past and is advised to keep his big nose out of it. Going toe to toe, Larry Dann and Eric Richard show their stripes and deliver knockout performances. "Shut up Alec, I'm fed up with you and your moods," Cryer mutters, and Peters suddenly flips, taking him into the office. "Don't you ever dare talk to me in front of the prisoners like that!" "I was out of order; but so were you, I don't know what's got into you lately." "I'm not the one who's changed, Bob. You have. You've become a guvnors' man – brownnosing the senior officers, stealing a job here, a job there. You write briefing papers for Conway, you do the overtime budgets, you even do the duties for sergeants and inspectors!" "And you're afraid I'm going to penalise you? Give you the worst duties? I'll tell you what it is, it's jealousy. You cannot handle the fact that I'm doing a job that you turned down." "You're just not the man I used to know, Bob."

Tony Stamp's anxious look in their direction as war breaks out highlights the essential role of the skippers in maintaining morale and discipline. These qualities are examined further when Julian Jones drops another regular into new surroundings. This time it's Cathy Marshall, due for a sergeant's board, who slips back into the mantle of acting sergeant: an uneventful, on-off role she had adopted in the past, which felt like an attempt to give her something distinctive beyond her DV background. The problems of that non-rank emerge in *Your Shout*. At the changeover of shifts, the boys of C Relief head to the pub to celebrate the impending fatherhood of their sergeant. Told by Brownlow that her role is "a question of projecting yourself, giving a sense of authority", Cathy is also advised to "relax and smile", and waves them off as they go. She settles at the CAD terminal and dispatches Tony to the first outstanding call. But the woman who made it turns up to complain about the police's slow response, which has given her ex-husband time to abduct their children. It turns out to have come in twenty-four minutes before the shift change. "It's down to the previous relief then," says Tony. "It's down to us if we didn't notice at handover," Peters corrects him, and wants to know why Cathy didn't check. Meanwhile, C Relief's booze-up gets so rowdy that a complaint is made. Norika Datta turns up to warn them to keep it down. "That's a nice tie," she compliments the loudmouthed PC 'Lucy' Locket. "What's the motif, SAS or something?" "Well you're close, it's the DPG. The only difference is, our motto is 'Who Cares Who Wins?'" Tuck into that alphabet soup and you will discover, much to your surprise and non-delight, that the DPG is the Diplomatic Protection Group; the very same Met unit that nurtured both Sarah Everard's killer Wayne Couzens and the serial rapist David Carrick, and had a review of its toxic culture instigated as a result. As *The Bill* demonstrates better than most TV series, everything is connected to everything else.

Cathy grows more anxious as the search for the kids intensifies. When another complaint is made about C Relief's pub do, Quinnan encourages her to dob them in to Monroe in retaliation for dropping her in it. She does so and instantly regrets it. "Oh come on, they're asking for it! They're always the ones that give Sun Hill a bad name." "They're like a bunch of hooligans!" agrees Delia French. "It's the sergeants," Dave maintains. "They're too young. I've got as many years in as Martin Welsh. He's a nice guy and all that, but he's not a leader. If the lads don't see you as skipper, then basically you've got no hope." His message isn't lost on Cathy. Peters convinces Monroe to let him warn C Relief instead, and can't believe that Cathy got him involved: "You don't point Mr Monroe at anyone unless you mean to bury 'em! If you wanted to reimburse C Relief you should have come to *me*, that way we can keep it within the family." Quinnan makes an ill-advised joke about how Brownlow will soon have Cathy back on the beat, and her patience snaps: "It might help if you gave me a little more respect!" "Yeah well that's got to be earned, hasn't it?" The kids are located and Cathy can breathe easy, but not for long. Brownlow pops in to give her the good news: with Sgt. Welsh on leave, C Relief is short of an acting sergeant. "I thought that would make you happy," he notes in surprise, as she tries hard to put on a game face. In *A Corporal of Horse* she dons her war stripes and goes into battle with their macho culture, which is causing concern at senior level. Cryer gives Brownlow the figures on their "batting average." "Not exactly the West Indies, are they?" "They consistently have the worst arrest rate in the station. There's an ethos sir, it persists, that they're the top guns." "Ironic considering these figures." Conway's argument that "each relief has its own character, it helps to build a sense of identity," does not impress the Super: "I want that identity changed."

Cathy discovers that Locket has driven another officer's car that day despite being uninsured on it. When she confronts him he snaps, "Look you jumped-up little cow, don't play sergeants with me!" She has no more credibility with C Relief's guvnor Inspector Bruce, the laissez-faire polar opposite of Monroe. "Got himself into a bit of a mess – and, you're obviously taking the matter seriously," he adds reluctantly. She finds out he has already been told about it, and realises he was going to do nothing. Seeing Brownlow, she asks to be considered for a new domestic violence unit, rather than pursue a role she's not suited to. "Well it's difficult being an acting sergeant," he sympathises. "You're neither one thing or the other; you're a corporal of horse." "Organising and disciplining officers, it doesn't come naturally to me." Lynne Miller stands out in one of the show's most remarkable experiments, putting Cathy into a role where the only familiar faces are people doing nine to five jobs, who interact with every relief: Viv Martella in CID, Ron Smollett as collator, Bob Cryer as duty sergeant and Brownlow and Conway upstairs. The latter's efforts to subdue C Relief remind us that the rest of the time, we are only seeing a third of their overall responsibilities. This kind of innovation was only possible in the half-hour era, when the short story format gave a freedom to try different approaches. When the show returned to the hourly slot in 1998, plenty of episodes thrust one character into alien surroundings, undercover or on attachment; but the shock of the new never applied to Sun Hill itself. Given the declaration of one producer to the cast at the start of this brave new world, that he was going to "make you all stars",[24] an hour of prime time television in which half the officers roaming the station are completely unknown to the viewer would have been a difficult sell.

The missing third relief rears its head in the show's first ever Christmas special, and first hour-long episode for four years, *Vital Statistics*. Stamp passes Quinnan the good news from "the gobby ones" in B Relief: "It's official – B Relief are the superstars, and we're the stuff on the shovel." "This isn't an arrest factory, sir," Monroe protests to Conway about his relief's inferior collar rate, fifty per cent less than its rivals. "Maybe that's because my relief are so red hot, the villains keep their heads down when they're on duty." Conway, a man fixated on quick victories, wants him to up his game: "When you think there's a PC in Avon who's doing a hundred and twenty in a year? A hundred and twenty, Andrew, in *Avon!* This is *London!* The streets are paved with crime! You tell your lads to get their fingers out." The smarting Tony informs Dave that he has made a bet that they can top the ten arrests B Relief managed in their last shift. A man on a mission, he grows steadily more agitated as he screens calls for arrest value and tries to nick anything moving. After he stops a man with a sack returning to his allotment, Monroe wants to know if he does any more: "The complaints figure's one thing that doesn't need bumping up." Ever the optimist, Tony takes keen interest in a black man carrying a bag before Dave warns him firmly, "No." Two kids are caught stealing from a timber yard and the area car is detailed to bring in their mother, much to his disgust: "Free taxi rides for slag now!" "You're just prejudiced," says Dave. "They're all human beings, you know." "That's what's so depressing." Mum

[24] *The Bill Podcast* 04: Andrew Mackintosh, 2017

insists her sons are under the age of criminal responsibility and she can prove it by fetching their birth certificates, which entails another ride home and back. "Go via Tesco, shall we?" asks Tony as he waits by the car. "Get your shopping in?"

He finally admits to his partner what is at stake: at the disco that night, the losers dance the conga, "Buck naked... I'd had a couple of drinks! Bottle out if you like." "I don't remember bottling in!" retorts an equally panic-stricken Dave. The shift turns out to be one of the least dramatic in memory, the highlight a destructive rampage by an OAP in an electric wheelchair who injures both Hollis and Datta. This battery-powered brawl feels like another anecdote that came straight down the pipeline from Christopher Russell's police source. Once the plug is pulled, the geriatric thug is brought in. "I can see he'd terrorise the whole estate, providing the lifts were working," Peters concedes, wondering when anyone is going to bring him a real arrest. At least it's a prisoner, not the relief's inspector, who now earns the ultimate brickbat; the slovenly conduct of his neighbours "doesn't give you the right to behave like a Dalek." Hearing of a shout at the Cambridge Arms, Tony is at first unimpressed – "Hoo-yah, make my day; yuppie punch-up" – but when he learns that a group of rugby players are involved, it seems his prayers have been answered. However, they are diverted to search for a woman who has been abducted, and get an overdue lesson in their real priorities. "Thank you," says a relieved Monroe, told they have found her alive. "Let's hope they've also arrested someone so we can put a tick in the little box," he jibes at a sour Conway. The Cambridge Arms has been cleared up by TSG; the Full Tony beckons. That evening he and Dave emerge cautiously from the changing rooms, particulars disclosed. "This is what's meant by 'dress optional', is it?" Conway demands as he catches sight of them. Their colleagues cheer them inside – and at the last moment, with the original broadcast approaching 9pm, the camera pans down to reveal there is no bluff in the buff.

BLUE TERROR

There are years on *The Bill* where certain writers come to prominence, and in 1991 the name that has the biggest impact is Russell Lewis. It's his work that gives this era its unique charge, and provides further proof, if it were needed, that it was the mass produced era of the mid-Nineties that sanitised the show. The original hourly series may have supplied more extreme content, when the programme was licensed for it; but there's an edge in Lewis's stories that marks them out from others, a feeling that danger and violence can erupt at any moment. In *Safe as Houses*, at the tail end of 1990, CID is tasked with babysitting supergrass Lennie Powell on the eve of a gangland trial. Their arrogant guest can't believe his shabby safe house has no TV, just an overly wordy paper. "If you're so desperate to look at a pair of cold tits, there's a birdbath in the garden," a droll Dashwood reveals. Desperate for a cigarette, Powell declares, "I could murder a snout." "I expect Mick Whelan's thinking much the same thing," Carver reminds him. Powell tells the young DC, disgusted at having to do deals with the opposition, that he's "a face, son – then and now." But there's no rose tint to Lewis's view of the good old gangsters of yore. Taking over for the night shift, Tosh tells Viv he met Powell during his West End days on the Serious Crime Squad back in the Seventies. "Lennie did a nice line in under the counter kiddie porn... He's one of the old school, he is – your original habitual criminal. Salt of the earth, that's a load of cobblers. A slag's a slag, whichever way you look at it." When Powell can't get Viv to make his dinner for him he launches into a tantrum, smashing up half the kitchen: "*I want some grub!*" Using his vast experience of screaming hungry toddlers, Tosh placates him by cooking half a dozen eggs. His strength revived, Powell makes a move on Viv in the bathroom, promising like Tony before him that, "It'll only take a minute." Much more impressive in that timeframe is Nula Conwell's performance, which switches effortlessly from cornered victim to angry avenger. "Listen you lowlife!" Viv yells, grabbing him by the arm. "Don't you ever, *ever* try that again!"

Powell is headed for the nastiest of falls. Burnside has brought in extra security, which comes in handy when the house is attacked by thugs. Tony Stamp among others, revolver in hand, collars them in the last vestiges of that tough early *Bill* that tooled up its regulars. Shielding the target upstairs, even Tosh Lines is packing more than an extra Mars bar. The troops are stood down and officers arrive at dawn to escort their man to court. "Be lucky, Alf," says Powell, moments before he is blasted to the pavement. "I'm all right!" Tosh calls to Viv, dazed by the ocean of blood covering his shirt. Burnside radios in to warn them "it's a fit-up, sit tight!" – a few seconds too late. The fallout results in another station-based cheapie, which exposes the fissure between CID's two volcanoes. In *Caught Napping* the Serious Crime Squad, headed by the fearsome DCS Petch, takes over the incident room and orders CID to halt their business while they inspect their paperwork, scenes that will be repeated a decade later. Reid arrives to find her department being turned upside down, and the stain spreading. Wiping his feet on the lesser ranks, Petch is all smiles and charm with his opposite number Brownlow. However, he points out that an informant being shot dead while under police protection is not a regular occurrence: "You're aware that the CPS have had to drop the case against Whelan and the rest of Powell's former associates? His liberty has been restored." Whelan's firm took three months to find Powell's original safe house, and one day while he was in Sun Hill's care. "Doesn't inspire confidence, does it?" Suddenly keen on team spirit, Burnside suggests that he and Reid agree that they stood down the extra troops together. She doesn't take the bait, reminding him she was brand new at the time, but refuses to throw anyone under a bus, telling Petch she won't "indulge in wild surmise when there's so much at stake. You must find your own answers."

Burnside insists he is "not losing any sleep over it; storm in a teacup." But his bravado vanishes when he tells Roach they must be on the same page. "We stood the troops down, didn't we?" "No, you gave the word!" Ted insists, wide-eyed with suspicion. "As I remember it Ted" – correctly, if you watch the earlier episode – "you asked me if you could stand them down and I agreed." The DI is of course trying to offload his responsibility. Burnside's constant one-liners are sometimes in danger of turning him into a comic figure. What Lewis always bears in mind, more than any other writer, is the menace that underpins the charm. "There's no one in this department doesn't owe me. Time to call in a few favours." Roach recognises an attempt to drop him in it: "If I agree to this, that's it for me – I'll have done my legs once and for all!" "You done your legs long ago, Ted." His aim to "cloud the issue" fails; asked who gave the stand down order, Roach points the finger at Burnside. "I'm not lying for you," he tells the DI. "If you've done nothing wrong, you've got nothing to worry about. Or are they getting a bit too close for comfort? Whelan got you in his back pocket?" "Don't push your luck, Ted. You gonna run and tell Reid? You done me up like a kipper, the pair of you!" "Well maybe she can't stand bent coppers either." "*You slag*!" Burnside roars, shoving him against the wall, and they have to be pulled apart. When the DI is interviewed, the tricks of the trade have deserted him. Certain the rubber heels have made up their minds, he lounges back casually, treating it as a joke. Then he goes on the offensive, suggesting that as Whelan is one of the funny handshake brigade, the Met should be looking higher up for the culprits. He defends the calls he made, but is told that "the force is changing, Mr Burnside. The attitude that you've displayed today is sadly outmoded."

The rancour between the two big beasts is making everyone in CID suffer in *Hammer to Fall*. "It's been brewing since Reid took charge," Viv tells Dave. "Neither of them are exactly what you'd call new men, are they?" But a chance to nail the much-sought Whelan emerges, via a gang feud with his business rival Vic Palmer. The latter passes word to Burnside that Whelan has a delivery due. The DCI wants Burnside to repair the damage with Roach and pairs them on surveillance. "Old cow. I bring home the bacon and this is her idea of a reward? Stuck on a roof, freezing me cods off with Paddy McGinty's goat for company." "One thing I won't be sorry to see the back of," Roach says acidly. "Your cheery Cockney humour." Burnside accepts he was wrong to pressure him, but declares that "attack is the best form of defence", and they achieve a reconciliation of sorts. CID bust a drug deal involving Whelan's couriers; but, determined to catch the top man, Reid has a tip-off fed to him that Palmer was responsible to spur him into revenge. She tells Greig it is best to leave Roach and Burnside out of it, given it would be "hard for them to stay objective" about Whelan – a reasoning he takes with a pinch of salt. She is unaware that the duo, law unto themselves, have gone for a drink with Palmer. Whelan and his heavies burst into Palmer's club and march them all outside, to take a final drive, before Reid arrives with the cavalry just in time. Reminding a shaken Burnside that he is now in the clear, she makes it plain she would never have let the bully boy Petch take down Whelan: "Nobody walks into my department and treats my officers the way they did." The DI has to concede she may be his equal in ambition and ruthlessness. "Seen the guvnor?" Greig asks Roach as the clear up begins. "Just passed him," says a puzzled Ted. "Nah, the guvnor –

Reid!" The long-term irony, though not intended, is that the head Petch finally does get on the block is that of Meadows – freeing him up to take Reid's job. The boys' club restores the natural order in the end.

When Lewis takes the multi-stranded approach in *Night and Day*, he invests it with the same brutality. Phil Young is sent to a snooker hall where an amped-up punter who has lost money nearly takes his head off with a cue ball. Phil has seemingly calmed him down when he suddenly lays into him with the cue. Subdued by back-up, he is taken in and blows his nose on the custody record before he is dragged to the cells in a foul-mouthed tirade. "I'd prefer it if he was completely legless, it's when they're half-cut they're the worst," says Cryer. The next day Delia French spots a prowler reported by an old man and chases him into an underground car park, where her radio packs up. "Don't work down here love, it's just you and me!" a menacing voice rings out. She ducks a flying bottle: "Can't you see me? I can see you." The OAP has followed to help her and the villain drives straight at them as he escapes, injuring both. At the nick Delia demands to know what happened to her back-up and doesn't accept Phil's story of transmission problems. "I will do the same for you one day. I could have been killed, you *bastard!*" The outraged Ackland follows her into the ladies': "You're a probationer and don't you forget it, you need all the friends you can get! You carry on like this and they're going to have you handing in your papers before six months is up, believe me, I've seen it!" "I was scared." "Well what did you expect when you joined, sunshine and flowers? Welcome to the real world Delia, 'cos different to what they tell you in training, the cavalry isn't always going to come and bail you out, just don't bleed all over us!" Delia breaks down in tears as she reveals that the old man who helped her is on life support. The mysterious prowler and his motives are never seen again; the frontline is not just a savage place but, at times, an inexplicable one.

In the end, the bleeding comes from what we all thought was the safest quarter of Sun Hill. *Cry Havoc* opens with a search for the local "pillhead" Gary Mabbs, wanted for glassing someone in a pub. Still bustling around like a poorly strung marionette whenever he is out of doors, Alec Peters goes to aid June, who has spotted Mabbs slipping into a flat. When Peters intercepts their target, he chooses the wrong moment to try the 'give it up son' routine. The psychotic Mabbs, high as a kite, refuses to come quietly. Peters turns to use the radio, a knife is produced – and June sees the result as she approaches. Blades, more than guns, are a sensitive issue in a pre-watershed slot; there is no close up of the stabbing, but that is where the restraint ends. Peters collapses in front of June, blood pouring from his gaping wound. The stains are still smeared across her uniform while she waits anxiously in hospital. Marshall finds Cryer in the locker room, musing on how fate is catching up with him. "I'm getting too old for this. First Tom, now Alec... That could just as easily have been me out there. Maybe somebody's trying to mark my card." Throughout this year we see a disinterest from the general public to officers being harmed, but Lewis ups the ante, showing the utter delight in some quarters when a blow is struck against 'the filth.' "One-nil, one-nil, one-nil, one-nil!" a crowd of yobs chants at Monroe and Maitland as they pass through the estate. In the mood for a fight, Maitland turns on one of them, who cravenly backs down. "Gary Mabbs should have been smothered at birth," declares Conway. When Burnside searches his mother's flat, he realises that the apple hasn't fallen far from the tree. "Your boy has put one of our lot in hospital!" "I hope he dies screaming." This triggers perhaps the most quoted of all Burnside-isms: "Stick her on," he instructs Sue Ford. "What's the charge?" "Being in possession of an offensive mouth."

But the stabbing of Peters is only the start of the dramatics – and an overlooked member of the cast gets his moment to shine. Replacing the killed-off Mark Powley, Jonathan Dow arguably inherits his role as the law-abiding woman's bit of Fuzz. The amiable Barry Stringer, who possesses no extreme opinions or grudges, is there to get on with the job; it was that normality, under pressure, that Dow was keen to explore.[25] But, out and about with a defective radio, a blissfully ignorant Stringer is put through it after he nearly runs down the fleeing Mabbs. Fearing he is injured, Barry pursues Mabbs into the derelict Battersea Power Station and across its hundred foot high girders, with Stuart Urban's ambitious direction, Roy Easton's inventive camerawork and stunt co-ordinator Nick Gillard's skills combining to create one of the most daring sequences ever seen on

---

[25] *The Bill Podcast* 31: Jo Dow, 2018

TV. Twice Jonathan Dow lurches over the edge of a sheer drop in one shot, with only hidden harnesses to protect him. In the pursuit of action, it could be argued that Barry becomes Superman rather than a normal bloke under strain. Taking two vicious beatings from Mabbs, not only does he keep going, but joins in playing Philippe Petit – rather than, say, waiting for Mabbs to come down. They breed 'em tough in Brum; that or Barry's had advance warning that performance-related pay is in the offing. The performances on screen push the boundaries Lewis is straining against in his work. The young Marc Warren brings another level of intensity to the disintegrating Mabbs. When he finally has Stringer helpless, suspended in mid-air while he pulls out the netting keeping him alive, the terror on Dow's face is authentic. His saviour is a guard dog that charges onto the gantry and attacks Mabbs, sending him plummeting to the screaming death his mother reserved for Peters. Aesthetics give way to real, human weakness when Stringer hauls himself to safety. Dow is entirely believable as a hyperventilating wreck who can't believe he is still intact. "Me shoe... I lost me shoe down there," Barry gasps at Tony. "He pulled it off... as he went. It was new."

INTO THE ABYSS

Russell Lewis plays a significant role in the major storyline of this year: the decline and fall of the lowliest cog in Sun Hill's machine. Having auditioned for Dave Quinnan, the bit part of Phil Young may have seemed small recompense for Arin (credited as Colin) Alldridge. There is, however, no better example of how *The Bill* can shuffle someone who is right at the periphery into the limelight. Introduced at the end of 1989, Phil is usually to be found slopping out the custody area and offering the occasional tart one-liner. His softly spoken manner gives little away, but as time goes on he offers firm opinions out of nowhere, hinting at an inner bitterness that takes his colleagues by surprise. Then, in Arthur McKenzie's *Attitudes*, he comes to his fellow PCs' notice when he beats them at cards and cashes his winnings straight away. "You shouldn't have joined if you're not prepared to take risks, son," he parrots Steve Loxton's mocking words back at him. "He's due some problems," Loxton mutters as Young walks off. "Don't worry, he'll get 'em," promises Stamp. Phil's vengeful colleagues try to hand the young upstart every rubbish shout going, and are chewed out by Peters for an attempt at victimisation. Cryer gives

Young a warning: "Don't ever play cards on my relief. Especially for money, it's divisive." The sardonic Phil takes away a different message: "Don't win." In an echo of *Woodentop*, the young rookie gets a rite of passage when he has to attend a dead body sealed up at home, albeit with Bob as a guiding hand. "A road we're all travelling, Phil," he is reminded. But this particular 'stiff' is a world away from the hideously decayed specimen that Jimmy Carver and June Ackland stumbled on. When Cryer opens the curtains, Phil moves forward to gaze admiringly on the old man: "He's so peaceful." "That's the way to go – in your seventies, in your own bed, in one piece."

Five months later, as a wave of sickness spreads through the relief in *Loophole*, Phil tells Cryer he is feeling ill. Unable to pinpoint any physical symptoms, except a general tiredness, he is urged to "get a grip. If we all clocked off every time we felt minus one, this place'd be as empty as a church." June watches Dave and Steve wind him up for trying to skive off, and asks Cryer if he is all right: "He was the one who found that fifteen-year old who committed suicide last week." "So?" "There is such a thing as delayed shock." "Well, if he doesn't learn the nasty side of this job now he never will," Cryer declares bluntly. "Look June, *I'd* like to have a nervous breakdown but I'm sure if I did they'd cancel it at the last minute!" In one line, he demonstrates why he will never experience such struggles – and, more importantly, why he'll never understand anyone who does. Patrolling an estate, Phil chases two boys up a staircase and is soon reduced to exhaustion. Steve asks him to rendezvous at a nearby scrap yard, but isn't there when Phil arrives. Dave radios him to look inside. Climbing the fence, he is trapped by another guard dog. His colleagues turn up to laugh at their prank, but when they lever the gate open he fails to see the funny side, launching himself at Steve. "Just calm down, it's only a joke!" Dave insists as he pulls him away. Phil later tells Monroe he will have to go sick, that "everything just seems an effort" since he dealt with the suicide of a teenage girl. "You've attended fatals before, haven't you?" "Yes sir... but not like that. I don't like to do it, but I need to take some days off. I'm no good to anybody like this." Contrary to expectations, the puritan Monroe is the only one to take him at face value, and lets him go, defending his decision to the bosses.

The extent of the sick list prompts Brownlow to set up a course on stress detection for management. This is a laugh out loud notion for Conway – been there, done that, had a hissy fit after one day – until his opposite number in CID cheerfully endorses it. Dave and Steve are left bemused when the Grinch asks how things are going: "Maybe he's lonely." The joke becomes blacker as the show observes the gulf between the efforts of officialdom and the real case developing under its nose. As Brownlow launches his scheme in *Stress Rules*, Young and Marshall are heckled by a gang of youths. Going over to confront them, Phil causes trouble rather than defusing it. Playing the ringleader, the teenaged Rene Zagger issues career advice that he himself will heed in later years: "Join the Met: free hat, good pay, throw your weight about. Make a prat of yourself on a daily basis!" "We're not out here to make enemies, Phil," Cathy reminds him afterwards. "No," he sneers, "we're out here to be loved and cuddled!" "Perhaps you shouldn't be out here at all." When the gang is brought in for attempted robbery the leader makes a run for it. Phil grabs him at the custody door and lays into him before his colleagues intervene. Cryer later asks what happened: "If you carry on like that, you're going to end up in serious trouble. You lost control, didn't you? Police officers get wound up, but they do *not* lose control. Because if they do, they stop being police officers. Is it getting to you, Phil? The job?" "It's more than a job, Sarge." "That's what they say in the ads," smiles Bob. "It's what we find out! I can't look at anybody without asking myself what they're up to! That's off-duty, that's with mates! If you do your job you get abuse, if you don't half the public's on your back." "Not easy, is it? But you've got to hack it if you can." "And what if you can't?" "Then you're no use to us."

The cracks become gaping chasms in the next episode, Russell Lewis's *They Also Serve*: the great experiment in minimalism that chronicles the boredom of a group of reserve officers trapped in a van on permanent standby. The episode is renowned for its eleven-minute take that covers the entirety of the first half, as camera operator Alison Chapman slithers seamlessly back and forth among the cast. But it's not so much an ensemble piece as an extended reading from the Gospel of Phil. "I reckon we should bill 'em," Young declares of the demonstrators they are expecting. "Soon see who's got ideals then, wouldn't you? Demonstrate by all means, but pay for the privilege. I'm not talking about the British, I'm talking about the Fifth Columnists!" He invokes the 'Tebbit Test', the marker of true citizenship dreamt up by Home Secretary Norman Tebbit the previous year: "You get the Windies over on tour or Pakistan, your ethnics aren't in the crowd rooting for England, you know. You can't have it both ways; you can't be British one minute when it suits you, and the next minute giving it 'Come on Windies' or whatever." Bemused by his eagerness to get stuck in, Stamp sets him wise. "There'll be no fun going on out there. I did Wapping mate, I know," he adds, referring to the bitter stand-off between print unions and the real police that put paid to *The Bill*'s first home at Artichoke Hill five years earlier. When the WPCs muse sadly on how respect for the police has declined, Phil vents again: "How many times have you waded in to stop some member of Joe Public getting a pasting? And how many times have they done the same for you? They couldn't give a monkey's; they'd cross the road rather than help us." Datta points out that many of them have to live alongside the perpetrators and are scared of the comeback. "Too many wets, that's the problem," he snarls. "When the muck and bullets are flying it's me that's going to be in there, see the results first-hand. I don't come into it six months later when it's all nice and civilised in court and the jury goes, 'Ah, don't look too bad, what's all the fuss about – next?'"

Phil's tirade gets only semi-ironic applause from Quinnan, and the strength of the episode, at the risk of breaking the record, is that it rewards both the long-term and the casual viewer. What can be seen in context as a destructive spiral is also, in its own terms, the unfiltered view from a job that diminishes faith in humanity faster than any other. The chaotic, overlapping dialogue recalls the fly-on-the-wall feel of the early days. The positioning of Ackland and Maitland in the front, long-suffering parents of the bored offspring acting up behind them, is no coincidence. No minor joy is spared, from Norika stuffing cotton buds up the nose of a dozing Dave, to Reg butchering a Marx Brothers gag. We even get Graham Cole's pitch-perfect impression of Christopher Ellison, as Tony recalls Burnside's courtship of the departed Frazer and suggests that he's a romantic at heart: "'Ere, I brung you some flowers, you toerag! Now get yer kit off!" Beneath the banter, there is a profound sadness to the depiction of Phil; a man not on accelerated promotion like some youngsters we see, but on accelerated cynicism. Worse, it's an overblown, posturing cynicism: the adolescent babbling of someone trying to fit in by proving he knows the score better than anyone else, when he doesn't know the half of it. Later he delivers another broadside about "some poor plod getting the stuffing kicked out of him, for what?" Maitland, little older than Phil but responsible, not jaded, beyond his years, quotes the rulebook at him, on the need to uphold the Queen's Peace. "Believe that, do you skip?" "Yes Young, as a matter of fact I do. And if you don't, if you let that truth slip, then you might as well put your papers in, 'cos you'll just be going through the motions. And believe me, there's nothing worse or more despised in this job than a timeserver."

But *They Also Serve* is not a purely minimalist exercise. Halfway through, our heroes clock off for a break and meet other PCs who have been in the thick of it. Dave suggests that the TSG should be left to handle these demos as they're kitted out for it. "I mean it's a joke, isn't it?" he says, rolling up his trouser leg to reveal the wooden pad on his shin. "What's that gonna stop, eh?" In the ladies', Delia tells Norika and June that things are kicking off, and an officer has been stabbed. "It's outrageous, we don't get paid enough for this," the latter declares. Suddenly a young black recruit emerges sobbing from a cubicle: "I just want to go home!" she cries on Delia's shoulder. Like many of *The Bill*'s most effective moments, she is a ship that passes in the night. What could have been a low-key piece of theatre is elevated to genius by the ending, in which the fears that have been kept off screen suddenly arrive. When the unit is stood down, the officers head home in high spirits, but then they pick up a PC fleeing a mob which surrounds the van, smashing in the windows and pelting it with petrol bombs. The newcomer is briefly set alight, and he is the lucky one; as they escape, Barry looks back through the open doors to see a burning man flailing around in the street. Twenty one minutes of tedium give way to forty seconds of nightmare: the oft-quoted ratio of a police officer's life, ninety nine per cent utter boredom and one per cent sheer terror, put up on screen. It adds extra bite to the preceding debate on the rights and wrongs of protest, which as we have noted has become the main stick with which to beat the police; either they crack down on it brutally or are feebly complicit in it, depending on the cause in question. This is *The Bill* at its finest, putting the nature of the job above the 'who did what' details of a crime. It's not just Phil Young, but also his more balanced peers, who have an eternity to brood on the worst of human nature and virtually no time to defend against it.

Buried in the episode is a significant moment, while Norika has stuck on her headphones to get away from the chatter. Phil asks what she is doing at the weekend and offers to help decorate her flat while her other half is away. "Nah, I don't think it'd be a good idea," she concludes. "You know what that lot are like." When Maitland puts Phil in his place, she is the only one to stick up for him, arguing that he just wants a little more appreciation. That small gesture of kindness is one she regrets, as Phil latches onto her and draws her into his torment. In *Out of Order*, he arrives at work to see Norika engaged in a mild spat with the teacher boyfriend that a sceptical viewer might have thought she made up to get her out of an awkward come-on from Jim the year before. At parade, Barry and Steve banter on the secrets of pulling birds, the former insisting that the gift of the gab can get you anyone. Norika is sent out in a panda with Phil; "Ooh, I didn't know there were any gentlemen at Sun Hill!" she coos as he opens the door for her. He notes that she's never been out with anyone from the nick before. She voices her fears about "canteen cowboys" and he insists, "we're not all like that." "Not you as well!" she chuckles. "You're all the same, aren't you?" "Give me a chance, come out with me one night," he pleads. Having been in this territory before, she tries to make light of it in the same way. Later they pursue two muggers and Norika chases one into a derelict warehouse. In the darkness she is set on and shoved against a wall. Only when her attacker is thrown into a pool of light does she realise, to her disbelief, who he is – a presentable young man in uniform.

Still in shock, Norika walks back to the car on tenterhooks to rejoin her predatory partner. They carry on as though nothing has happened, but finally she snaps and threatens to report him to Monroe. "You need sorting out; there's something wrong with you." "Look, I've had a bad time recently. I don't know why I did it, but I couldn't help it." "You're pathetic..." They almost blow the arrest of the mugger who evaded them earlier, and George Garfield has to tackle him instead. Back at the station Phil sees Norika speaking to

Monroe, who then calls him into his office for a word. Going down in flames, Phil snarls *"Bitch!"* in her face as he walks past; being different from the other blokes isn't such a plus after all. Much to his surprise, Monroe merely wants to know if there are any problems he would like to bring up before his next assessment. "I'm fine," he smiles, failing to grab hold of his last olive branch. He has, however, succeeded in spreading the misery. June finds Norika hunched over against her locker, sobbing. Told that Phil tried it on, June declares, "I hope you gave him a smack round the chops!" before realising it is worse than that. "He didn't actually do anything, did he?" "Yeah, well he tried..." Norika whimpers. "I can't work with him anymore." She wavers over whether to make it official, a familiar tale of a work culture that punishes troublemakers. The episode shows how abusers choose their victims well; that smack was never an option for Norika. Lacking the big personality of some of her colleagues, her quiet demeanour is a weakness to be exploited. Phil tries to apologise to her in the yard and is pushed away. In his own locker room he declines the offer of the pub and is left alone, clawing the air in desperation.

Russell Lewis applies the crippling blow to Phil's damaged psyche in *Losing It*, an episode I first saw on a YouTube upload of a grainy UK Gold recording; once seen, never forgotten. When Young calls on a woman who has not been seen for weeks, he has to break the back window to get in. The smell hits him first, followed by the sight of cockroaches and maggots swarming over a sideboard of rotting food. Trembling, he ventures upstairs, the faint buzz of a single fly a clue to what lies in store. When he opens the bedroom door, he is engulfed by a cloud of the genuine article, wrangled especially for Arin Alldridge.[26] A closer look at their meal on the bed sends him fleeing downstairs to cough his guts out. "Never mind old son," Tony later tells a shivering Phil, "nice big fry-up when you get back to the nick!" By now he is way beyond the bants, and the only one concerned for him is Norika – her fear seemingly suspended, in a slight lapse in continuity. "It's always me," he mutters. "Why me, what have I done?" He announces that he's going home, but as first on the scene that is not an option; he must return to the funhouse. The dead woman has form for soliciting and is a registered drug addict. "More than her fair share of pricks, then,"

---

26 *The Bill Podcast: Losing It* Patreon Commentary, 2023

quips the (female) SOCO. Carver finds a tape recording she made before her death. The camera zooms in slowly on Phil's gleaming face as they listen to a reedy, despairing voice begging her mother to forgive her. "Try not to hate us... Please pray for me. I love you. It's for the best. Pray for me; me and the baby." Outside Phil tells Norika what we all know: "I can't hack it." She urges him to talk to someone – but when she enters her room at the section house, fresh out of the shower, she discovers that he hasn't looked far for a counsellor. One of Lewis's inspirations was Sidney Lumet's bleak 1973 crime noir *The Offence*, in which Sean Connery's veteran copper disintegrates while investigating a series of sexual attacks. The fly-blown corpse Phil discovers could easily slot into the montage of nightmares Sgt. Johnson recalls on the way home from work. Likewise, the exchange between Phil and Norika evokes Johnson's rant at his wife about the horrors he has seen – horrors she cannot, and does not want to, understand.

Norika sits cautiously on her bed as Phil muses on the dead woman, asking whether it hurt: "It's not meant to, is it? Pills and booze – like going to sleep... How would you do it? Kill yourself?" He reminds her this is the second suicide he found. "The first wasn't even our age. They must have just said, 'that's it. No more; I'm gone.'" "You can't let them drag you down with them!" Like the twelve-year-old he is inside, Phil asks hopefully, "Will you go to bed with me?" When she orders him out, he insists, "I love you, you know." "You don't know me!" Reassuring her he is not a virgin as people joke, he maintains, "I'm not like the others, jump on anything that moves." Then he switches to the formal ID he must attend with the dead woman's mother. "What am I going to say tomorrow? How do you prepare somebody for that... horror? How can she possibly recognise her, she hardly looks human!" Feeling he is at fault, he says he should have done something. "How, how could you have saved them?" asks Norika. "You didn't know them, it was *their* choice, nobody made them!" He backs her into a corner and she holds out a finger, reprimanding that twelve-year-old: "I want you to go, now." Instead he produces a ring and pops the question: "I've got nobody else! I'm so alone, I'm scared!" "You're scaring me." He claims her boyfriend mistreats her, then starts to question her desperate attempts to make tracks. Jim Goddard's direction builds a rat-a-tat exchange of close-ups until he lashes out, slapping her in the face. Shocked at the blood pouring from her mouth, she asks him to go to the first aid box and locks him out, collapsing in tears. Arin Alldridge and Seeta Indrani both impress, expertly delivering one of the most chilling sequences in the show's history. Afterwards, it falls to Jim Carver, self-appointed defender of Norika, to give Phil's door a sustained kicking. "I know you're in there, you gutless tosser! You touch her again, I'll break your neck! You're dead, do you hear me, *you're dead!*" Phil stands impassive on the other side, gazing into the abyss. Jim's supposedly bloodcurdling threat is nothing he doesn't know already.

The end comes soon after, in *The Square Peg* – to which your author must declare a hefty interest at the outset, as his favourite thing broadcast under the title of *The Bill*. One top-tier Russell gives way to another as Christopher takes over writing duties. The hero of his own story makes only a fleeting appearance, giving a cheerfully oblivious Reg Hollis a lift into work. At parade, Phil numbly accepts his beat, sent off by an exasperated Maitland. "At least he looks smart," Monroe points out. "From the shirt collar down, yes sir." When a shout comes in he is mysteriously silent. What Russell bears in mind, and conveys so brilliantly, is that this is a normal day for everyone. In the area car, Loxton and Quinnan discuss the Shield training course up for grabs. "There's got to be more sport in that than you get on division," argues Steve. "I mean when you analyse it, fifty per cent of our work here is crap." His point is proved when they are assigned what should be Phil's call, to get a drunk down from a tree. "ETA, two minutes!" announces Dave; his rendition of the *Thunderbirds* theme, with authentic Supermarionation, fails to inspire his partner. "Nursing a dog's breath," Steve mutters after the drunk hits the deck. "Philly should be doing this, it's his ground." As time goes on, the theories on his whereabouts are revealing. "Anything on offer on five beat?" asks Monroe. "Bored housewives, rich widows?" "No way could our Phil be OTS with a merry widow," Steve assures Dave. "I dunno – still waters run deep." "Him? He's probably gone walkabout on another planet; where he came from." Reg saw Phil leave in his own car and suggests he has taken it to be MOTed, having noted his tax disc was out of date. "Has he, by God?" says the vengeful Monroe, ordering the search cancelled. This is the best insight Phil's colleagues can muster; their world was never his. Steve and Dave are dispatched to the Jasmine Allen, where a woman has spotted a man in his car with the exhaust on and a hosepipe in the front. They break the window and drag Phil's corpse out – a surreal final scene for Arin Alldridge to shoot on his twenty-sixth birthday. The motor Reg dismissed at the beginning as "one expense after another" has paid the way for Phil in the end.

By the time CID arrive, the body is being taken away. "I'd rather not leave one of my men lying in a public place," Monroe tells Burnside coldly. "So that's Phil Young," Cryer notes briskly as they walk off. "Finished and gone." "Doesn't say much for our powers of man management, does it? These lads and lasses are our responsibility." "To a point; but in the end they have to be responsible for themselves, everyone does. If they won't talk to you, what can you do?" It was Cryer who planted the seed in Young, not knowing just how fertile that soil was. His dismissive attitude is an attempt to draw a hard line, between the certainties he can deal with and the demons that he can't; even Uncle Bob has his limitations. He and Monroe find Phil's locker empty and his room neat and tidy, uniform and warrant card on his bed with the 'M.P.' logo blazoned across it: a last attempt to be the model officer he never was. Cryer opens an unsealed letter whose brief contents echo the tape recording Phil heard: "'Dear Mum and Dad, I did my best. Love, Phil.'" Back at base, June follows the day's other casualty into the ladies'. "How do you know how I feel?" snaps Norika. "It's not fair, I mean he's dead now, and he's still on my back. He's still affecting my life, there's going to be an inquest..." "There is nothing you could have done about it! He was a very strange man, he was mentally unhinged. He found two suicides in the space of a few weeks, he had this thing about you, he's got a *really* strange attitude to women! He assaulted you!" "Maybe I should have told Monroe; maybe he could have helped him." "Yeah maybe he could have suspended him, maybe he could have sacked him! Maybe he'd have got a pat on the back from his friends!" "But that's the point, innit?" Norika yells. "He didn't have any friends, so he picked on me!"

Learning that there has been a death on duty, Brownlow is momentarily dazed. "You'd better inform Area. Nothing wrong in his last appraisal, was there?" he asks Conway, hinting at a need to cover their backs. "There was no suggestion of any suicidal tendencies, no." Brownlow rings the parents to let them know he is coming round. En route he observes that his driver has delivered plenty of death notices. Out of nowhere, Tony Stamp emerges as the star of the episode, with one of the most outspoken views ever uttered on the show: "Suicide's different. An old-fashioned word, but to me suicide's wicked. It's the ultimate selfishness." "That's a robust point of view," replies the ever-diplomatic Super. "I don't think it's one I shall be putting to the parents, though." He arrives at their pleasant suburban house and is shown into a living room where Phil's mother is waiting in silence, broken only by the incessant ticking of a clock. He sits down to talk to her and the father, a stoic white-haired man in a grey jumper. Told their son has died, they run through all the palatable explanations: "Smash-up...? Somebody shoot him...?" before Brownlow reveals that he took his own life. Shaking her head, the mother insists, "He wouldn't do that. Not our Philip. He couldn't! What have you *done* to him? He was fine till he left home!" Brownlow tries to comfort her with the most ideal of all lies: one that the teller believes to be true. "Mrs Young... in all his time at Sun Hill, Philip never let anybody down, in any situation. You can both be very proud of him." In one of those piercing throwaway moments that Christopher Russell did better than any other writer, the buttoned-up Mr Young, who has never had to have a meaningful conversation with his wife about anything, tries feebly to comfort her and she turns away in scorn.

In the parade of shootings, explosions and other bursts of violence that sent officers to a terminal end in *The Bill*'s history, Phil Young's exit stands alone: even from the suicides in the show's rather frenetic later years. The topic itself is one where television usually treads gingerly, well aware of the strictures on how it is handled. Suicide refocuses the drama inwards, away from the colourful escapism of blaggings and car chases, to ask more complex and disturbing questions. Phil was there for all the high drama of the previous two years; he was one of the pallbearers at the funeral of Ken Melvin, killed by something visible that was beyond his control. But who's going to shoulder Phil's coffin when the time comes? Certainly not the officers his mother blames for putting him in there. Yet that seems too linear an explanation for his downfall. The horrors of the job may warp some people; but what gives this storyline its haunting power is the implication that, like Sgt. Johnson in *The Offence*, those horrors touched something in Phil that was warped already.

The final two scenes are stark, penetrating masterpieces in their own right. In the locker room Steve asks Dave, "Why there? Why on *our* ground? So we'd find him? The ultimate wind-up, the ultimate revenge for all the times we wound him up?" It recalls the suicide in Russell's earlier *Sun Hill Karma* who holds on long enough for Viv to appear, then lets go – wanting not just a witness but, perhaps, an accomplice: someone to leave a final imprint on that proclaims, *You made this happen.* Viv's, of course, was the anguish of a blameless woman failing a stranger; this time there is blame to go round. "He was cracked Steve, all right?" says Dave feebly, trying to assuage his guilt. Without a word Tony pushes past them and leaves, slamming the door shut. But when he meets Norika in the corridor, he is full of voice – and refuses to conform to the idea that lessons must be learnt. "Don't start any of that 'we're all guilty' crap. It was his decision. He drove himself, parked very neatly, and did it." In a painful irony, the lesson Norika does learn is the same one she gave Phil: that someone else's choice remains just that. Tony's short epitaph for him contains no platitudes about how he was lost or misunderstood; instead he doubles down on his view of suicide as moral cowardice. "There's nothing wrong with being different, so long as you've got something else to offer. Something in *here*," he clarifies, pointing to his chest. "Phil Young didn't. He should never have been in the job." Norika supplies the obvious, but devastating conclusion: "Well he's not now, is he?" They walk away, leaving the doors swinging behind them – and in a remarkable moment of stillness, the camera lingers on those doors for a full five seconds as the sound fades to nothing. Phil Young gets a final requiem as powerful, in its own way, as the entire episode devoted to Ken Melvin, before the end theme kicks in with the strongest punch it ever had.

PC NASTY

However controversial Tony's opinion, he is still given the chance to air it; and what makes him such a valuable character, in Christopher Russell's episodes in particular, is his ability to say the unsayable. Whenever his colleagues reach a handwringing liberal consensus, up he pops to play devil's advocate. His response to the torment of the dead Graham Butler's parents, that they should stop whining and pick themselves off the mat, is only a sample. Russell supplies more food for thought in *Cause and Effect*, in which an employee at an animal testing lab is kidnapped by activists and threatened with death.

In the midst of a gripping debate between Burnside and the immovable ringleader on the ethics of animal research, we cut to Stamp and French searching for the kidnap victim. "It's the hypocrisy that gets me," Tony suddenly declares. "You can't tell me they'd all refuse antibiotics if they'd got a temperature of a hundred and five, or plastic surgery if they'd got their faces burnt off." In *Every Mother's Son*, Ackland meets a middle-aged woman living as a recluse, a pariah on her own estate because her son killed a much-loved resident. "She discovers her son is a murderer. Can you imagine what that must be like? And she thinks it's her fault." "Well, it is her fault — partly," argues Tony. "Do you think people are born murderers? If you're a parent you've got to take some of the blame." During a tree-planting ceremony to honour an Asian youth knifed to death, he sits in the car with Hollis, moaning, "It's rubbish, all of this. What good's that tree gonna do anyone? It'll have more effect on the ozone layer than anything round here." "Yeah, well I expect the dogs'll like it."

If Tony is the outspoken member of the relief, then further beyond him on the fringes is Steve Loxton, the definitive 'PC Nasty'. Tom Butcher saw the term written beneath a costume fitting photo, before anyone had settled on a name for the character.[27] It suggests that the role was conceived as a blank slate, onto which any undesirable quality could be etched; but this is by no means a bad thing, indeed it's an advantage of *The Bill*'s all-year round format. Pete Muswell lived up to the 'nasty' label more openly back in Series 2 — but then he had to, in a run consisting of only twelve episodes. In the half-hour era, without the need to make an immediate impact, the writing can bed in Loxton and then explore various shades of him: usually the shadier ones. The lean, mean intensity of the character is enhanced by the constraints of this era. With no time for a deeper exploration of the chip on his shoulder, like we got with Muswell and do so again with Smithy at the end of the decade, Steve's opinions are simply *there*: emerging to surprise his colleagues in the random, disconcerting way people reveal unpleasant traits in real life. Moreover, his background makes him an outlier in the parade of dodgy coppers. The rest are Londoners born and bred, situating the dark side of the Met close to

---

[27] *The Bill Podcast* 46: Tom Butcher, 2019

home. Many TV characters who hail from Don Beech's feared "frozen North" are painted as whimsical or downtrodden; Steve is neither. The departure is especially obvious in his early episodes, when Tom Butcher's Manccent is at its thickest. When an Asian man arrives at Sun Hill to complain to Monroe about "intimidation", Steve is unfazed. "Me first sergeant used to clip me round the ear if I didn't get a complaint, reckoned I couldn't be doing me job properly!" Hollis points out that the man he targeted happens to be a magistrate. "What are you getting your knickers in a twist for?" snarls Loxton. "If every Paki we shouted at complained we'd all be out of a job, wouldn't we?"

Steve's agenda and ambitions are alluded to in his opening episode, *Police Powers*. "We'll have to watch that Loxton," Cryer observes in the new boy's first seconds, as he drags a hooligan off a football pitch. At Sun Hill he reassures his hapless opposite, who is nursing a head wound, "Don't worry George, I had a go at a couple of them for you." When Tony warns him not to make an enemy of Bob Cryer, he replies with trademark contempt, "Bob's your uncle, right? Well I'm not going to end my days as a Sun Hill plod." These are the shadowy vignettes the show pulls out of the hat time and again with Loxton. Hints of a profitable sideline emerge when he wanders into a pub to introduce himself. "You'll be seeing me around from time to time. So if you get any bother... give us a shout." "That's all right mate, I don't get bothered." "Well let's hope it stays that way, shall we?" The landlord watches him go coldly – then turns up at the front desk to tell him to back off. "Try it again and it's official!" At a video store, Steve spots a copy of the new Bond film. "*Licence to Kill* – I've not seen that," he says, an odd oversight for a man who goes rogue every time he's on duty. He goes off air for a "call of nature", in fact a call of the gee-gees; but when it's other people's money he is more cavalier. Asked to place an accumulator for Sue Ford in *Photo Finish*, he is relieved when a steward's enquiry denies her the second winner – and Dave forces him to hand back the tenner he never put on. But the customers cop Steve's disdain for the rules too. In *Up the Steps*, he gives evidence in court on his arrest of a man who he collared before for urinating in public. He is accused of meting out justice in kind at Sun Hill, which Peters denies took place when it's his turn in the box. "Never arrest vicious drunks with a string of past cons, do you Sarge?" Steve asks later. "Give them the benefit do we, pat on the shoulder?" "You can avoid having a pee in their cells, anyhow." The pro-police judge lets the case go to trial, but Steve is warned he may not be so lucky next time.

Steve is back in court in *Crown vs Cooper*, the trial of a man who slashed him with a knife after he was told to attend his crying child, left sealed in a car on a hot day. Dismissing Cooper as "rubbish", he hardly bothers to compare notes with the anxious George Garfield, who arrived on the scene later. "Lying little turd," he sneers as Cooper protests his innocence. On the stand he is lured into voicing his vitriol: "I thought he was pathetic, sir. Well he's got to be hasn't he, treat a kid like that. I mean a man like that isn't fit to be a father in my opinion!" The defence reads out the catalogue of injuries sustained by Cooper in the arrest, producing alarmed looks in the jury. Steve's account begins to crumble, and George's evidence contradicts his. Outside, George challenges him over his story: "For all I know you might be fitting him up. You might have knocked him about just a bit too much, and then planted the knife on him to cover yourself." This unleashes a rant on Steve's pet obsession – loyalty. "Shall I tell you what happens to coppers who don't stick by their mates? Very soon they find they don't have any mates, that's what. Who's gonna come to his rescue in a tight corner? Who's gonna back him up? No-one. And a copper with no back-up, you know what he is? Dead meat!" When the not guilty verdict is read out, Steve hurries from the courtroom in advance of Cooper's cheering relatives. He walks past the two barristers as they arrange to meet for dinner, throwing them the faintest of looks: good game, good game. Outside he sees Cooper's boy crying his head off, locked in a car as before, while the family celebrates in the pub opposite. He straightens up and puts on his hat – and the story ends with a final, disgusted look that could either signal vengeance, or resignation that he can't touch his target. That ambiguous ending is typical of the balance the show maintains: it was a deserving man who got Steve's undeserving treatment.

Steve's bullying of the fragile Phil Young fits into a wider issue explored in the second half of the year: what makes and breaks a copper? A yob brought in for trashing a shop in *Bending the Rules* has an unusual item in his effects: a Metropolitan Police warrant card. He turns out to be DC Malcolm White, from Burnside's former nick. "I hardly recognise you, Mal," the DI mutters of his lank-haired colleague. "You look like a right dosser." Insisting that White is a "family man, straight as a die", he thinks they can convince the shopkeeper to drop the charges. White finally roars out the truth: he was part of "the *Millwall* Firm! Two and a half years, I was in... Operation Kith, Kick In Their Heads." He and others were handpicked from across the Met, to avoid the risk of being IDed by the gangs they infiltrated. "I spent more time with those... than I did with my own family. I've seen and done things, make your old lady *sick!* Do you know we even did over a copper once?" he reveals, more in boast than shame. The wife he knew once is long gone; in contrast to the failures of Yorkie Smith and later Mickey Webb as undercover hooligans, this is what a success story looks like. The plot evokes the famous *Colditz* episode in which Michael Bryant succeeds too well in his attempts to be repatriated by feigning madness. "I sometimes wonder whether these kinds of operations are worth the risk," Brownlow tells White's superior. "Well that's for the Home Office to decide, isn't it sir?" The Super reminds Burnside that, "being a copper is not a mitigating circumstance." "The man needs help, not nicking," the DI insists - the reverse of his normal philosophy. Monroe visits the shopkeeper to explain the special background of the case. The latter points out that when he objected to a police eviction of his neighbours earlier that day, he was told "'the law is the law is the law', that you don't make it, only you carry it out. It would appear that things are not quite as simple as that."

These double standards are critiqued again in the debut of Matthew Wingett, younger brother of Mark, who first sent in his script under a pen name. Potential accusations of nepotism are fronted up in the title, *Thicker Than Water* – and with results this good, other cast should have actively tried to get their relatives onto the payroll. Wingett, twenty-three at the time (making the twenty-seven year old Russell Lewis a positive veteran), produces a staggeringly mature and nuanced piece of work, on perhaps the touchiest of all police subjects. Barry Stringer and Steve Loxton are called to a domestic that takes a different turn when Steve recognises the husband, Mike Gibbs, as a mate from Stafford Row. "Go on, sort it out!" the bloodied wife yells as they head to the kitchen for a chat. "You still want a special badge for black eyes, do you?" On the assurance that things are now OK,

Steve exits with a reluctant Barry, promising not to blab to Gibbs' mates. "We watch each other's backs, you know that," he lectures Barry, proving his point at a snooker hall where he leaves him to cope with two unwelcome guests before popping up to scare them off. But they are called straight back to Gibbs, whose wife is lying injured on the stairs. "If you're worried about Nancy talking she won't, she'll keep schtum, she's all right like that," he pleads. Told he has to come down the nick, Gibbs turns nasty, threatening Steve with a bottle before sense prevails. Once more, the sight of a warrant card on the custody desk paralyses everyone. Steve faces the prospect of giving evidence against a fellow officer and friend. "Don't worry," Dave Quinnan assures him, "you know as well as I do that the wife usually bottles out in these cases. Without that the CPS haven't got a thing." The ugly spectacle of the police joining ranks continues right the way up the chain. "As far as I knew, Gibbs was a reliable officer," his own chief super declares. "Nothing on his yearly assessment to indicate psychological problems," he adds, echoing Conway's assurance to Brownlow after Phil Young's death. "I'm absolutely sure the enquiry will find no quarrel with the senior ranks at Stafford Row."

Meanwhile Steve is desperate to make excuses for Gibbs, suggesting this must be a one-off ,when all the police's experience of domestics tells them the opposite. "Do you want to see his face all over the papers?" he asks Barry. "See the courts nail him up 'cos he's the job, *that's* what'll happen!" In the interview room, Gibbs' mental struggles trickle out as he speaks to Quinnan. More telling than his words is the squirming demeanour of Quinnan, who clearly wants to be anywhere, doing anything, rather than talk to another bloke about emotional issues. For a chirpy chappie, no one played brooding discomfort quite as well as Andrew Paul. "I couldn't hold onto it... it's like my mum, my dad, before they got divorced, all that shouting, screaming... I promised myself when I was a kid I'd never do anything like that. I hated my dad. Suddenly I'm just like him." Dave suggests he get professional help. "See a shrink, you mean? I thought that was for nutters?" "I didn't say that." "No, but we all think it though, don't we?" The other half of the story emerges as Datta talks to Nancy. "It started a couple of years back... You just sort of adapt. You learn to expect it. Mike was always touchy; he couldn't unwind. The first time it happened, he didn't get home till God knows when. I launched at him and he just went berserk. I read about it in the papers the next day, there was a kid killed on a bike. Very messy. He wouldn't admit anything was wrong! You don't believe it's happening, you try and tell yourself all sorts of things like, 'He's laying into the villain, the one that got away with the community service or a stupid fine.'" Recalling Cathy Marshall's excuses for the beatings she took from her CID husband, the story illustrates a worrying truth: that the job is a constant presence in the lives of everyone around an officer, even if they want no part of it.

Nancy comes in to make a statement, but backs down in front of the suits from MS-15. "She decided she'd been assaulted by a staircase," Norika informs the lads drily. "Dave Quinnan was right," says a triumphant Steve. "Blood is thicker than water." "Oh yeah, whose blood?" "Nancy's not stupid. Where's she headed if Mike gets sent down? A single parent family on a council waiting list? She knows what she's doing." Gibbs' confidence that he is only looking at disciplinary proceedings – "Not court, you need witnesses for court" – highlights how the police's bad apples know exactly how far to push the rules they enforce. But his wife's change of heart is no obstacle to MS-15: "A crime's been committed. Mrs Gibbs' statement would have been the icing on the cake, that's all." Dave informs an astonished Steve of "the new policy. The DVU can take it to court regardless." "They're gonna have him? Even without Nancy's statement?" After Tony Stamp's comment about being an ethnic minority, here we get further evidence of the sense of persecution embedded in the police: the feeling of being hounded from above, any wrongdoing pursued far more doggedly than that of the public. Given the actual conviction figures, however, the double standard they perceive may not be the one the rest of us see. "It can't be much fun, going up against a mate," Dave observes. But Steve's much-vaunted loyalty lasts only as long as he can keep a colleague squeaky clean – and avoid being tainted by association. In his black and white world there's job and slag, and never the twain shall meet. "Mate?" he queries, shutting his notebook. "Got it wrong. He's no mate of mine."

If Steve's watchword is loyalty, his eternal goal is action, the defect that distinguishes him from the Petes who came before; and he hopes to earn it via a transfer to a firearms unit. "He's not getting anywhere near firearms if he's got a short fuse," warns Conway, who evidently eases up on him. When Steve turns up for his basic firearms training at Lippitts Hill a year later in *Shots*, it's with the approval of the CI, who is there on a tactical course with Bob Cryer. The latter is astonished to see Steve, and to learn he has applied for our old friends, the Diplomatic Protection Group. "They want him, but they'd prefer him with a pink card." "So that means Mr Monroe, and Mr Brownlow, have supported his application?" "So have I, as a matter of fact. There's nothing on his record to say he shouldn't carry a firearm." "I wouldn't give him a sparkler on Guy Fawkes Night – but that's not down to me." Bob's judgement on which officers to trust with a gun is, we see a decade later, not foolproof – but on this occasion his lack of faith is justified. Not only is this the show's best 'behind the scenes' episode, it may be J.C. Wilsher's greatest contribution in the decade he spent on it. It says everything for *The Bill*'s format that it can offer its most potent comment on policing in a story with no crime, no Sun Hill, and only three of the regular cast. Steve takes part in a simulation where he guns down a fleeing suspect in the back, and defends his choice with the same nonchalant machismo he applies to all situations. "I was firing to protect a member of the public and prevent the suspect escaping." "That's what you'll tell the coroner's court?" "That's enough to square it, isn't it staff?" Told that the inquest will hear that the man's shotgun was unloaded, Steve isn't thrown, even when challenged by his fellow trainees. Pointing out Cryer nearby, he brings up his recent experiences with the delicacy they deserve: "See that geezer over there? The one with the big hooter? One of our skippers. He blew away a slag who had an empty shotgun – and walked. Morning, skip!"

The early Nineties marked a turning point in the police's use of firearms, when they were taken away from regular officers and assigned to specialist units, and Wilsher examines the impending change. Cryer and Conway are shown a diagram of the existing back-and-forth structure for deploying AFOs from reliefs. "This is a situation where speed of response is of the essence; where there may be lives at stake. Is this structure doing the business for us?" The lead instructor, McKenna, unveils the new procedure, in which a patrolling Armed Response Vehicle is immediately assigned to a shout. In the live demonstration that follows, the gunmen in a house surrender with one challenge. "Easy peasy if everyone sticks to the script," remarks a doubtful Cryer. His fears increase when he listens to Steve raving about the ARVs over lunch: "Pack a tasty bit of firepower, don't they? Those H and K self-loading carbines are the business." "Well I'll say this about having Armed Response Vehicles: at least it reduces the chance of giving pink cards to cowboys." Steve brings up "your bit of bother", i.e. shooting dead an unarmed man, and dismisses it as nothing to lose sleep over; simply their bad luck. "It's that all right," notes Cryer drily. "Look Loxton, we'll compare notes on losing sleep when you've done the job for real." He gives Conway and McKenna his straight opinion: "I've never been impressed by Loxton ever since he come to Sun Hill. I don't trust his honesty or his judgement as a beat copper. I think it's Loxton first, the public, his mates, nowhere. I wouldn't give him a whistle, let alone a gun." Conway suggests that Cryer is somewhat out of touch with events on the relief, and McKenna insists he can only go on Loxton's performance. The next day, the officers test the ARV's weaponry on the firing range. Once the instructors confirm that Brownlow is well off the premises, they hand Derek Conway the accessory missing in his life: an aforesaid Heckler and Koch machine gun. Sun Hill's dyspeptic John Matrix reins in his killing spree at first, but then takes out a woman and child, and not to make a point about vigilantism, like Harry Callahan in *Magnum Force*. When it's Cryer's turn he politely declines, saying he's learnt his lessons already.

Views are sought on the new system and Conway is all in favour: "I've had it drummed into my skull over the last few years that the police are a social service. We play politics with the local council, we have multi-agency initiatives with education and social workers, and we're also supposed to go on dealing with everyday crime and public order. Well that's quite enough for my lads to be getting on with, without tooling up and playing the SAS." But as Cryer listens to this argument, he is preparing his own, and it's delivered with all the wisdom we would expect. "I'm not knocking the new system; I hope it gets results. But it is one more step down a particular road. Now each step is a good move in itself, but we could end up going somewhere we don't want to go. That road leads to two separate forces: social workers in uniforms, and tooled-up paramilitaries – and that's where ARVs are taking us." Could there be any better descriptions of what the police mean to a present day public? It could be said that those two forces are fused together in visual terms; the social service role is wrapped oddly in the commando-like image that has evolved by necessity since 9/11, kitting officers in increasing layers of body armour. Russell Lewis's observation of the Brighton police in his research for *Grace*, rows of "almost paramilitary garb coppers" working at hot desks,[28] highlights the dissonance of a job that is simultaneously more office-bound and more detached from everyday life. Unsurprisingly, Bob's views go down like a lead balloon. "You're not saying we should put our lives and the public's lives at risk so a slag can be shot by his home beat constable?" another inspector challenges him. It's pointed out that ARVs are still under the control of officers at the scene, and Conway brings up the hostage situation from *Cold Turkey*: "Or did we get that wrong according to you?" "I'm not claiming to have the answers to all this. I'm talking about what worries me, after a long time at the sharp end." Conway suggests the new system will take away the psychological effect these incidents have on non-specialists, a clear dig at Cryer. It's the standard response of power to an unacceptable message: attack the messenger instead.

Meanwhile, Steve Loxton's group learns about the firepower it will be up against. In a demonstration of various types of shotgun rounds, he blanches at their pulverising effect. "The last round is a rifle slug: a single, solid projectile. That would take out your breastbone, your heart and a section of your spine – effectively ending your interest in the proceedings," adds the sergeant, with the gallows humour drawn from Wilsher's research of the police. In another exercise, Steve guns down a man pointing what turns out to be a folded umbrella. The other recruits are sympathetic, observing that it was a split-second decision. Then, watching a video of a gunman ambushing officers, he fires too late and seems to have frozen under pressure. Meeting McKenna in private, he admits he screwed up: "I'm a good shot, I can do the business on the ranges. It's just I've had to think about real-life situations: about shooting at people. I thought if a scrote needs taking out I'll do it, no bother. I don't feel that way now. I'm just not confident I won't freeze or panic out there." He withdraws

---

[28] *The Bill Podcast: Forget-Me-Not* Patreon Commentary, 2021

from the course and Conway and McKenna suggest Cryer has misjudged the man. "You know my definition of real courage?" says McKenna. "Not going around firing guns, but knowing when you're not right for a job and speaking up about it." "You got him down as a bastard and you just won't change your mind," says Conway. "Oh, I've changed my mind," admits Cryer. "I've decided he's a cunning bastard." Sure enough, on the bus back Steve's true motivation is revealed. "I started thinking about gunshot wounds," he tells the female trainee next to him. "I don't want to get wasted, or spend the rest of me life in a wheelchair, for getting between some wog politician and his voters. If I hear a rumour of armed suspects from now on, I'm taking deep cover and shouting for an Armed Response Vehicle. I gave McKenna the sob story about how I was too nice to shoot people; came out smelling of roses. Mate of mine's having a party Saturday night – you wanna come?"

It's the purpose of these books to examine how *The Bill* looks at policing, not to use the show itself as a vehicle to debate policing issues. But *Shots*, more than any other episode, lends itself to such a debate. One could hardly look across the pond and argue that the wider circulation of firearms leads to a safer society; but does their restriction to the hands of specialists in the UK police create the two-tier system that Cryer is worried about? Wilsher posits the dangers inherent in elitism, in people thrust into powerful roles without the purest of motives. Conway's mention of the SAS brings to mind the surge of applications they received in the early Eighties, following the publicity of the Iranian Embassy siege and the cash-in movie *Who Dares Wins*. They found themselves turning away a lot of psyched-up men wanting to get stuck in, and one can imagine the police was Steve's acceptable fallback. "This is what I joined the force for," he announces eagerly as the crackdown on defaulters is launched in *Empire Building*. "Any action's fine, riot'd do me nicely," he adds, getting a look of disbelief from Garfield. People who pay up "take the fun out of it. I'm still looking for a ruck, me." Wielding a gun is simply one more high; and if that isn't enough it has to be obtained by other means. It doesn't take a genius to look at the disaster stories attached to the DPG and see the potential trouble in those who carry firearms but rarely have to use them: a combination of power and boredom that leads to abuse in all walks of life. One can't examine the Couzens and Carricks, the extreme of the extreme, without considering the barrel that produced them. The inquiry in their wake highlighted the Met's firearms units as the worst of the bad apples: excessively macho, unanswerable to authority, and in the DPG a belief, just as 'Lucy' Locket's apathetic creed implies, that they were seen as poor relations of the rest. Steve Loxton supplies a gaze in that direction, without going all the way. Michael Chapman observed that the show's setup while he was in charge, of self-contained stories that could have their transmission order reshuffled at the last minute, prevented it from making any of the regulars an outright villain.[29] It might be viewed as a literal copout to make Steve indicative, rather than emblematic, of the dark side. But *The Bill*'s format of individual plays gives us glimpses not only of different worlds, but of the worlds beyond them, on which 'our heroes' rest.

Verdict: To spell out what is probably clear from the preceding analysis, 1991 is my single favourite year of *The Bill*. This is a show at the absolute top of its game, one foot in the gritty past of the hour-long episodes and one in the variety of the half-hour era, sampling the best of both. Much as Series 3 did, it ventures into rich, sophisticated territory and mines it effectively, focusing on heavyweight subjects like police corruption but also police burdens and pressures. So high is the standard that multiple gems aren't even covered here; e.g. *The Negotiator*, not so much an episode as the opening to a pub joke: "Reg Hollis, Trigger and Waynetta Slob get themselves trapped in a cold store..." Or *Skint*, the tale of George Garfield's money woes; another largely crime-free affair that drops in on his birthday party and stays to examine the flirting and the punch-ups, recalling the observational feel of the early series. This is a world with depth and texture, one that does justice to the complex landscape of real policing. What becomes obvious from this year in particular is that the twice-weekly format was *The Bill*'s ideal state, preserving the balance of individual and ongoing stories. But, to reiterate a point from the end of the last volume, when a TV show hits perfect conditions there is always a change lurking on the horizon; and in another year's time it will arrive.

---

[29] Colbran, Marianne, *Watching the Cops: a case study of production processes on television police drama "The Bill"* (2011), p. 171

REVIEWING THE BILL: 1992

First Broadcast 2 January – 31 December 1992

Script Editors: Zanna Beswick, Gina Cronk, Diane Culverhouse, Michael Le Moignan, Chris Penfold, Rachel Wright. Producers: Richard Handford, Pat Sandys, Tony Virgo, Peter Wolfes. Executive Producer: Michael Chapman.

Key Exhibits:

1. Illegals
Written by Christopher Russell. Directed by Laura Sims.

2. Lost Boy
Written by Dave Simpson. Directed by Nicholas Laughland.

3. Chicken
Written by Julian Jones. Directed by Christopher Lovett.

4. It's a Small World
Written by Barry Appleton. Directed by Bill Pryde.

5. The Paddy Factor / The Wild Rover
Written by J.C. Wilsher. Directed by Christopher Lovett.

6. Principled Negotiation
Written by J.C. Wilsher. Directed by Gordon Flemyng.

7. Man of the People
Written by Christopher Russell. Directed by Richard Holthouse.

8. Up All Night / Snakes and Ladders
Written by Tony Etchells. Directed by Mike Dormer / Michael Simpson

9. Part of the Furniture
Written by Christopher Russell. Directed by Udayan Prasad.

10. Snap Shot
Written by Tony Etchells. Directed by Mike Dormer.

11. We Should Be Talking
Written by Duncan Gould. Directed by David Attwood.

12. Cold Shoulder
Written by Tony Etchells. Directed by Haldane Duncan.

KICKED UPSTAIRS

If 1991 was an unusually stable year in terms of the regular cast, then 1992 is anything but. The last year of twice-weekly episodes is also the point at which Michael Chapman, renowned in lore as 'the Admiral', began to clear the decks with his line-up of regular cast, beginning first with Carolyn Pickles. Assigned to resolve the feud between Kim Reid and Frank Burnside from the tail end of 1991, Tim Vaughan (still writing under the pseudonym Victoria Taylor) takes things further in *The Best Policy*. After a bloody armed robbery, pressure comes down from AC Renshaw to get a result and Reid is happy to let the DI take over. A chance remark by Tosh makes him realise he is being set up to fail. Roach advises him to play the long game: wait for the stolen goods to turn up on the black market and trace them back. But after a dawn raid produces nothing, the pressure increases. Dashwood, the CID Oracle, is always wise after the fact: "I could have told him the raid'd be a no-no.... What, and get my head bitten off for giving good advice? No thank you. She wants him transferred, or she wants out. Reid'd have him in a traffic warden's job given half a chance. You know what they say, when you get above the rank of sergeant? Never let police work get in the way of your career."

Burnside then goes after victory at all costs in Vaughan's next episode *Dinosaur*, leading to his most famous and definitive act. Cornering his snout, he takes him into a pub toilet and administers a ducking to force info out of him while a guilty Carver watches the door. One of the beauties of *The Bill* is that it can be read in different ways; an ensemble piece about life in a police station is also, on a more selective level, the story of one man's loss of innocence. The baby-faced Carver of 1983 has become tired and cynical, yet retains flashes of his idealism. Outside, Burnside is challenged by Sun Hill's own Frank Serpico – who witnessed a head-flushing of his own in the eponymous film, surely the inspiration for this scene. "Don't ever do that to me again, guv. You were bang out of order in there!" "Oh, and what they did wasn't? A man of sixty goes out shopping with his old lady, meets up with them and loses the use of both legs! He'll never walk again! Now you listen to me, Jim. Never mind about what the governors say. What the public wants is a bit of muscle. Helps them sleep at night. If you can't see that, you're in the wrong job, pal."

Pressure induces different reactions the further up the chain you go, as we see when Reid is called to a meeting with MS-15 at Scotland Yard. Convinced it is about an appeal hearing on a case of hers, she goes on the offensive, telling Renshaw and Commander Huxley that she would like to know if she is under investigation, and distancing herself from rumours of misconduct at Sun Hill. The bemused pair clarify that they are discussing a vacant superintendent's post. "There are boards coming up next month. If you applied... who knows how lucky you'd be?" Reid's bashful smile acknowledges the cosseted world she has joined. Burnside, meanwhile, is taking the ethical route to triumph. Another raid turns up two shotguns used in the robbery, but the snout who begged him for protection is found kneecapped. "Don't you think we should share some of the responsibility?" hisses Carver. "We got the information out of him in full view of a known pub, now what do you expect?" Without a shred of remorse, the DI replies, "What I got." Redefining the term 'flushed with success', he visits Reid and is told to leave the report on her desk. "No," he declares, shutting her door. "I'm worth more than this. You're not giving me the brush-off." Aware she is off to bigger things, he sneers, "So whose back are you going to be climbing on next, then? Do you know what gets me with you people on accelerated promotion? You never get your hands dirty. Not even when you're rubbing someone's nose right in it." The unfazed Reid asks, "If you know so much about the way it's done, what's stopping you?" "Self-respect." She gives him a pitying look as she leaves. Vaughan demonstrates how officers at every rank are driven by scrutiny from above, and success is ultimately founded on ugly actions like Burnside's: giving him, in a twisted way, the moral high ground.

Reid is awarded a grand send-off in *Somebody Special*, another episode sprinkled with Christopher Russell gems. "Twenty-eight quid?" exclaims Burnside as he surveys the piles of ten and twenty pence coins gathered in the whip-round. "I don't think that's too bad actually, she has only been here a year," says Carver. "I can do you a bent car radio for twenty," adds Dashwood. "I thought you'd just have me shipped out sideways," Burnside tells Reid as she clears her office. "Well if it had come down to you and me, I would have done," says the genial DCI turned Super. "I wasn't about to disappear in a puff of smoke like Gordon Wray, I can assure you." "You're not rushing off, are you? The troops will want to mark your departure later." "With a footprint on the backside in certain cases, I'm sure," she notes drily. Burnside slips into a stupor as he listens to Brownlow's farewell platitudes about her forward thinking and initiative. She opens her leaving gift, a task dumped on Carver at the last moment. His shortcomings as Secret Santa are exposed when she pulls off the wrapping to reveal a silver tankard. "Well I didn't know what else to get her!" he protests as Burnside mouths something at him. "We always give people tankards, don't we?" "No Jim, thanks very much, it's very nice," Reid assures him. "I shall put it on my mantelpiece; next to my pipe." The party ends abruptly when the rest of CID leave on a job, forcing him to stay and be mother. "Would you like another Scotch, ma'am?" "Yes, in that," she snaps, passing him her tankard. When the blokes return in high spirits after a success, they pass Reid carrying her belongings on the stairs. "Bye, Frank. See you in court, perhaps." "You'll have to catch me first," he mutters as he slips away.

One can't shake the feeling that Reid, like Christine Frazer before her, was an experiment in female leadership brought to an abrupt end when the gimmick had worn off. It's fanciful to read too much into background processes, but on a symbolic level it's telling that her exit storyline is crafted largely by a female author who in fact wasn't one. Having enquired about her future on the series, while trying to juggle the demands of filming with motherhood, Carolyn Pickles' reward was a promotion for DCI Reid, in recognition of all the good work she put into the character: which, coincidentally, removed her from the show. The following ten years of stable and virtually all-male casts in the upper ranks suggest that the producers were happy to have hit on a winning team for whom the issues of childcare and maternity leave would never be a factor. When Reid returns for one final appearance in her new role, a Superintendent in the complaints investigation department, it is to supply further commentary on the gulf between the troops and the out of touch guvnors. "You've never had much faith in the system, have you Frank?" "You're a necessary evil," Burnside replies graciously, on the role of MS-15. "I'd rather have you than some raving loony council committee." As far as he is concerned, she's made the logical move; keeping an eye on other coppers' misdeeds is part of the brown-nosing that takes high flyers to the top. Somehow, the female boss is too much of a breed apart to be retained for very long.

Whatever the circumstances, Pickles does at least walk out of the door; more than can be said for the next in line, Larry Dann, in another hangover from a story begun in 1991. Tim Vaughan is once again on script duties for *Addict*, which sees Alec Peters return to work after his stabbing. The echoes of Tom Penny three years earlier are strong; also confined to light duties, Alec has to desert his post in CAD when a helpful Hollis starts banging on about criminal injury compensation. The sound of an ambulance siren, taking away an OD-ed youth, induces the shakes as he tries to down a cuppa. Finally, when he sees Conway, the truth emerges: "You sit there in hospital, drugged up to the eyeballs, pissing into a bag, and you realise: I'm a statistic, that's all any of us are. It occurred to me that when I do finally jack this job in after thirty odd years, the only thing I'm going to come away with is this scar." Conway tries to impress on him that it is just a job; but, like Tom before him, Alec recognises it as a toxic way of life. "I feel like I'm an addict. I don't want it, yet I can't do without it. I'd give up tomorrow if I thought... what else can I do?" One can only imagine the reason why producer Peter Wolfes watched this scene and then felt it necessary to call Larry Dann up to his office and inform him that his performance in *Addict* was "the laziest I've ever seen."[30] Was more scenery chewing expected from Alec Peters, international man of passion? Such criticisms suggest that, in the constant focus on the future, the producers sometimes took established faces for granted. In this case, one can also detect a blurring of actor and character: as though Dann was as pliant and unambitious as the man he played, and could be talked down to just as easily. The fudged exit that follows has all the signs of a production team getting rid of an inconvenience, having lost sight of one of the cast's most consummate professionals.

Come 1992, the friction between Cryer and Peters over the former's role as duty sergeant has got worse. In *Mates*, Bob goes undercover to help bust a suburban brothel, and for all the jokes he has to endure afterwards, realises what he is missing. Full of advice as always, it goes

---

[30] Dann, Larry, *Oh, What A Lovely Memoir* (2023), p. 204

unappreciated by Alec, who is running the operation and insists that Ackland interviews one of the prostitutes arrested. But she and Bob agree that it's a waste of time for WPCs to talk to girls who regard them as annoying mums. Cryer has a word with Quinnan and gets him to take over. Then he visits Brownlow, who is keen to discuss Peters, bringing up his recent sick record; it becomes clear that he is trying to manage him out, suggesting he hasn't fully recovered and should seek professional help. "If anyone wants to see the job psychologist, it's me!" retorts Cryer. "This duty sergeant's job is beginning to drive me round the bend." Brownlow assures him he's been very successful. "Too successful – I didn't join the job to be a politician! I *have* reconsidered; I've spent months considering." This reflects Eric Richard's own feelings about a change of scenery he wasn't enjoying, and in the resulting game of musical chairs someone has to lose out. The dispute is resolved in brutal fashion in *Chicken*, perhaps the most memorable of all Julian Jones's gut-punch episodes. Told that Cryer wishes to return to the relief, Peters observes tartly, "I wasn't aware there was a vacancy for him to return to." Brownlow reminds Peters that he was first choice for the duty sergeant post and puts it to him again. Peters dismisses the idea that there are any lingering effects from the stabbing: "It was really only a flesh wound. It's just one of those things that happen. It was months ago, I've forgotten about it."

Furious at Cryer for "stitching me up with Brownlow", Peters refuses his offer of a drink and Bob has to contemplate another six months in post before someone new is recruited. "He's a desk jockey!" says the brash newbie Boyden, already making his presence felt. "Bob Cryer is a pedantic pain in the arse. I tell you, I wouldn't be duty sergeant, mate," he informs Peters in the gents'. "It's a civilian's job. It's for old coppers that are past their sell-by date." "That's why he doesn't want the job." "A has-been! Lost his bottle." Monroe enters and breaks up their bitching session. In response to a spate of trespassing by children on the railway line, he orders Peters to liaise with British Rail over repairs to fences. Alec dismisses it as "a waste of time, if you ask me", and is hit by one of the headmaster's greatest takedowns: "I didn't ask you – and that's not the attitude I expect. Perhaps you should keep an eye on the company you keep." Two kids shove a trolley onto the live rail. After the power is cut, a cheerful Steve Loxton tells June to clear it. "Oh, get stuffed!" "Chicken!" "I touch that mate, I could be Kentucky Fried!" Still in a huff, Peters hands out his own brusque orders to June, telling her to ignore the truants and get on with other work. Then he and Barry Stringer respond to another shout involving kids playing chicken on the line. One boy tries to cross at the last moment and is shocked by the current, then takes the full impact of the train. Barry glances away in horror as Alec stares, from beginning to end. Afterwards he is all blunt efficiency, informing the paramedics: "I don't think you'll be needed. An undertaker and a couple of refuse bags are all that'll be required." He visits the boy's mother at work to break the news, accompanied by her next-door neighbour. "I don't know if I can do this," the latter whimpers as she approaches. "Martin's her only child!" Peters gives the boy's mother the facts, hard and implacable, before showing her his effects to ID. Seeing the shoe knocked off in the collision, she howls in despair in her friend's arms while he looks on, the model of professionalism.

Back at the station, Cryer apologises for going behind Peters' back, but Alec doesn't care; the mask he has kept on finally cracks. The resulting monologue evokes the trauma of Yorkie Smith in *Fat'Ac* and arguably surpasses it. Whereas Yorkie was a young man discovering the worst the job can throw at him, Peters is an older man who thought he had made it to the far side unscathed, by doing just enough and no more. But the damage catches up to him in the end. "I was thinking about Gary Mabbs. I can always remember him holding the knife," he reveals, proving that his claims to the contrary were to fool himself more than anyone else. "The next I remember is the blood on my shirt. But the moment in between – the vital moment... Today, when the lad got hit by the train... somehow Stringer managed to turn away. I didn't. I watched. I saw him hit. And when I went down on the track, I looked at his body. His torso – his head was... Of course I went to tell his mum; and all these faces around me. All I could see was grief, pain. And all the time I was thinking: *There's no way you're gonna get my job*. I mean, that's really sick. But it's true. Just now, I was thinking about Mabbs. I always remember what he said. He said he was going to kill me. And I was thinking... in some ways it's almost as if he did." Volume 1 of *Reaching a Verdict* observed that the key to Alec Peters was that there were no depths to mine. What Larry Dann conveys so brilliantly, eyes wan and mournful behind those big owl glasses, is a depth that has been created in Alec against his will. If you can't "lose it", as Yorkie hoped to do, then pretending it's not there won't work either. It was in *Fat'Ac* that Cryer proved he was effectively three sergeants in one; now that is made official, as he becomes the last survivor of the original trio. Peters sees Brownlow to discuss a holiday: "It's the timing, sir. I'd like to take it the week before I start as duty sergeant."

What could, and perhaps should, have been our last sight of Alec Peters is instead followed by a few half-hearted cameo appearances in suit and tie before he vanishes into the ether. This is merely one example of the odd phenomenon that plagued the show for a decade, even into the Richard Handford era: the 'Pencil Exit', named after those times in *Crossroads* when someone popped out of the motel to get one and was never seen again. Larry Dann's was by no means the first – both Ashley Gunstock and Kelly Lawrence had vanished abruptly in the Barlby Road days. A better, but no less abrupt departure from early 1992 is that of Natasha Williams, such a memorable presence as the assertive Delia French. When someone's contract was terminated, their final appearance was often dependent on a quirk of scheduling: an episode recorded long ago in which they might only be a truncheon carrier. *Acting Detective* does at least give Delia a central role, forced to go undercover with no notice to replace a Nigerian drug mule put in hospital after the packets in her stomach burst. Pressed for an update on her condition, Burnside reveals that "she won't be using her return ticket." Since "June Ackland blacked up's not a lot of use to me", he asks Delia and she accepts, but without the bravado that was always her strongest trait. Her fears are borne out when both surveillance teams lose the taxi taking her to the dealers, in part because of the show's most groan-inducing cliché, the reversing lorry. Some quick detective work by Tosh narrows her location to the street and a desperate Burnside starts the search, his future slipping away too. In a typically bold move, her cover blown and backed into a corner, Delia chucks a case out of the window. The cavalry burst in just in time, but the ordeal isn't quite over. The laxatives she was given to pass the drugs suddenly kick in, and she is sent dashing upstairs. Whatever Williams' final scene lacks in dignity, plenty of longer-serving actors who came after her could only have dreamt of such a potent exit chute.

FINDING YOUR LIGHT

In the balancing act needed to supply two-dozen actors with decent material from as many writers, some came off better than others. One of the best catered for was Lynne Miller, who continues to impress as Cathy Marshall gets her third change of scenery in as many years, when the DVU placement she had expressed a wish for becomes reality. Before that, she has an uncomfortable taste of another kind of domestic violence in *Trials and Tribulations*. A key witness in two trials, she finds her car has been vandalised and her flat trashed. The story anticipates June Ackland's future ordeal in *Target* when Cathy has to endure prurient questioning by Meadows and Burnside on her private life. "Like my ex-husband? Wouldn't come within ten miles, not after last time... If you want to know who I'm going out with, there's no-one, I haven't had a boyfriend in ages. I haven't slept with anyone in ages, is that all right sir?" Cathy gathers her things from her ruined flat, keeping up the carefree bants with Dave and Barry. In the kitchen, she pulls apart the remains of her cupboard doors in fury. Recognising how brittle she is, Tosh invites her for a drink. She muses that when she saw the damage, "I felt sick, physically sick. I could hear them larking about in the other room so I pretended everything was fine. 'Cos that's what you do if you're a good copper, isn't it? You pretend. You don't let anything show, not anger or fear or love... oh god Tosh, why do we do it?" "Because we believe in it, I suppose." "Yep," she concludes, sipping her drink, and that is as much insight as we get into the workings of a woman who plays things close to her chest. The last few minutes turn into a conventional thriller as her stalker is revealed: the wife of the man she is testifying against. In a struggle Cathy proves the pen mightier than the sword by overturning a bookcase on her assailant, and is still on an adrenaline high at the end. The woman with painful experience of being a victim is getting better at fighting back.

The placement stretches across a trilogy by Russell Lewis, who as we have noted was no puller of punches. They are visible on screen in *Better the Devil*, alongside an array of belt marks and cigarette burns: streaked across a woman in her underwear who giggles as photos are taken, as though posing for a particularly niche calendar. "She wasn't a loved kid," notes Cathy's supervisor, WDS Morgan – not the one who later joins Sun Hill. "I get on his nerves and you know, fair enough if I've done something bad or upset him," the victim Lesley says blithely, used to a world where fists solve problems. "But he does it even if I've done nothing now. I know I'm stupid but that can't be right, can it?" She insists that "he's always sorry, I mean it's him who cries, it breaks my heart sometimes!" – and Cathy gives a hollow smile as she hears her past excuses echoed back at her. When she spots a ring on Lesley's finger from her boyfriend that matches one taken in a spate of burglaries, her default mode starts to clash with the caring role she is supposed to offer. Morgan is hopeful that Lesley will make a good witness, but Cathy has to agree with Greig that this is doubtful on her past form. He tells Morgan he is "one of the few here who is behind your unit", but urges her not to waste CID's time. When he and Carver visit the couple's "charming flat", the ring given to Lesley as "a token of what we mean to each other" is found to be hooky. "On my mother's life..." "Your mother's dead," she cuts in. The fittingly named Ray Bird protests that putting his hands up will make him a criminal. "Well you're doing the work, you might as well have the job title," says Greig. Cathy's successor as collator, Ron Smollett, has dismissed her attachment to Stafford Row as "another of her nine-day wonders... She'll chuck the towel in before the end of the first round." Even June, her ally, points out that "the relief are calling you 'suck it and see Marshall.'" She is dismayed to hear that Cathy is serious about this move: "There'll be nobody left to have a decent gossip with!"

In *World to Rights*, Cathy sees things from the legal end as a woman gives evidence in court against her abusive husband. Leafing through photographs of her injuries in front of a room of strangers, she mutters, "It's me," and is told to speak up. Tony Stamp suggests that the placement is not going how Cathy intended. "Well you can never tell with her," observes June, acknowledging that her fellow WPC is a closed book. Though found guilty, the husband's claims of seeking treatment for his alcohol problem are enough to give him a suspended sentence. Back at the office, Cathy is given the job of making return calls to women who have left secretive messages: a glimpse of the confidential support network that must have been tested to its limits in the Covid lockdowns, to say nothing of the emergency alert test to mobile phones that included the ones people need to hide from their partner. She visits a woman who sounds in immediate danger and finds her nursing a bandaged hand, which her boyfriend held down on the electric ring after she refused to sleep with a loan shark to cancel a debt. When loverboy returns unexpectedly, his partner claims that Cathy is "the catalogue woman", but he blocks her way as she tries to leave: "I think you smell a bit porky!" Pinned to a wall, Cathy strikes back with a well-placed knee and arrests the scumbag. "Come on, result like this, body on the sheet – you know you miss it," says Stringer. "Yeah, like a hole in the head." She gets no plaudits from Morgan, only a severe reprimand: "You disregarded all the guidelines, the safety procedures? The last thing you do is go round to the victim's home if you think there's any chance the assailant might return. You should have passed it to the relief, got an area car round there, you are not in uniform now! If you can't keep a sense of detachment then maybe the unit's not for you."

Cathy's mind is made up in the final instalment, *Punching Judy*. A man arrested for hitting his wife, who was lying unconscious for twelve hours before an ambulance was called, becomes a murderer when she dies in hospital. Cathy herself is engaged in another case which shows the many facets of domestic violence. After two stories above in which it was interwoven with other crimes, a different and equally potent form is revealed when she talks to a middle-aged Asian woman about her husband. "He doesn't hit me... notes. He leave notes. Cruel, wicked things to hurt me. He says he will kill me with poison so he can marry someone else, someone who can have children, he wants a son! He means it. He works in college, laboratory technician you see. It would be easy for him to... The notes he writes, they say 'Maybe it's today' or 'When I get home, you'll be dead'. Sometimes I sit in the living room all day, I'm so scared to find what he writes. There is a student at college, a white girl. He says I'm old, I'm fat, I'm ugly, everything she is not. He says he will bring her to live at our house during holidays. I say, 'over my dead body.' He says, 'Yes, it will be.' We're very strict about divorce, you see. Easier for him if he kills me." Cathy assures her this can be prosecuted as mental cruelty, but she has to leave her in the canteen and returns to find she has gone. When Cathy learns of the dead woman, she passes the good news to Quinnan and Loxton, with a reminder that they were called to a domestic there days earlier, and took no action. "Still, don't let it upset your refs, eh?" Quinnan is straight after her: "That is not fair! You know we have to take some of these things at face value. Most of them don't even want us there at all! They don't want saving, they want leaving alone!"

In the locker room, Cathy tells June that on the relief she could at least judge if she had made the right call on a situation. "I'm withdrawing my application. I don't want to waste any more of their time. I'm a beat copper, it's what I'm best at! What I've learned in DVU is best used on the ground, where it's most needed!" The strength of these longer-running storylines was their ability to put a character in new surroundings and then return them to the status quo, while still developing them as a person. Cathy's various ping-pong moves over the last few years tell us about her limits, but more importantly remind her where her strengths lie. As Russell Lewis has observed, from his time shadowing the police for many programmes, domestic violence is the most constant crime they encounter.[31] If Cathy can best tackle the problem at the sharp end, then her exit from the DVU leaves the pitch clear for another WPC to become the specialist.

Other long-serving characters went through not just fallow months, but fallow years; luckily the sheer volume of output meant that they got their time in the spotlight at some point or other. A promising first year for Alistair Greig is followed by a quiet two, overshadowed by the *Sturm und Drang* of Burnside and Roach. But in early 1992, there is a sudden rush of episodes in which he plays a central role. Most memorable and hard-hitting of these is *Lost Boy*, which not only gives Greig an origin story but slightly redresses the balance after a year of female victims reduced to sexual playthings. The search for a missing boy, Stephen Watson, is proving fruitless and the police suspect he has gone looking for his friend Lee Garside, who left home months ago. Lee's parents don't want to know, and the father eventually reveals why: "He's selling himself." Greig is tasked with finding the two boys, based on his experience with the Vice Squad in Central London. "We think you'll be able to look under the right stones – if Lee is on the meat rack." When he learns that Steve and June are his back-up, his response is emphatic: "I don't want Loxton on this case. He's not right for this sort of job. This young boy, if he's thirteen there'll almost certainly be a ponce involved. The macho approach is

---

[31] *The Bill Podcast: Forget-Me-Not* Patreon Commentary, 2021

out; Loxton's attitude is all wrong." He insists on taking Dashwood, and Steve's hopes of a night out in the West End are crushed. "In this operation we're going to be mixing with the gay community, looking for their support. I can't afford to take along anyone with the wrong attitude." Never failing to disappoint, back comes Stonewall Loxton with the immortal reply, "You what? I've got nothing against shirt-lifters." "Sensitivity's not one of your strong points, is it?"

When Greig reaches the centre of town with Dashwood and Ackland, they visit a man who used to be his best snout: a rather arch nightclub manager, just the sort who would grind Steve's gears. He recognises the photo of Lee, who he caught plying his trade and threw out: "He sometimes acts as hook for a ponce called Matthews. He's likely to be trolling round Victoria." Such is the notoriety of the place that it's referenced in a later episode, when Ted Roach tries to speak to youths at an arcade. "Bog off grandad, go to Victoria if you're that desperate!" snaps one – prompting another of Tony Scannell's classic raised eyebrows. The remainder of *Lost Boy* unfolds in the station itself, a remarkable piece of filming that allows real life to carry on around it, with commuter bustle and platform announcements. It's all too appropriate for a story about what goes on in plain sight of the public, if they just turn their eyes to the corners. Greig's team is rumbled by a face from his past. "What the hell are you doing, Alistair?" asks a long-haired scruff played by Peter Lee Wilson, later to return as Claire Stanton's CIB handler in the Don Beech saga. "We're in the middle of a bloody operation here." The rough-and-tumble band watching the station from an upstairs office, led by Robert Glenister's bearded, woolly-hatted DI Baker, look more like vagrants than policemen. Specialist units, be it vice, drugs or hooliganism, must blend into the seedy worlds they investigate. Realising they are targeting the same villain, Greig asks to come in on their obbo but is told that Mike and June must remain off the plot. "The officers down there have all been specially trained for this sort of work. In fact I think you helped train a couple of them, Alistair." Out of his element, Mike learns some bleak truths about the business – which must have been learnt from a real police adviser in the course of researching this episode. Down on the concourse another pimp is talking to an employee. "Looks fond of him, doesn't he? You see the way he's stroking his chin? He's actually feeling to see if he's started shaving yet. He's worth more if he's still a chicken... twelve to sixteen. Younger than that, they call them spring chickens. Some of them are only three years old."

Baker tells June that Matthews is "making over a thousand quid a night from these boys. That's after he's sampled the merchandise himself, of course." Once their employers are caught, most of them go into care but don't stay there, given that they have already run away from home. "Half the time they're back here in a few months. When you live like that for any length of time it's difficult to form a normal relationship. It takes time, care... love, for want of a better word. These kids haven't got that. So they just drift back." Matthews turns up in the throng of people, as do Lee and the terrified Stephen. Greig has to push his undercover role to the limit when Lee approaches him, asking if he's cottaging. With the promise of "a real chicken", he is taken to meet Stephen, then Matthews, who tells him the action will take place "in the back of my motor. I'll be watching. I want to keep an eye on this one." He gets Greig to dump the money in a rolled-up newspaper, a transaction that caught the eye of the British Transport Police while filming. Then they head to Matthews' bachelor pad, a van outside the station. The moment Greig is inside with Stephen, he lifts the burden etched on the boy's trembling face: "I'm a police officer, and I'm here to take you home." Matthews makes a run for it and is taken down mob-handed. June asks Stephen how he got ensnared. The grooming process is visible in the cigarette he tries to smoke and discards. He is equally unimpressed by the Scotch he was plied with: "Tastes bloody horrible... Lee called me; said it was great up west, said he'd meet me off a train. Why did he do it? He was a mate... They got me in this flat. There was videos and that... fags, booze, whatever you wanted. But then it got horrible. Matthews, he made me do things. I said I wanted to go home, but he wouldn't let me. He locked me in this room, said he'd beat me up if I ran away. He said he knew my address, and he'd find me and kill me."

I once asked Andrew Mackintosh about his memories of this episode, which strikes a chord with me partly because it's set in a place where I've spent so many hours peering at departure boards. But the subject matter is also familiar, courtesy of hundreds of case files waded through in past jobs in social services archiving. While they do not, thankfully, qualify me as an expert on child trafficking, I can say I know more about it than I want to. It becomes obvious why Greig made his way in the job by policing this world: his is a calm, straight-ahead temperament that takes the memories of the damaged young at face value and listens. It's also why, in his long-term value to the series, he is worth at least two of the many mavericks he serves alongside. When the one-liner merchants have come and gone, he is the sort of man that those in need depend on for rescue. Baker asks him if he misses his old job. "This kind of operation, yeah." "Of course you're only remembering the good bits," the DI observes. "When you've been working twenty-two hours a day, you're dead on your feet, nothing's happening, you wonder why you do it at all. And then something like this happens. I wouldn't work for any other section." Many cop shows are happy to rub our noses in human depravity, but through its focus on the police rather than the crime, *The Bill* also points to an upside: the courage and perseverance of people doing harrowing work to make a difference. At the same time it's not naive enough to think that one victory wins the war. The title is something of a feint; Stephen is the Found Boy, while Lee, last seen rushing off through the station, is the lost one. At the end Greig and Dashwood spot another group of teenagers touting for business. "Just carries on, doesn't it?" notes Mike grimly.

Two episodes later, Greig is to the fore again in *Somebody Special*, taking the lion's share of the story as Kim Reid's leaving do goes on in the background. PC Garfield brings in Nicola Purdy, a "twenty-four carat slag", for shoplifting and stabbing a security guard, but points out that she has valuable local knowledge. Greig sees an opportunity to recruit a snout on the troublesome Fairways Estate. "Nicola Purdy, turn informer?" scoffs Burnside. "She wouldn't give you a hanky with snot on it. I've always managed to keep out of gobbing distance." He lets Alistair try, but doubts he will be able to "build a relationship." "Well it's better than pushing people's heads down lavatories," says a rebellious Jim Carver. With the cell door open, Greig goes in for an informal chat, and Christopher Russell reprises his 1989 classic *Greig Versus Taylor*. Once again it's a near two-hander between policeman and criminal – and once again, Greig's dead straight approach wears down the opposition in a way that no amount of threats could. Bronagh Gallagher makes Purdy as formidable an adversary as

Taylor, her Northern Irish brogue not half as thick as those fearsome Pat Butcher medallions hanging from her ears. Insisting that she "only scratched the wog", she scorns the charge of GBH, but is told that she is looking at Crown Court this time. "I'm just trying to understand; treat you like a human being," Greig assures her. "You sound like a bloody social worker!" He asks if she has considered what it's like to be locked up. "Ooh, you're scaring me!" Having lost one child to care, she may lose her five-year-old too. "Look what do you want, do you fancy me or something?" she demands. "I've told you: I just don't like the nick 'em and bin 'em approach."

Greig discovers that Purdy has a boyfriend and suggests she may miss him too. "We do find that's one of the major problems when men go down: the loss of physical contact." Nobody else in CID could make such an appeal, especially to a female prisoner, as a sincere point rather than a coarse joke. "So this is a stable relationship? Wherever he goes, he'll be there waiting for you when you come out? Eighteen months is a long time." "You said six!" she protests, suddenly alarmed. "Six *minimum*, Nicola," he clarifies, holding back the vital blows for the right moment just as he did with Taylor. After he brings up the drug situation on the estate, she realises he is angling for a grass, but as he leaves she snaps, "What can a prat like you do anyway?" – a classic buy sign, proving that she wants the deal. Greig makes no false promises, saying he can't predict the judge's decision but can try to slim her sentence. She balks at the idea of grassing on drug dealers, but could provide info on stolen goods. If recruiting informants is the bread and butter of CID, then we saw the Burnside way, all bluffs and entrapment, in 1988's *Snout*. Everybody handles the jungle differently; where the DI swells up to intimidate opponents, Greig blends in harmlessly till he is ready to strike. Russell doesn't take the simplistic route of casting him as a saint among sinners. When he returns with news of a shop selling bent gear, Burnside is astounded that Purdy came across, all for the sake of hanging onto her boyfriend. "What chance has a slag like that got of finding anybody who thinks she's special?" "None whatsoever," says Greig, "but we all have to dream, don't we?" Just as ruthless in his own way, his bluffs last longer: playing best friend rather than bully has more mileage.

Greig's desire for a new informant is motivated partly by his rise in the ranks. The departure of Reid prompts a round of pass the parcel in which Greig is shifted to Acting DI and Burnside to Acting DCI. The latter gets a pep talk on his new role, Brownlow style: "It means taking an overview – strategy, innovation, thought." "Rest assured, sir. I shall grasp the challenge with both hands." Meeting Greig in the corridor, Burnside observes, "Anyone would think I was standing in for God." "Whereas I am, of course," comes the brilliant riposte. Greig soon learns that God's shoes are very hard to fill. The show's other veteran writer, Barry Appleton, returns to the office politics of CID that were always such fertile territory for him in *It's a Small World*. Tosh watches Greig making a phone call in what has become his office and notes that this Acting DI gig has changed him. "Someone'll pull the rug from under his feet and bang, he'll be back in the land of three stripes before you can say 'Sir Robert Mark.'"[32] Viv Martella storms in, fresh from being humiliated in court, and lays into her ersatz boss: "I lost the Vinci case. It was thrown out as a result of *your* advice! You told me Vinci was no longer a suspect, so I kicked him out. Then I should never have held a street identification two weeks later! It's not technical when you get a slagging-off from the beak! 'A total disregard of the code', that's what he said. You made a complete fool of me!" Smarting from this public attack, Greig holds a meeting to try and correct the idea that his promotion carries no real authority. "If there are any comments, criticisms, whatever – let's hear them now and clear the air." He singles out Roach, insisting that he call him 'sir', not 'Alistair'. "I'm not being pompous; it's a question of respect for the rank." Given the floor, the court jester makes full use of it: "Sir – you can rely on my complete co-operation. And if you need any advice, please don't hesitate. No, sincerely!"

Overhearing this blatant piss-take, Burnside drags Greig into his own office. "What the hell was that all about? You were letting Ted Roach take centre stage. He is finished – over the hill, played out, as far as promotion is concerned. He's got nothing to lose. *You* have got a future. Protect it!" He advises Greig to delegate: "If stamping your authority means being uncompromising, stuff 'em!" "I don't work

---

[32] A Metropolitan Police Commissioner of the 1970s who introduced reforming policies to tackle corruption, especially within CID.

that way!" "Well then it's time you did." Marching back into CID, Greig begins laying down the law. After dumping his caseload on Roach, he orders Tosh to "smarten yourself up. Your appearance is not becoming to a member of this department. I'd suggest a haircut for a start, and I want to see that suit cleaned and pressed. There won't be a second warning." Then it's Viv's turn, chastised for taking too many short journeys by car. "This office has become very sloppy. I want to see maximum effort from everybody." This charade has echoes of Roach's behaviour when he was Acting DI – kicking backsides to prove he is in charge, but failing to disguise the air of desperation about it. "Power corrupts," an angry Ted declares this time; but to those ill suited to it, it reveals their incorruptible flaws. If he didn't have the restraint to be DI, then Alistair doesn't have the presence. It's easy to forget that the latter has already received a blot on his copybook as Acting DI. When he has CID tackle armed blaggers without using back-up in 1990's *Lies*, a gun is left at the scene and found by a kid, who wounds another with it. DCI Bradby, himself covering for the on-leave Wray, tears him off a strip: "You know that anything like that should be at least two to one, or even PT-17. You didn't plan it correctly, that's how an inquiry might see it." This is the start of a slide that will pass to Greig the role of nearly man that was seemingly reserved for Roach. These polar opposites, denied power for different reasons, at least get to share an inheritance of sorts.

THE LONG HAUL

The planets are restored to their orbits when the demoted Jack Meadows arrives at Sun Hill to begin his eternal reign as DCI. The generally held view of Meadows is one of the subtler acts of reinvention performed by Paul Marquess in his 2002 revamp of the show. Positioned as the decent survivor of the old school, he works with Mickey Webb to bring down the corrupt Superintendent Chandler and suddenly his past sins are forgotten. When Sally Johnson returns as a private eye she is all smiles when she meets her old boss for lunch – her tenure under him having ended, like it did for the DIs before and after her, in betrayal, anger and recrimination. Odder still is Meadows' attendance a year later at the funeral of his "close friend" Ted Roach. Judging by their time as colleagues in the early Nineties, and Ted's return as a free agent in 2000, Jack would only show up to make absolutely sure he was dead, and wasn't about to climb from the grave swearing vengeance, one fist clenched for action, the other round a bottle of whisky. The Meadows of the Nineties is not a rough, tough legend watching the backs of his troops, but a careerist weasel ready to push them into the gutter at any moment. In his early days as a Super there are worse traits in evidence. Arriving at the scene of a lover's tiff that became a murder, he mutters, "Poofs, great." With the culprit in the bag, Brownlow wants to inform the media but Meadows is less keen: "It's not the kind of case I like to be associated with, to be quite honest. I don't think it merits the publicity. 'Gay love nest murder solved'? You know what the press are like." If only, you can see him thinking, I had got this result for the Blake murders; kids bring more kudos than queers. In *Plato for Policemen* he attends a seminar where the lecturer plays devil's advocate with his audience, to challenge their ingrained views on policing. While Greig tries to engage and rebut him, a bored Meadows asks "where this is getting us"; he sees it as a tick-box exercise to climb a ladder that he has no idea will be kicked away from him.

After two DCIs on their way up, it was a smart move to bring in one headed in the other direction. By now Meadows is such a familiar face that there is no announcement of his takeover. His first episode as a regular, *Re-Hab*, sees him put in his place by his successor at AMIP, Detective Superintendent Douglas, and the scorn comes from below as well as above. Passing him on the stairs, Garfield asks Loxton curiously, "He's not the new DCI, is he?" "Corruption," Loxton declares, and Meadows is after them in a fury: "You got a problem? Well you will have, if I ever hear you use that word again." The murder of a young drug addict has been confessed to by his father, a former robber. "Once a villain, always a villain," a cheerful Douglas reminds Meadows. Still feeling guilty for precipitating his fall, Burnside offers to help: "I know I've only been Acting DCI, but if there's anything I can do..." "Thanks," replies a grateful Meadows. "Is the DCI's office clear?" "Well, it's all in boxes, sir." "Well if you could clear all your stuff out by the end of the day, that'd be great." He delivers a lecture to his new team on standards that echoes the one from Greig: "I don't want my officers walking around as if they've just fallen out of bed. So, if you're interviewing a suspect you wear your jackets. If you're outside the station, and that includes the front office, you wear your jackets. Shirtsleeves will only be worn in here, or if you're not dealing with the general public. Ties will be worn done up, properly, at all times." The dismay on Ted, Jim and Tosh's faces as this news sinks in, and they all tighten theirs, is matched by Burnside as he has to do likewise. Brownlow meets Meadows outside his new office, struggling with a keychain. He assures him he has his full support, and that his door is always open. "You haven't got a key for this one, have you?" asks Jack feebly.

Meadows' efforts to distance himself from his past are obvious to everyone. When Carver racks up four complaints of harassment in a week, the DCI assures him he does not believe they are founded, but he doesn't want to see any more for the next month. "He can't afford to be associated with anything iffy with his history," Jim observes to Tosh. Predictably, however, it's that close friend of Jack's who gives him most grief. In *True Confessions*, a defendant withdraws his guilty plea, claiming that said confession was pressured out of him by Roach in return for the amphetamines he needed. There now begins a *"voir dire* – the trial within a trial", to rule on its admissibility. Ted drags the CID apprentice into the crossfire. Martella is often the victim of the changing attitudes forced on her superiors. The year before, while giving evidence, she reels off the suspect's convictions from her notebook and is hastily told to stop. When he is found guilty, a complaint is made by the CPS – and a naive rookie error turns out to be anything but. "What cretin did you ever see do that?" Burnside demands. "The first case I ever saw you in, guv. I was still on the beat." "Can't you *choose* what to remember?" he sighs. "Look Viv, times change. You do not have to imitate your elders and betters." Usually, of course, she is told just the reverse. This time Roach gets Viv to sit in on the trial for him. "You know what you've done, don't you?" Meadows rages at her later. "Hearing Lawson's testimony means that Roach'd be able to alter his own testimony if it came to a full trial. You know the sort of stink that'd make if the defence found out? What that would do to the credibility of this department? To our relationship with CPS? Get out!" He then hauls Roach in: "An officer only bends the rules if he's lazy, bent himself or to cover up a mistake. Mistakes I can cope with, up to a point, as long as you come clean with them. But laziness and corruption I have no time for! Do I make myself clear?" Though he is temporarily cowed, Ted knows that sermon is a little rich coming from Meadows; he got busted down because of the former and hasn't dispelled all hints of the latter.

Meadows' first outing as a regular sets the trend for what is to come. His predecessors were realistic attempts to portray the life of a DCI: strategy, paperwork, blue sky thinking. Jack is out on the streets leading enquiries as much as he is sat behind a desk. When another CID raid goes south and a post-mortem is conducted, Burnside is keen to go out with Roach to find his snout and leave the office duties to Meadows. But the latter gives him that task while he accompanies Ted, seeking out addicts in their hiding holes and questioning them. Simon Rouse may have been given this more active role as an incentive for him to stay on, providing continuity that was badly needed after so much chopping and changing. In the long run, it often reduces the DCs to functionaries, grabbing the bodies after their boss has done most of the detective work. Such problems were never envisaged in a show that started out very light on the ground in senior officers, but the expansion of that realm gave the show a whole new dimension, one which had to be kept fresh. To repeat the struggles of the modernisers Wray and Reid with the Neanderthal Burnside would have been to push a well-worn theme past its limit. Meadows' crime-busting is perhaps a necessary step towards the show's return to the hourly format, when just about everyone ends up 'involved', and compromised, in far more unlikely ways. At this point, though, it is still pushing the orthodox message. When Jack's subordinate tries to turn his short-lived role as Acting DCI into the real thing, the challenge ahead of him is clear: getting used to the still life. In J.C. Wilsher's *Overdue*, it's Burnside's turn to face the ordeal of a selection board, like Roach and Brownlow before him. "I don't think he'll get it," the new boy Alan Woods tells Carver as they sit in a van on obbo. "He's not the right flavour at the moment. He's... passé." True to form, Burnside is keen to get stuck into their job, but Meadows assures him the lads can handle it: "Crime management, that's the name of the game – the art of delegation."

Meadows started off his own board with a resume of his police career, a subject on which Burnside is understandably cagey: "I know the things I want to bring to light... and the bits I want to leave out." At the Yard he is met with the familiar combo of hostile admin followed by a three-man hit squad. The interview episode, another of *The Bill*'s sub-genres, wasn't Wilsher's specialty as much as the training episode, but both required a strong supporting cast in thankless roles: earnest, well-meaning people, there to bring out the flaws in our heroes. Like the course instructors in *Effective Persuaders*, the actors here do a sterling job. The lead interviewer is amiable and encouraging; then come the testing queries from his lieutenants. Burnside is softened with flattery about being an "active officer", before he is reminded what the role of DCI entails: "Delegation, supervision, control of resources. Budgeting. Not your style at all, is it?" He maintains that operational experience should be valued, and people have always been recruited from the ranks. "Yes, but this is a police service for the 1990s. Shouldn't you be more interested in change?" He uses Reid's street robbery scheme as an example of this, while conceding that the initial idea was not his. When Burnside is asked for his view of women in the police, the story reflects – and arguably, criticises – the show's past record. "A good woman officer is worth her weight in gold, sir. That's especially true in CID." "So how come women are disproportionately concentrated in the uniform branches? And at the lower ranks?" "Well, I expect they're discouraged by some aspects of police culture from fulfilling their potential. It's not a level playing field, is it? Canteen culture still discriminates, unfortunately." His attempt to recast himself as a feminist for one afternoon does not fool the board, who remind him he might have to serve under a female super, like he did with DCI Reid. "And you're telling us that was a model relationship, are you?" Burnside insists that any difference of opinion was down to a clash of personalities. "The job seems happy enough with Reid's attitude and personality. She got made up to Superintendent in complaints." "Yes, well I'm always pleased to see someone find their right niche," he snipes back.

Glancing at his watch, he realises the nightmare isn't over. "Some senior figures in the legal system have been talking about an officer corps in the police: graduate entry for inspectors and those above. What is your view on that?" "Well if it came, I'd have to live with it. But I don't like the idea. It would make your average constable feel like a second-class citizen. And he or she would have no great prospect of advancement in the job. I don't think an academic qualification can tell you whether someone's got the right stuff or not." "Be better placed to make that judgement if you had a degree yourself, wouldn't you?" Burnside explains he has never been able to take time off to pursue it – only for one of the board to reveal that he managed it in his own time. "Well I find that totally admirable, sir," he replies through gritted teeth. "I'm just not the scholarly type." By the time he leaves, he has been torn to shreds like those who came before him. Most drama appeals by depicting situations we never face in real life, but an interview story is quite the reverse. To see the gulf between who someone wants to be, and who they really are, exposed so brutally is something we can all identify with. Burnside has a debrief with Meadows, who has spent all day running round after the former's snout, again proving that the DI is too close to the villains: "In future, keep your distance. It's the modern way." Christopher Ellison again brings out that subdued quality in Burnside when he finds himself on the losing end. "Trouble is, once you get a bit of a reputation in this job people are all too willing to think the worst. I mean would you believe it, there are stories going round that I shoved a prisoner's head down the khazi! They got it all wrong, anyway. He wasn't a prisoner." Meadows gets a call and gives the DI a four word summary: "Better luck next time. Maybe they thought you just weren't quite ready." "Yeah... well by my reckoning I'm a bit overdue," Frank mumbles. He finishes his drink and leaves quietly, taking his frustrations with him.

THE GILDED CAGE

The difficulty of leadership is one of the most enduring themes of the show. Nowhere is this better demonstrated than in *Man of the People*, which marks a day of salvation for Charles Brownlow: "After five long years, I'm finally going to be able to shut the door on Hollis... He's only held onto the Federation job for so long because nobody else wanted it." Convinced that the day's ballot will see him off, the Chief Super celebrates by inviting Conway to join him in the staff canteen for lunch. "We're rather out of step here at Sun Hill in clinging to the privilege of a senior officers' dining room. Other divisions have done away with theirs some time ago. Today's as good a day as any to take the first step away from remote elitism." "But I *like* remote elitism!" Conway protests. "I like having my dinner in peace. I don't want to share a gunged-up sauce bottle with the likes of Loxton or Garfield!" With no fanfare for the Common Man, he scowls at his boss as they tuck into their cod and chips. Hollis is less certain of his imminent demise, loitering to make sure his rival, Stringer, doesn't try and canvass the electorate. "Today is vital, one vote could make all the difference!" Conway warns Brownlow to beware the devil you don't know: "Do you want a Federation Rep with common sense? Hollis is a clown, you can ignore him. You won't be able to ignore Stringer." "For God's sake Derek, stop sulking!" In the half-hour format each second of onscreen time was precious, little details needing to be justified; and this episode makes the best ever case for them. The long zoom out from Brownlow and Conway to an otherwise empty canteen, as the former insists that "the them and us attitude is outmoded", is brilliant enough. Even better is the glimpse of Datta's reading, abandoned earlier as she made a speedy exit before her masters could sit beside her: Dirk Bogarde's wartime-set novel *A Gentle Occupation*. Stamp refuses to dine under the imperial yoke, and a delegation descends on Barry. "There are certain issues that need looking at," he admits. "Sector policing, changes in the shift system." "How about the rights of plods and plonks not to be spied on?"

Once the polls close, Brownlow swoops on the ballot box and carries it to his office. The votes, plus one crumpled Skittles packet, are emptied in front of Reg and Barry and the count begins. After Barry, the diffident challenger, scrapes through by fifty-eight to two, the relief are instantly on his case about the canteen. He visits Brownlow and, though visibly nervous, puts over the position of his members: "They've asked me to inform you that they're in favour of the status quo. They feel that retaining the existing catering facilities would allow all ranks to relax in the appropriate manner. This being a disciplined uniform service in which the differentials of rank have an important part to play, they don't want the edges to be blurred." 'Them and us' is ingrained in everyone; the only thing worse than the bosses never being around is when they are. Barry later tells Reg where his extra vote came from: "Didn't seem right voting for meself. It's nothing personal, is it? After five years people fancy a change." Keeping a sense of proportion, Reg observes that "it is history repeating itself. Being kicked in the teeth by an ungrateful electorate. Winston Churchill had the same trouble in 1945." The ending is the greatest in the show's history, from its funniest ever dynamic. Whichever double act he's put in, Jeff Stewart is the straight man, in that he never, ever changes. It's the reactions of his partner that sell the joke, and nobody does it better than Peter Ellis. Tension grips Brownlow's entire body as he enters the car park to find his nemesis waiting for him. Reg observes that divisional newspapers have been a great success and he wants to start one at Sun Hill, with himself as editor. "Shall I pencil it in for tomorrow then, sir?" Brownlow glances forlornly at the sky. A massive crack of thunder greets him as he walks away, shaking his head; even the Earth weeps.

Reg passes his accumulated wisdom to the new man when Barry faces his first real challenge as Rep. Conway posts a notice about policing demos, for which A Relief will have to give up their Saturdays on the next three long weekends. Amid cries of outrage, Barry is warned by his meddling predecessor that he needs "some fire in your belly if you're going to see the governors on this. Otherwise they'll walk all over you if you let them." Garfield passes as they discuss their strategy, and for one moment the Reps of Past, Present and Future are all in shot. Reg explains the basic principle of collective bargaining: "Aim over the top. If you're angry, be furious. If you want two pence, ask for ten pence! It's all part of the negotiation process, you see?" The psyched up Barry marches into Conway's office and starts ranting at him: "You won't get people's co-operation in the future, and I'm speaking on behalf of the sergeants here too. No-one is going to accept this!" His rhetoric bounces off Conway, who asks what alternative he can propose. A chastened Barry is pointed to Monroe, who dispenses gentle wisdom: "Being the Rep isn't about shouting everyone out. It's about being the sort of person who can go between ranks: talk to the PCs, then talk to the management. Understand both, and be understood by both. Let Reg choke on it, Barry; and the relief. If you can get Mr Conway on your side, you'll achieve more in one day as Fed Rep than Reg Hollis did in *five years*." This has the ring of authenticity from Colin Tarrant, who in real life became the cast's rep when issues cropped up. Barry sees Conway again, and this time is so meek and accepting that he is about to leave without offering a single challenge to his scheme. It's the latter who suggests they discuss it, recognising a need to play the game. They agree a compromise: if the relief can decide the numbers of people on duty between themselves, they each get one weekend off. "But

Barry... what happened to the negotiations? I'm flabbergasted, I'm lost for words!" "That's the general idea, Reg."

Reg's foray into the world of journalism sucks in most of his fellow officers, even though they have no influence on it. "As far as I can see, Reg is writing the whole paper himself!" complains Stamp. "Quite sensible," says Quinnan, "he's the only one who's gonna read it." Forced to supply news from CID, Tosh is advised by Roach to "make it snappy, make it grabby, make it up." Brownlow, meanwhile, was paying attention every time "work" forced Burnside to leave one of their interminable meetings. When his loyal secretary Marion announces grimly that Hollis has arrived, "the appointment we moved from last week", she adds, "How long before the urgent phone call?" "If you leave it for more than three minutes, I'm going to find some very urgent typing that needs doing before you go home, all right?" Unaware that Garfield has slipped a top shelf mag into his envelope, Reg passes it to the Super – "I just wanted you to see the way my mind is working" – but the latter doesn't bat an eyelid as he pulls out the offending item: "Full colour printing. Rather ambitious, don't you think?" Both Brownlow and Conway are stuck with their nightmares, and humanised as a result, proving that the slow drip of adversity is as effective as a big burst in providing insight into a character. During this year the show delves deeper into Del Boy, implying that his misery has deeper roots than the man next door; his stagnant career may be as much the symptom as the cause. Of Mike Dashwood's transfer to the Arts and Antiques Squad, he remarks, "If he wants to spend his time fondling *objets d'art*, that's up to him; it's not what I joined the police for." Voicing the thoughts of his colleagues and the viewing public, Brownlow asks curiously, "What *did* you join the police for, Derek?"

That profound question is explored in more depth in *Hands Up*. Christopher Russell always seemed to relish writing for Stamp and Conway: unsurprising, given that bellyachers supply the best dialogue. Emerging from a Yard lecture on management structure, Conway asks Brownlow wearily, "Will there be an interpreter next time, sir? How much does he get paid for making the obvious unintelligible?" On the top-heavy problems of the service, he observes, "There's too many Chiefs and not enough Indians, there has to be, doesn't there? Otherwise the Indians wouldn't have anything to look forward to. Promotion's the only reward the job has to offer." "Well you don't sound very rewarded, Derek. To be perfectly frank, you never have done." "You're a red-hot PC, brilliant on the street, and what do they do? They promote you! And they carry on promoting you until they find something you're completely useless at. Then one cock up too many and they retire you early on a full pension, it's crazy." "You telling me you'd rather be a constable back on the beat, are you?" "To be honest I would, sir." Putting his money where his mouth is, Conway tells Stamp that he's coming out as a passenger in the area car. "It's only a whim; I am allowed, you know." "Of course, sir. Nice to have you onboard," says Quinnan unconvincingly. Their despair mounts as Conway embarks on a nostalgia trip. "What's the crumpet like round here? When I was your age I used to park up the RT car by the local Tube station of a morning; watch the dolly birds going to work. Mini-skirts, hot pants... you ever do that?" He gets them to drop him at a market and they make tracks "before he changes his mind." He hears a crash and discovers that a sign has been lobbed through a shop window. He soon finds the culprit, a drunk with a plaster cast over one arm. "Right, that's the one-armed drunks taken care of," notes Boyden in CAD. "Wonder what he'll go for next – one-legged grab and flees?"

But his problems are just beginning. The yob's lawyer points out that the description given by the shop owner places the cast on the wrong arm, and insists on an ID parade. "Where am I supposed to find eight people with their arms in plaster?" Conway demands. "You could always send out snatch squads to the local hospitals," ventures Cryer. "What I did when I had a case like this before," adds Maitland, "was I brought in eight volunteers and... broke their arms." When even he is scoring points, you know the Chief Inspector is in trouble. Without a victim, as the shop owner has gone on holiday, Conway throws his toys out of the pram: "Forget it. Stick him on for the D and D. Drop that as well if you like, give him a commendation for all I care. I don't want anything more to do with it." While his whinging has much in common with Stamp, Conway's real soulmate in the lower ranks is Ackland: both of them rootless and dissatisfied, looking for more out of the job and failing to get it. Where her frustrations are milked for their dramatic worth, however, his play out as comedy, and are no less real or affecting for it. After PACE has battered him into submission, the puns begin. "Shouldn't worry about it, sir; he seemed 'armless enough," Maitland notes. Meadows has caught a robbery suspect and asks if he wants to sit in on the interview: "Just thought you might like to chance your arm again." The final insult comes when Brownlow drops in at the end of the day. "I thought you were enjoying the simple life downstairs, Derek." "Downstairs, upstairs – the job's not 'simple' anywhere, sir," he muses as he draws on a cigarette. "Quite; money's better up here, though. At least you're not out on a limb, hmm?" Conway gives him a dead-eyed stare as he leaves.

Conway is under the microscope again in *Force is Part of the Service*. Loxton has brought in a black man, Malcolm Jackson, for questioning over an alleged robbery and given him a bloody nose in the course of restraining him. His protests threaten to ruin the cosy impression that Brownlow and Conway are giving of the rebranded service to the council's police committee. "Well there's a new generation coming to the fore, isn't there?" remarks one member. "They talk about the policemen on the beat getting younger, but when you see the top brass on television some of them look as if they're only in their thirties!" The irony isn't lost on Conway, who quickly fakes a smile. He sees the "floorshow" beginning in the custody area and ushers them away, but when the genuine robber is caught, Jackson wants to make a complaint. Monroe is straight with him about how long it will take and the questioning he will face, and seems to have deterred him – but after returning home to mull it over, he phones to reveal that he is going ahead. Conway tries the first line of police defence by digging up dirt on him, but there is none. "It's one thing getting an assault allegation on somebody we've charged, but this sort of thing does PR no good at all," Brownlow declares. "Well I'm sure there's something we can charge him with sir, if you think it'll help." "Don't be facetious, Derek." While the evidence may not support disciplinary action, it could be enough to try in civil court, which requires a lower standard of proof. "And Sun Hill won't earn any brownie points by letting the job in for twenty grand's worth of damages," notes Conway. He is dispatched on a charm offensive to try and talk Jackson out of it. "Is this afternoon soon enough?" "If that's the best you can manage, yes," replies Brownlow icily. "And bear in mind: a soft answer turneth away wrath."

Suited and booted, Conway enters the high-rise dump Jackson calls home and tries to accentuate the positive: "Well you certainly get the views from up here, don't you? Right across London, more or less." "Yeah – except for the good bits." Pointing out that the address wasn't his choice, he clears the pile of takeaway junk in front of the TV. Although stories of blue-on-black strife tended to recycle the same beats, here a young David Harewood at least gets to play more than 'wronged and indignant'. As he talks blandly of his career as a mechanic, we get the sense that Jackson is a hopeless case: a drifter who accepts the punches life has thrown at him. He had hopes of starting a business, but was made promises by his boss that never materialised. Conway is quick to empathise: "Believe me Malcolm, I've been there." Jackson lost his home, then his wife and child. "But you know, that's life, you've gotta keep going I suppose," he adds with hollow briskness, as though repeating a mantra someone has told him. Only after exploring his life story in detail does Conway move onto the complaint, asking what he really wants from it. He agrees to withdraw it. Loxton and Garfield are called to a pub brawl and take a leathering, showing what kind of reception the police have to prepare for. Monroe, however, warns Steve not to treat complaints like medals. "That complaint stays on your record even though it's been withdrawn, and if you get a complaint that goes the full distance, the investigating officer will look at that record and he'll draw conclusions. Be advised." Loxton was lucky to get handy with the right man. "What did you make of him, as a matter of interest?" Brownlow asks Conway. "Jackson? He's a loser – I can spot 'em." Their entire relationship is summed up in the kindly look the Super throws at his oblivious deputy.

MUTUAL DEPENDENTS

With the battles between police and courts less frequent this year, it's the police versus the criminal that takes centre stage – a more nuanced and at times, less combative relationship. Philip Palmer's *Suspects* is a great example of the reward that comes from viewing the show in order: a totally unheralded episode that turns out to be a minor classic. The ever-thorough Greig has the house of a robbery suspect, Bartlett, cordoned off by PT-17 officers. Their phlegmatic inspector is prepared for a siege – "No skin off my nose, get the caterers in" – but Bartlett gives himself up after his terrified girlfriend Karen walks out past the heavy artillery. When a search reveals nothing, it looks as though Greig has severely overreacted. "You can't be bothered looking for the thieves can you, you just go down your list, 'He'll do'!" snarls Karen. "Who can we stitch up today, let's plant the phoney evidence, lads!" Greig receives a head butt from her lover, and is in no mood to discuss it at the nick. "Touch of the old Glaswegian martial arts," Roach informs Meadows, "the man was under arrest and handcuffed." "Have to use a blindfold next time." "Nah – he'd still lose." Greig is taken to one side by Bartlett's solicitor Wilkin, who is trying to persuade Bartlett to plead guilty. "I told him he hasn't got a ghost of a chance, not against the forensic you've got lined up." One puzzled look from Greig later, he adds, "Thought as much. See you in court, chum." He puts in a claim for unlawful detention and Meadows realises that Greig's evidence is thin on the ground. Then a tip-off puts someone else in the frame. Annoyed that his most able man is pulling people who are 'likely', the DCI suggests he is falling into bad habits. "Bartlett can't afford to go all the way, a court case would cost him..." "It won't get that far. You're gonna apologise to Bartlett, smooth things over with that sophisticated charm of yours." Greig tells him curtly he is being released: "Just like that? You get me up at gunpoint, chuck me in a cell, and when you're fed up of mucking me about I'm free to go? Till the next time!"

Greig gives a lift home to Bartlett, who insists that an apology is owed to Karen. "It doesn't matter to me, I expect to be picked up, but she finds it hard." "She should learn to expect it." "She shouldn't have to expect anything, she hasn't been a thief!" Karen is taking legal action through the high-priced Wilkin, which Bartlett isn't keen on, and we realise she is the driving force – he only wants a quiet life. "Having Wilkin did you no favours," Greig tells her. Alarmed at this comment, Bartlett follows him out and reassures him he will get her to drop the action: "Am I in the clear, are you taking me off your list? I'm no fool; if I stay the wrong side of you, you'll do me. Whatever happens, I'll go down." The bemused Greig insists he doesn't work like that. "I don't bear grudges. Come on, do I look like I'm that kind of bent copper?" "All coppers are the same, I've had me share of it. I haven't always gone down for the jobs I've pulled – but it evens out in the end." "Not in my book." This scene echoes one from an episode called, funnily enough, *Suspects*, back in Series 2. At the London Docks, a gnomic exchange between a kid on a bike and Galloway speaks volumes: "My brother got stitched up by the Bill; got six months for doing up a Paki in a newsagents." "Was he at it?" "Oh, yeah." "Well," the DI concludes, throwing his cigar in the water, "there you go." Ex-copper Barry Appleton voices the generally held belief of the job: that the deserving are caught in the end, even if it requires creativity at times. To paraphrase Eric Morecambe, they're nicking all the right people, but not necessarily in the right order. Even Bartlett, the criminal, sees a justice in this – an attitude that leaves Greig profoundly disturbed. It suggests that he is a lone figure trying to uphold the rules, while all around him dodgy practice is the norm. "I really want you to believe this: I have no intention of fitting you up." "Don't make me laugh, it's the game, isn't it? I'm one of yours."

The common threat of legal action in the past two episodes highlights the rise of compensation culture in the early Nineties, aided by the miscarriages of justice that had been exposed in the past few years. If villains can't shake their image and end up being hassled forever more, then the bent perception of the police also sticks, and can be exploited by the other side. The lawyers start to dictate the agenda in *A Friend in Need* (another title recycled from the hour-long era – as is that of the very next episode, *Whose Side Are You On?*, both written by the same author, Duncan Gould. The seemingly bottomless well of proverbs that *The Bill* drew on for titles did, after all, have its limits.) Quinnan is facing a civil action and a complaint from a hoax 999 caller who claims he was assaulted during his arrest: "Our pal Garrod decides he deserves a few quid for being so legless he falls over and cuts his head!" The complaint is averted, but when Dave calls at the police solicitors the woman he speaks to suggests they may not fight the action: "It would cost at least twenty thousand to defend the case in court; more like two or three times that. And there's absolutely no guarantee of winning. We're talking about the civil court. There's none of your 'beyond reasonable doubt' in civil courts. Juries are instructed to decide on the balance of probability. The jury will know that Garrod got six stitches. Would you bet forty thousand pounds that a jury would believe you? People think policemen lie these days, you know." "A bloke walks free for two crimes and I've got to watch him get paid for it?" says an astonished Dave. "I've wasted a whole day and picked up a complaint on my file, just so a villain can earn himself a couple of grand for falling over!" "It's a matter of economics!" "No it's not, it's much simpler than that. It's a matter of I'm a copper, he's a villain. I nick him, he gets off suspended; I get a complaint, he gets given a couple of grand! If that's justice you can shove it!" he roars as he leaves.

Policeman and criminal reach an accord, of sorts, in J.C. Wilsher's *Principled Negotiation*. The late great Pete Postlethwaite stars as a blagger of years past, Ray Goller, who is brought in after a raid on an antiques shop, carrying a slashed set of ladies' underwear. Seeing him in custody, Ted Roach insists that he's no knicker-snatcher. "You talk about him as though you were old pals," says an irritable Burnside. Ted speaks to Goller alone, with the tape off. "You wouldn't lie to me, would you?" "Well of course I'd lie to you, if it was a bit of work – but it's not." It's personal business, and we learn how personal when Martella brings in the woman whose underwear was stolen. "There's no way it can be Raymond Goller! He's my dad." "This is beginning to sound like the women's page of *The Guardian*," remarks Burnside. "Are we going to have to add incest to injury?" Viv observes that the daughter is scared for Goller, not of him. When Goller's car is found trashed it becomes obvious that someone is putting the frighteners on him. Burnside hopes this news will "wind him up nicely", but Roach has other ideas: "There's a time for the stick, and a time for the carrot. Let him walk now; he understands favours, I'll get it out of him." The DI wants to know how big a pal Goller is, and Ted tells him a story: "A wage snatch goes down. One of the bandits turns out to be a bit of a psycho. He half-kills a security guard with a pick handle, beats the stuffing out of his girlfriend, and threatens to do the same to his mates. Ray is under pressure to put this guy in order. One way is to kill him. Now rather than do that, Ray gets into negotiations with a young DC who badly needs a good collar. Matters are handled with discretion and efficiency on both sides. The DC puts a dangerous nutter in the bin. Within strict limits, there's a basis for trust and understanding."

Roach accompanies Goller to his upmarket house, which is being used as security for the bank loans he needs for his business. He bought gold in an overseas deal which turned out to be a scam, and "my creditors were expecting their money at noon today. There isn't any." Ted suggests he can help, but Goller asks what will happen to his reputation when "it gets around that I call the law in? Don't try and kid me Ted, I'm not Salman Rushdie. How much protection am I going to be worth in the long term?" After receiving a threatening phone call about his daughter, he went round to her place to find her slashed underwear lying on the bed. Viv is sent to babysit her while Burnside joins Roach, promising Goller and his girlfriend that they can get the loan sharks to roll the debt over. "You're all the same," she scoffs. "You're like eight-year old boys fronting each other up on the playground. You all think you're in the last reel of a John Ford movie, don't you? Cowboys is the word!" "She's got A-levels," Roach informs Burnside after she has swept out. Viv, meanwhile, assures the daughter that her father is "with two officers who are highly skilled in dealing with aggravation. They have to be; they cause enough of it." But their front proves ideally suited to the task at hand, in a further demonstration of how *The Bill* never lets one character hog the right approach. In the same way that Honest Al can make a pig's ear of it now and then, his shadier colleagues aren't just written off as dinosaurs. There's a time and place for their brand of inflated machismo.

A car pulls up with two heavies and two suits, and the latter are introduced by Goller to his friends from the Old Bill. "There hasn't been any misunderstanding here, has there?" they ask, suddenly on their guard. "People think we're always on duty," says Burnside, finally able to have fun with his bent image rather than mending it with his colleagues. "Can't even have a drink with an old mate without some slag getting anxious... Oi, Wickhead!" he shouts as he looks out of the window. "The name is Wickford." "There's an ugly-looking scrote out here molesting the gnomes. Tell him to stop." Wickford hastily calls off his thugs, who are decapitating the statues in the garden. The regard Roach has for Goller puts another twist on the relationship between the police and their clientele, who sometimes build up a professional respect for each other. The favours that pass between them can't always be boiled down to corruption, but that belief has its uses. After the visitors have gone, a delighted Goller reveals that "they think I'm bunging the pair of you." "A misleading impression," Burnside points out, which Ray is willing to make a correct one. "Right at the present moment I'm boracic, but if you bear with me..." "We didn't hear that, Ray," Ted cuts in coldly. "You haven't got the point, have you?" "You owe us Ray – but we don't want readies in a brown envelope. We want information." "Now Ted'll tell you Mr Burnside, I've never been a snout. That's well-known." "Which is why you'll make a very good one," Roach chips in. "Ray understands really, Frank. He knows what he owes. He's just getting used to the idea." The dismayed Goller realises that, having rid himself of one pair of predators, he has sold his soul to another.

If the debut of both Jack Meadows and the new Sun Hill in 1990's *A Fresh Start* are a turning point in the show's history, then another comes when Meadows is installed as a regular. *Re-Hab* follows the final contribution to *The Bill* from its most important writer, Barry Appleton. In terms of the number of scripts delivered, his half-century of episodes is still some way off the top of the league table, but the first third of those came during the hour-long era, making up half of its total. Given the chance to put his stamp on the show, he made the most of it. If the blueprint for *The Bill* came from Geoff McQueen, then Appleton turned it into a finished design. To a solid procedural backbone he added a layer of adventure that was starting to fall out of vogue in TV: honing a story round unusual scams and schemes, in the tradition of the great thriller writers of the Sixties and Seventies like Brian Clemens and Robert Banks Stewart. His episodes often focus on 'high-end' crime: gangland feuds, jailbreaks, armed robbery, terrorism and industrial espionage. Appleton's police experience also gives him an instinct for the bizarre: the turnip top in *Country Cousin* who causes a punch-up in a belly-dancing joint and still won't tell Burnside what he's bought for his wife when he leaves; the dope smuggled to a remand prisoner inside a cup of tea in *Fort Apache – Sun Hill*; and the trail of dismembered pets in *When Did You Last See Your Father?* that turns out to be the work of an escaped panther. And during his episodes there is a slow, believable growth of characters in both uniform and CID: in particular Cryer, his values tested by his delinquent son, and Roach, always being knocked back. No one did more, and perhaps only Christopher Russell as much, to make Sun Hill a living, breathing place.

Appleton's last two episodes home in on a favourite character also on his way out, Mike Dashwood. Mike is getting itchy feet when he attends a sales pitch by a security firm in *It's a Small World*. The audience is mainly people like himself: coppers wanting a change, nearing retirement, or drawing their pension. Convinced by a polished talk, they are sure they can flog the company's burglar alarms and earn a hefty commission. This is a world Appleton had explored many times, of upmarket hotels, 'defence contracts' and investments that are not as sound as they appear. Mike is suspicious, thinking they wanted security consultants, not salesmen. He runs into an old colleague, Len Dorton, about to retire and ready to invest his five grand. Mike urges caution and delves into the firm's international credentials, with the help of the Fraud Squad. He uncovers the criminal past of the men in charge, but his interest in the scheme was genuine. On his return he tells Greig he is thinking of leaving the force: "People are getting promoted, I can't even get a transfer!" "Would you have gone for it?" "If I was someone like Len Dorton with a lump sum burning a hole in my pocket: yeah, I'd probably have gone for it, hook, line and sinker. Coppers... never believe we can be conned." The crestfallen Dorton muses that he nearly lost all his savings. "It's not just the money. It's the fact I've been a copper for thirty years, taken in by a couple of conmen. It's my pride that hurts... bastards." Mike warns him of the publicity if he testifies. "I'll go all the way," he promises. If TV consultancy is one route for the ex-copper, the most common is security work – and another, as Appleton doubtless saw around him, was to fall victim to the crooks they spent their lives trying to put away. The Acting DI tries to keep the restless Mike out of trouble by declaring that "rank isn't everything. This job's about getting a good result, not promotion." "You being straight? Or honing your management skills?" Greig's reply comes with one of Andrew Mackintosh's trademark enigmatic smiles attached: "What do you think?"

Going Soft is fittingly titled for a story that has the makings of another all-action spectacular and goes a different way. Mike is sent to the home of a magistrate to pick up a search warrant and finds her bound and gagged in the living room – moments before a gun is shoved in his face by one of two balaclava-clad robbers, who we soon realise are not professionals. She has an asthma attack and they have to find her inhaler. She recognises the man as the son of her old cleaner, urging him and his accomplice not to "put your lives at risk." "Lives? What lives? That's why we're doing this – to try and start one!" With their hoods off, his girlfriend reveals the gun is a toy. "He wouldn't have hurt you. We're broke and I'm pregnant. Eddie just wanted the best for me. When my mum found out, she threw me out." Mike promises he will do what he can for them, and leads them outside. He then announces his intention to plead on their behalf in court. Given that Appleton wrote more gun-toting villains into the show than anyone else, this is an interesting note to conclude on: that sympathy starts to win out in the tragic stories the police uncover. Don Henderson, who brought the oddball copper George Bulman to life in three separate series over the course of a decade, was himself a policeman before he began to feel sorry for those he dealt with and quit the force. Roach, who failed his firearms training in Appleton's *Hold Fire* because he didn't want the power of life and death any more, is furious. "Come on Mike, they're villains!" "They're kids." "Kids? Holding a police officer and a magistrate hostage?" "It's an imitation gun." "Oh and you knew that when you faced it? All we see is a masked gunman, what are we supposed to do? Give them the benefit of the doubt? You guess wrong and you're dead. What matters is the *intent* was there!" "Was it?" Unmoved, Mike walks off down the street – echoing the final shot of Appleton's earlier hour-long episode *Suspects*, which lingered on Dashwood alone. Appleton later acknowledged that he should have written even more for Jon Iles, who he thought was "brilliant" in the role.[33] But as the writer headed for pastures new, one of his favourite leading men would not be far behind him.

THE MASTER JUGGLER

1992 is a year dominated by the misadventures of Matt Boyden, introduced at the end of the previous one. Boyden is a figure indelibly associated with the show for me; whenever I caught an episode during the Nineties, he was there behind the custody desk, greeting each new arrival with a sour look and a cutting one-liner. Looking at that decade as a whole, it's arguable that he was the show's single most valuable character. Certainly he comes along at the right time, giving the uniform branch a vital injection of energy. By this point the original Holy Trinity of Cryer, Penny and Peters has given way to the Holier Than Thou Trinity of Monroe, Cryer and Maitland. Boyden supplies the duff note in the choir: a man who does the business on the surface while grabbing every perk he can get. From day one he is

---

[33] Crocker, Oliver, *Witness Statements: Making The Bill (Series 1-3)*, p. 86

trying to be one of the lads, his glib manner at parade earning him a quiet word of advice from Monroe. Stamp gives Boyden a guided tour of the ground. Easing him into his new role, he helpfully points out the spot where Penny got done for drink-driving, then the road where Peters got stabbed. "Bit accident-prone, the skippers on this relief," comments Boyden, the show poking fun at its recent track record of catastrophe. He didn't know when he was well off; a decade or so later and that tour would be a fully fledged Chamber of Horrors, in which he would become an exhibit. Mike informs Ted that A Relief's new sergeant has come from Romford. "I don't blame him," remarks Roach, before we learn that he was stationed there himself. Once Boyden's name is mentioned, he adds, "Small world." Boyden has been transferred following an incident with a married WDS, which isn't yet over. Dividing his time between manning the custody area and breaking up with her by phone, the template is set for his most enduring trademark.

The role of custody sergeant is forced on Boyden sooner than expected when Peters strains his back and has to be taken to hospital. He is unfazed when his first customer, a tottering drunk, passes out: "Height? All right then... length?" Challenged by Monroe about the lack of evidence of arrest on the custody record, he can't believe it when Hollis and Ford warn him the boss will check up on this: "What is he, a maniac?" So begins one of the show's longest, most entertaining battles. Boyden invents the details and quickly tells Stringer to put them in his notes before Monroe gets to him. "He won't care if we say he was hanging from a lamppost by his ankles dressed up as Batman. All that matters is we're both singing from the same page of the hymn book," he chirps, in a higher-pitched voice than the impatient drawl Tony O'Callaghan later settled on. "Hell Matt, your juggling is not what it used to be," says Roach when he turns up to find chaos in custody. But Boyden's debut episode, *Balls in the Air*, surely owes its title to another pastime. What makes him one of the show's biggest assets is that, like the departed Tom Penny, he can be played for both laughs and drama, and at the root of both is the same thing: his eternally restless zipper. His conquest from his old nick was also courted by Roach, the source of some needle. Ted assures him there are "no hard feelings at all, Matt. As my old dad used to say: what's given to a friend is not lost." When Boyden helps him solve a case, Roach says he owes him one. "No Ted. We're square." But this gentleman's agreement disintegrates the following year, by which time Boyden has already sailed close to the wind.

In *Illegals*, Tosh and an immigration officer break up a wedding between a Nigerian woman who has overstayed her visa and an elderly man co-opted into the scam. Outside the town hall, a bored Garfield asks Boyden if they're here to provide back-up: "Yeah. Could have been bridesmaid if you'd asked." Seeing the devastated woman emerge, Boyden coos, "Ahhh... Ask custody to have the bridal suite ready, would you?" Their next call is to a bored housewife whose missing car has been found. Boyden watches as she does everything to tempt George in for a quickie, short of disrobing on the doorstep. Being George, he looks a gift horse in the mouth and leaves with nothing. "Well you made a right pig's ear of that. She was on a plate from the moment she opened the door. The leg was there, George – leg and a half, open door. Dressing gown tied, but loosely. I've known probationers could have read all that, and done something about it. Obviously you've never been taught the facts of life on the beat, my son. We're policemen – it's there for us! If they want it from a uniform, what's wrong in providing a public service, eh?" What could have been a throwaway scene instead softens the audience for the punch that follows. An anonymous denunciation letter names an illegal immigrant running a minicab firm. Tosh organises a raid, the eager Loxton suggesting they should target a kebab house nearby that has "a lot of new faces." George ponders whether Tosh enjoys this work as much as Steve does: "Nah – sheer necessity with him. He's filling up the country with his own kids, isn't he? He can't afford to let the rest of the world in." The limits of Steve's zeal are exposed when one of their targets legs it over the back fence: "Stuff that, these are new trousers." Slapping the cuffs on another, he adds longingly, "Just wish they'd put up a fight sometimes."

Boyden snoops in the upstairs rooms and finds a startled woman on her own. Giving Tosh the all-clear, he has the prisoners loaded and sends George off to scout for the missing man. Back in the house, he sits the woman down on her bed. "Are you legal?" he asks coyly, a line that will acquire a whole new meaning in his future conquests. "I don't like to see young women in trouble. I like to help them. Would you like me to help you? You know I'm a police officer. That means I can help. I can sort things out for people." His advances are halted by the sudden arrival of Tosh, who lets them leave with a suspicious look. Later he walks past Boyden as the latter brags to George: "Even you couldn't have failed. She knew what the game was, she just sat there waiting for me. Beautiful black hair, skin like velvet; all dark and creamy..." "You make her sound like a pint of Guinness!" snaps George. Cathy pays her a visit in her cell, assuring her innocently that "we're quite human", as the woman gives her a hooded stare. But the reckoning comes when Tosh drops in on Boyden for a little chat. "I just wanted to tell you I had you sussed. I know what you were thinking." "It happened like I said. I nicked her and she put herself on offer." "She was offering nothing. We all know you're the man with the golden Y-fronts, you never stop telling us. But if you're ever out on a job with me again, you never use *this*," he snarls, prodding Boyden's uniform, "to get what you want." "Getting too old for it yourself, then?" "I'm getting too old to give a toss about your career, pal. But if you want to put yourself down the pan I'll happily pull the chain. Received – sergeant?" Boyden gives the faintest, grudging nod as the episode ends. According to plan, this story would have ended in his removal, disgraced, after mere weeks on screen. Instead this darkest of all his acts is allowed to lie dormant for years as he becomes a semi-loveable rogue, his skirt-chasing sometimes played for laughs. But the blueprint that has been established is never forgotten.

This episode demonstrates an important quality of *The Bill* at its best: that there need be no trade off in emphasis between the regulars and the situations they police. Future eras of the show seemed to believe there was, slanting the focus one way or the other, but this period proves that character and theme can be given equal weight in twenty-four minutes. *Illegals* is a tale of Boyden's wrongdoing, but it's also a study of immigration, tackled with the sharpness, finesse and lack of preaching that typifies its author. In Christopher Russell's last full year on the show, it is more reliant on him than ever, and the results are better than ever too. *Illegals* harks back to his earliest work on *The Bill* in Series 2; perhaps the very earliest, *Home Beat*, in which Carver observed that people from the subcontinent were used to policemen as "bullies with big sticks", not the decent sort they could expect over here. But it was his next, *This Little Pig*, that saw another uniformed raid on a business housing illegal immigrants, much to the annoyance of Cryer, taking his troops away from "real police work." Seven years on it's still a hated job, handled despondently. "Busy week for denunciations," Monroe remarks to Stringer about the anonymous letter they have received, "that's the fourth. He's probably on a good earner and our pen friend's not, that's all it takes." When Tosh interviews the Nigerian woman, Monica, he finds out she has been working, as well as residing, illegally: "Cleaning offices; washing dishes; making beds." He notes that it's been a hard slog. The money she's earned has gone into paying for her fake husband, but when Tosh observes that it's a one-sided deal – "They've got your five hundred pounds and all you've got is a one-way ticket out!" – she still refuses to name names. He suggests she has nothing to lose, when she is probably playing the long game: keeping on the right side of the scammers in exchange for their help next time.

One of the best scenes Russell ever wrote plays out when Tosh visits "the bridegroom of the year", a wheezing alcoholic named Prentice who lives in a one-room hovel. "It's better than the gutter," he is told optimistically. "When you've had a drink, yeah," he mutters, putting down his bags of supermarket booze. Tosh warns him that he is an accessory to a crime, but he is confident they will never catch the criminal. "Most people know which side their bread's buttered. Junk people. Unemployable old tosspots like me. Someone offers you a few quid to do a lady a favour, well... Why do you have to give poor little cows like her so much hassle anyway?" "'Cos if every one of them's allowed to get away with it, this island is gonna sink." "Yeah, well they work their butts off don't they, the ones like her." In her interview Monica was reminded that her original visa denied her the right to work. With the legal market off the table, the black market reaps the reward: and as Prentice observes, there's a whole other strain feeding off it. "We all know there's thousands of illegals out there, thousands of young bucks who never do a stroke – fraud, drugs, more fraud, you don't catch many of them, do you eh? And they're all poncing off the state while they're at it." "Like you, you mean?" "I'm allowed to ponce, I was born here," he smiles, openly acknowledging the double standard. And even in a scene of tight close-ups, the grimy background speaks louder than words: the fate of the hard workers who escape the police will be to stay down among the junk people. Small wonder they are eager to rat on the few who show signs of climbing out. "Still, you have caught me little Monica; and screwed her to the floor. Good for you," Prentice concludes, raising his beer in tribute.

The story offers yet another spin on the issue when Lines and Maitland speak to a high-priced lawyer representing the detained drivers. He announces smoothly that his clients want to apply for political asylum. "Obviously no further action may be taken to remove them from the UK, pending initial interview." "If they needed asylum they should have applied for it on arrival, why wait till they get arrested?" demands Maitland. "Fear is a stronger motivator than logic." "Then it was fear that forced Mr Simsek to become a cab driver, was it?" The lawyer maintains that "my client has no knowledge of such employment", and that bail will be no problem: "Our community looks after its own, sergeant. I've already spoken to respected permanent residents who will stand surety if required." The police, like the immigrants, are stuck in a vicious circle, trying to enforce a law that isn't even applied consistently. Those who can work the system because they have countrymen ready to help may be successful, while people like Monica, out on their own, are not. "Makes the whole thing seem ridiculous," says Maitland. "All this huff and puff about an accident of birth. I don't know why we don't just build a few hundred tower blocks in Exmoor and have done with it." Cathy, whose own brusque attitude to Monica is that she knew the risks, reminds her she'll be able to see her family again after nine months away from them. "We have four children," she replies coldly. "My husband has no job. I earn one hundred pounds a week here. Would you be glad to see me?"

Russell pulls off the same balancing act in *Street Cleaning*, lifting the lid on another hot topic through the eyes, and mouths, of the principals. A furious man turns up at the front desk with his daughter, abused and spat on for not handing over money to two homeless men. The blame is pinned on an organised gang of bogus beggars that targets London in the summer, when tourism is thriving; some have relocated east to Sun Hill following a crackdown in the West End. George mentions Billy, the man with a dog who usually works the Tube station, doubting he would ever spit on anyone. "Perhaps he's trained his dog to do it," chips in Steve. Cryer puts together a plainclothes squad from the relief to search for the gang, Conway stressing that this "is not an excuse for harassing life's unfortunates. Genuine beggars are not our target, OK?" But as he speaks he gets a venomous look from the man who, as ever, goes against the bleeding heart crowd. "Sorry sir, but when you say 'genuine beggars'," asks Tony, "is that like saying 'genuine shoplifters' or 'genuine burglars'? I mean begging is an offence, after all." "Are you saying none of them are genuine?" June later challenges him. "There's not a single family breakdown in the whole country, not a single hostel that hasn't got room?" "So how come they're only homeless in the summer? You don't see many of them on the streets in the winter, do you?" "You've obviously been looking in the wrong direction, mate." They meet a well-known tramp, Harold, who Tony views with affection, giving him a few quid to tide him over. "He *is* genuine. He's the only truly homeless person in Sun Hill." "Oh, *the* local tramp, you mean? Like everywhere's allowed one, and he's it? You've got some very quaint ideas, Tony. You ought to have been a village bobby."

Stamp's separation of the deserving and the undeserving poor by their bus pass rights has a sentimental basis – which we see after Harold is found badly injured, thrown down a staircase by two of the gang. "I suppose it was because they'd taken his place," says a woman who works nearby, "where he's sat for years." At the hospital, Tony tells June how Harold ended up on the streets: "He was at home on leave in the war. House he was in got blown away by a V2. His wife and baby with it. He's not set foot in a house since." But she has a rather different account of his life story: "I heard he became a tramp to avoid the call-up and just went on walking." After they are told of the life-changing injuries he has sustained, she adds glumly, "Sorry. I think I preferred your version." "Don't make a lot of difference now, does it?" Jeered away by a group of winos, Steve offers George his thoughts on the street drinking community: "It's a pity we can't recycle them along with the bottles." They find Billy, the man with the dog, earning his money with wry patter, not threats. "Is that what they offered you, Billy? A solo flight down the up escalator?" "Look, if I wanted to be involved I wouldn't be a dropout, would I?" He was evicted from his usual pitch by two men who "came round taxing. Like you said, taking me money. The next day they told us to bog off." Nothing is immune from market forces; as in *Illegals*, the parasites feed off the sympathetic cases and both are lumped together by the system. When Cryer manages to track down the gang and they are lifted in one go, it gives the relief a badly needed morale booster – after a disaster caused, once again, by Golden Balls.

ONE FOR THE TEAM

Alistair Greig isn't the only character to get an overdue turn in the spotlight in 1992; in a good year for Gs, George Garfield is also developed further after a quiet couple of years. *Fair Play*, the first of thirty episodes over the next decade from Mark Holloway, gives George an origin story of his own. It also demonstrates that he is still a long way from being best mates with Dave. At a community fair George catches up with the guest of honour, his former amateur boxing rival Mal Grant, who went on to hit the big time. "I always said 'Garf, you got to learn to relax; you train too much and win too little.'" Quinnan, however, is ready to land some blows in the present. First he warns Grant his car is parked illegally and pressures him to move it. Then a bag of pills drops into view and Dave scoops it up. George arrives and has to reinforce the rules: "If PC Quinnan has reason to believe..." "'PC Quinnan has reason to believe' – Garf, is that you in there? I need some help here! Screw special favours, I want some respect!" Grant gives his old pal a black eye and assault is added to possession. Back at the nick, George maintains that Grant is no user, and asks him for permission to approach his doctor to prove that the drugs were legally prescribed. Then he learns another painful lesson about what his uniform means to some: "OK... how much? You know, you want me to buy you a drink. I've got it, you need it!" "Don't insult me, Mal!" "Why are you doing this then?" Grant explodes. "Just a little power trip, is it?" George is dismayed to learn that the drugs are steroids, as the image of the man he admired begins to crumble. "You never understood about wanting to win," the latter murmurs. "Boxing was just a part-time thing for you. You had a day job."

Monroe takes a firm line when told that George doesn't want to press charges for the assault. "He's in the police now; I think someone better remind him of that. I'm not having someone thumping one of my men in front of a crowd of people and then walking away scot free." George tells his inspector it would "be like hitting a man when he's down", but is told it "isn't your decision. I want a statement of what happened: an assault on a police officer." "Yeah, but that's it! He hit me because it was me. Somebody that he knew; somebody that could have helped him but didn't." "The people who saw him do it don't make that distinction. The people you work with don't. If you can't wear that, you'd better think very carefully about your future in the job." Ironically it's Dave who has encountered this dilemma of late in *Decent People*, going undercover in his former role as an electrician and meeting an old mate who offers him dodgy credit cards. He puts this 'hypothetical' scenario to Cryer, whose advice is that "the officer's got to decide whether he wants to be a copper or not." Dave makes his choice and gets spat in the face by his friend's wife, then head-butted by the man himself. But for George there is added pain in turning on someone he idolised for achieving greater things than he could. It says everything about how he views himself, as an average Joe trailing two steps behind supposedly better, brighter people. "Do you ever wish you could keep your life in separate little boxes?" he asks Norika. "Home, friends, work, family, just keep them all apart. That way you might not end up feeling like something that just crawled out from underneath a stone." Dave points out that Grant has been using drugs for years: "He probably was when he beat you." "Yeah, he was always better than me though," says George, humble to a fault, or several.

That trusting nature leads him to a nasty fall in *Up All Night*, as Tony Etchells kicks off a major storyline. Graduating from a black eye to a head injury, George is rushed into casualty after trying to stop a fleeing burglar. Tony and Dave, who found him and brought him in, are reassured that they did all they could. "That's not strictly true, is it?" the former reminds the latter. In fact they were already at the hospital, joining in a party with the nurses, when the call for urgent assistance came through. "We both know what happens if this gets out." "We're not the only car on the relief, where was everyone else?" protests Dave. "You don't let a mate down." "You think I don't know that? I used to work with this bloke at Bow Street, right. He let a probationer get a kicking because he didn't go to an urgent assist. You should have seen it when the relief found out. The bloke's selling life assurance now.... I mean we didn't even like this probationer!" It's feared that the man who whacked George did worse to the absent

Boyden, who was in the area but isn't answering his radio. Then he pops up from nowhere, radio magically working. "He was there, wasn't he?" Cathy mutters to Dave and Tony back at the nick. "In a dead spot? For half an hour? He was there." George tells June they were on patrol together when Boyden departed, saying he had "something to see to, and he'd see me later. He just walked off." The blame has begun to fan out, Steve commenting that Dave and Tony took their time. "Give you a thorough examination, did she?" he sneers at Dave. A contrite Boyden turns up at George's bedside, now claiming he heard the noise and ran to help but went the wrong way. "Your radio was down... don't worry about it skip," the patient assures him.

But the truth emerges when a woman called Jackie Welland arrives at the station to see Roach, complaining about harassment from Boyden. It becomes clear from their frantic argument that she is another woman the two men have 'in common'. "You're still seeing him?" "Seeing him? He practically broke into my flat last night, I can't get rid of him!" "I told you not to get involved with him!" Roach meets Boyden in the corridor and snarls, "You are ruining my snout." "Is that what she is? Not doing too bad for a snout, is she? I think you'd better ask yourself who's using who. I'd watch yourself, because if she does make a complaint, then you and I are both out of order." When Roach admits he can do nothing without dropping himself in it, Jackie makes it official, opening the fault lines in both uniform and CID. Burnside reviews the latest in his sergeant's best-selling disaster franchise: "So you got involved with this snout on a personal level – found out Boyden's giving her one. You don't discuss work, I hope?" "Oh come on, guv. Look, the wives of villains are the best informants; you know that, you've been there yourself. You sail in, you put the old man away and then you work on the wife while she's vulnerable." "Yeah, but you don't have to become the surrogate husband. Next thing you'll be telling me you take her down Tesco's on a Saturday morning!" Then Meadows bursts in to add his own boot print: "Right little mess this, isn't it? In future you keep your ears open and your trousers shut!" But things are worse for Boyden himself, which highlights an interesting difference between the two. Ted will happily get his leg over, but hopes for a leg up as a result; the former on its own is what drives Matt to ruin.

Haggard and unshaven after his electric razor fails, Boyden's alpha male image begins to fray at the sides, just as Roach's does every other week. When he turns up at Jackie's home, Tony and Cindy O'Callaghan – no connection – enact a courtship for the ages, including the most romantic case any woman has ever heard for accepting flowers from a man: "Because I look stupid holding them!" "You were just a good laugh Matthew, and you weren't that for very long. I'm sick of being there every time you and Super Cop fancy a bit on the side! He's using me for information and you're just using me! It wasn't very good, OK? It wasn't very good with him and it certainly isn't very good with you!" Boyden reveals the depths he is capable of plumbing when he warns that the only way she will be rid of him is if she drops the complaint. She does so, but the damage has already been done. The coughs and chicken noises that he gets from the relief as they crowd round him at parade, birds ganging up on a cuckoo in the nest, soon give way to outright hostility. The furious Monroe demands a written account of his actions, and Brownlow is equally scathing: "You let down an officer under your command in a potentially life-threatening situation! You've lost that officer's respect and that of every other officer under your command! I don't have to remind you, do I, that this could end your career?" "Sir... I was considering a transfer," mumbles Boyden. "Well you will do it without my help. I'd think about clawing my way back here before running off to wreck some other relief. And God help you if you ever get involved in another incident like this!" Enduring the walk of shame past the assembled PCs, he takes refuge in the sergeants' locker room – but on opening his, he pulls out a pillow wedged inside and is showered with feathers. "Bastards...!"

With Garfield due back at work in *Snakes and Ladders*, Steve opens a book on whether he will punch Boyden's lights out before the shift is over. George cuts a morose figure when he appears, knowing he has been let down by more than just one man. "I know where you were," he tells Quinnan coldly. "You were at a knees-up in casualty. You got lost round the back of a staff nurse," he adds, in a line that could have fallen through time from seven years later. "I hate to do this to you lot, not play the hero and that, but I'm out there getting battered and none of you lifted a finger, did you?" The main dissenter, once again, is Stamp, who wants nothing to do with this vengeful atmosphere and holds Garfield back when he goes for Boyden in the corridor. Tony and Dave are assigned to CAD and a smirking June tells the latter, "I've just found out who your sergeant is. You laugh that off!" Cryer is astounded that Monroe will take no action: "Or would you rather I stuck Garfield on, turned him into some kind of hero, because that's what Loxton and his pals are looking for! Matthew Boyden's dropped himself right in it... I'm not fighting his battles for him." George is dispatched to a domestic call on the Cockcroft Estate and a bizarre pantomime develops. Dave wants any excuse possible to get him back in the nick, Tony the exact opposite, and they start feeding him contradictory orders. George announces that he's going off watch. "You can't keep me out forever, you know," he warns the raging Boyden. "I'm coming back in." Enjoying the show, Ted notes that Matt has "a crisis of leadership. The whole nick wants you out. You don't know what it's like in Sun Hill. Covering you in feathers is nothing. You're finished!" "I haven't even started!" snaps Boyden as he walks away: and sure enough, a year later he is going to enjoy the last laugh in this showdown.

As Dave and Steve gang up on him again, Tony reveals his true motives: "Do you want Boyden off this relief? If Boyden gets hit now then this whole thing's finished. But if we keep the pot boiling we can get rid of him! Why do you think I'm doing all this? I'm trying to stop George hitting him and this prat is putting money on it!" Another budget-saving episode, along the same lines as *C.A.D.*, goes further in the way it puts the characters under the lamp. A self-inflicted wound exposes a whole range of attitudes: not just the bloody-mindedness of Tony, but the outright insolence of Steve. "And why should I believe what you say?" he snaps at Boyden in front of the others, leading to a warning that if he speaks to him like that again, "I'll stick you on." In line with his belief in Victorian values, Monroe feels that a punch-up is a healthy way for blokes to resolve a dispute, like giving a lad a clip round the ear for stealing. "If a fight breaks out then by this time next week no-one'll remember what the fuss was about," he tells Cryer. "If you can't take what's happening, look the other way." Having learnt of the book from Roach, Boyden lets George know when he storms in, fist raised. "What kind of loyalty is that? You'd better do this, 'cos if you don't they're gonna lose a lot of money." George rushes out and shelters in the locker room – and in the finest moment of the story, the betrayal from all quarters sinks in and Huw Higginson brilliantly holds back the tears. Finally George composes himself and delivers the goods: but the moment is hidden from us as well as the other PCs, refusing to satisfy our bloodlust. Boyden is found in the CAD room with a bleeding lip, and twigs Tony's game: "You didn't want this over, did you? You wanted me to get transferred. Thanks. Sorry Dave, all over," he announces as the latter enters. "I reckon this relief's finally got a sergeant it deserves."

Even more the voice of sanity than usual, Bob soon gets to say 'I told you so' when this supposed release of tension only increases it. With morale falling in *Street Cleaning*, Brownlow asks him for his opinion and he agrees that Boyden was "way, way out of order. But that was a matter that should have been dealt with by senior officers, not his PCs. He's still here, so presumably the offences weren't sackable. Letting Garfield thump him didn't help the relief, it just split it." "With hindsight, I'm inclined to agree," adds a chastened Monroe. Of all the guilty faces among the PCs, the guiltiest is George's, feeling he has brought this on everyone despite his being the wronged party. Cryer gives the troops a pep talk, telling them he has assured the bosses he has complete faith in them. "I was right to say that, was I?" In the silence that follows, it's George who looks round at the others and then announces firmly, "Yes skip." Likewise, at the end when Dave and Tony suggest that the drinks are on Cryer, George counters, "Maybe we should buy him one?", showing an instinctive, dog-like devotion to natural leaders. He finds it hard to accept that Boyden is not and never will be one. Proving again the usefulness of opposites, one man's utter lack of guile is contrasted with a man who has an excess of it. Tension surfaces between them again when it's George's turn to get in trouble over a woman, in *A Scandalous Act*. When a house is hit in a drugs raid, he finds a girl played by a teenage Martine McCutcheon in an upstairs room. Unlike his sergeant he doesn't take advantage but he does know her of old, having arrested her for shoplifting. With Boyden again unaware of George's whereabouts, having sent the troops back to base, Garfield takes his prisoner to Sun Hill in a panda by himself. When they arrive she accuses him of indecently assaulting her en route.

Monroe lays into Garfield for his naivety, breaching a rule on the transport of female prisoners that is designed to protect him. Boyden is quick to say the fault is his, earning a sarcastic shake of the head from George. "All I can say is she must have a vivid imagination if she thinks George is giving her one," remarks Dave. "I don't think he knows where it is yet, does he?" says Tony. The wolves of MS-15 arrive, headed by a familiar face: the new Detective Superintendent Reid, who qualifies her bright opinion of Sun Hill to her DS when Burnside appears to greet her. Of the sunlit waste ground where George is alleged to have had his way with the girl, the DI notes, "Even the rats don't fancy having it off there!" After Boyden is questioned, he assures George that he told them nothing; but, in a textbook example of transference, adds, "I think they've sussed you've been giving her one." "I was just trying to be nice! Just because I usually wear a uniform it doesn't mean I can't be nice sometimes." "No, course not! But I understand..." "Understand what?" "How it is." In his own interview George reveals that he first arrested the girl, Amanda, when she was thirteen, and thought he could keep her out of trouble. "She's a bright girl, I didn't want to see her get on a downward spiral." Finally she admits that the evidence of sexual contact on her is from a boyfriend her father had forbidden her to see; George, once again, was a ready-made fall guy. "All right?" asks Boyden. "Yeah, fine Sarge; no thanks to you." Amanda tells him she is sorry. "Not half as sorry as I am," he mutters, realising that someone else's ulterior motives have sailed over his head.

The atmosphere is still uneasy when we reach *A Blind Eye* by Julian Jones. Called into Monroe's office, Boyden jokes that it sounds as though he is on probation, and is informed sternly that he is: "A transfer is still very much on the cards... The main difficulty I have with you, Matthew, remains your inability to command respect. You don't earn it by drinking half a yard of whisky with the lads or going at it like a fiddler's elbow with every pretty girl you see. It's not difficult; there's a rulebook. You make sure that you, and everyone on the relief, knows you're going to work by it." His point is illustrated when Boyden checks up on Stamp, making a visit to a day centre: "You've got biscuit on your chin... just testing." "Yeah," Tony mutters as he walks to his own car, "knew you'd skive off and take afternoon tea." The man who observed that Tom Penny could dish it out but he couldn't take it finds his successor equally lacking: "Oi, come here! If you think you can get away with a comment like that you've got another thing coming." Tony is called to assist George, asking Boyden if he wants to keep talking: "I'm sure George is getting used to being let down. Probably enjoy another week in hospital." "I'll speak to you later!" The two PCs are alerted to an old woman who is being mugged: the latest in a spate of attacks by a psychopath who seems to be in it for the beatings rather than the money. As they approach they see a man standing over her body, going through her purse. He is set on by a vigilante gang that puts the boot in – while Tony keeps his foot off the gas. "Get a move on, he's getting a kicking!" "He's getting what he deserves." Finally Tony crawls up to the scene and chases his heroes on foot. He quickly 'loses them' round the back of the estate, then learns there is a witness in one of the tower blocks and is just as quick to be first to speak to her. But her description changes everything: the woman passed out, a man came to help her and was then set on by the gang. "Like you they must have thought she was being mugged."

Stamp is already panicking when he gets more good news from the man's belongings: "It's a warrant card. PC Trevor Gale." "This is a joke," he sighs. Seeing the irony better than anyone, George berates him: "Even if that bloke had been the mugger, you don't stand there ringside and watch him get lynched. If this comes out you'll be done." Boyden has already passed news of the incident to Monroe, "not that you knew he was a PC at the time." In private he dresses down Tony over his insolence, telling him he's missed his chance to get rid of him. "You continue to throw your weight around and I'm going to do your legs so badly you'll never walk again. This relief's been allowed to go Humpty Dumpty. I'm going to put it back together again." One of the gang is caught and asks why "your mate let us off earlier." He repeats this accusation to Boyden, claiming that a big bloke "smiled and let him vanish" even though his asthma meant he couldn't run fast. Boyden tells Cryer, going off on one about Tony's hypocrisy, but is advised to play it carefully before making it official: "I'd certainly have a word with Stamp before I did anything else." "Oh yeah; I want to make him feel what it's like to make a mistake." In a quiet, dawning moment, Bob realises that Matt has no interest in being the better man. Boyden puts the charge to Tony, gets him sweating and heads off to see

Monroe. "We all make errors, we don't all get punished for them though. But believe me, there's always going to be someone at this station that won't let you forget." In the end he cements his place with the relief not by setting the example Monroe wanted, but by proving what is all too obvious: that none of them can set one either. "What are you going to do?" "Same as you, Tony," Boyden replies cheerfully as he knocks at the boss's door. "Turn a blind eye."

With his feet under the table, Boyden tries to assert his way of doing things in Russell Lewis's *Open to Offers*, when Quinnan's sparky past returns to haunt him again. A loan shark brought in for smashing up a pub, played with sleaze dripping off him by Tim McInerny, recognises Dave as the man who did a job for him last year. Realising that he was moonlighting, he has a hold which he threatens to use unless Dave gets the charges dropped. The first person to know, because he happened to be near the cell door, is Boyden. His advice is characteristic: "Front it out. Deny everything, let them prove it. If they say anything to me, I'll swear it was never mentioned." "Maybe I should pre-empt him, maybe I should cough to it voluntarily." "Dave, you're looking at a sackable offence. You put your hands up to moonlighting, you could be out of a job!" But Quinnan goes to the straight as a die Maitland, who with his blessing informs Monroe in turn, arguing that moonlighting goes on at every nick. "That's officers helping one another out, not sub-contracting their services to the local pond life," Monroe declares. He agrees to help Dave out of trouble on condition it never happens again, but the chasm between the two sergeants is revealed. "Shame that couldn't have been avoided really, innit?" says Boyden. "I could have found someone to alibi Dave for that particular day in question." Maitland asks a simple but profound question that should be on everyone's lips come the end of the decade: "Where does that road lead?" Boyden then questions why Dave went to him. "You know what he's like. He'd offer a drowning man a glass of water if that's what the rulebook prescribed." But a grey streak in the whiter than white Maitland is unearthed when he asks Monroe not to let Dave know that he spoke up for him: "I don't want to be thought of as a soft touch." Sun Hill's supposed boy scout is smart enough to recognise what Boyden cannot: the value of keeping a distance.

ARMED AND DANGEROUS

The biggest potential danger to the police station of the Nineties that J.C. Wilsher unveiled in *Citadel* appears on the horizon early this year, in the same author's two-parter *The Paddy Factor/The Wild Rover*. Carver and Martella tail a burglary suspect trying his luck with parked cars, including one whose owner is inside leaning under the dashboard, having just left a flat and loaded a holdall. The burglar is hit by two gunshots at close range and the car speeds off, leaving him twitching on the pavement. Elsewhere, proving that *The Bill* was usually ahead of its satirists, Stamp pre-empts *The Fast Show*'s Fat Sweaty Coppers by several years as he gives Quinnan his order for the Chinese takeaway: "I'll have a pancake roll, chicken chow mein, prawn crackers, fried rice with egg, packet of soy sauce and a large Coke." "Is that all?" asks a deadpan Dave. "Well, I'll be sinking a few later, so I've got to leave a bit of room." They get a shout to pursue the car and Tony wisely hands Dave the sauce, which splatters him as they drive off. An ambulance arrives at the shooting, followed by the new Armed Response Vehicle outlined by Wilsher in *Shots* the previous year. The command structure that the Met trainers promoted as a step forward also comes under the spotlight. Jim wants to turn over the flat the gunman appeared from in case there are more weapons inside, and is told, "You're the officer in the case pal, you set the objective. If it's feasible we'll do it for you, but it's your decision." This new state of affairs is commented on by Tony as he and Dave chase the car onto a ring road. An armed vehicle appears behind them and he is advised to pull back, given that the suspect is tooled up. "I wish I was; they changed the rules," he mutters. The police set up a roadblock and the car ploughs into a lorry, crushing the driver to death. The ARV men fear that Dave has got caught up in the carnage before he licks some of it off his finger: "Sweet and sour." In the boot they find two AK-47s: an idea which must have been inspired by the real life discovery of these weapons in a car boot after a police chase on 23rd May 1990 – eerily, the day after the broadcast of *Trojan Horse*.

The flat is raided and its startled occupants, an Irish man and woman, frisked at gunpoint. "You still think you can treat us like shite, don't you?" he complains. "Do your snooping somewhere else, we've got rights and we know it mister," she adds with mistaken certainty.

Maitland informs Jim of the weapons found, which make this a different ball game: "Kalashnikov assault rifles. That's not blagging gear." "No – we're talking politicals." The two flatmates, Paul Harris and Marie Sinnot, are arrested under the Prevention of Terrorism Act. The moment they are in custody, an attempt is made to turn Sun Hill into the fortress that its planners allowed for two years earlier. The officers are issued with firearms, signed for as per established procedure. "That doesn't make us a high security nick," a worried Boyden reminds Monroe. "No, but it'll only be for a short time. The anti-terrorist squad are on their way, they'll take them off our hands." As he gets a broadside filling in the custody record, Boyden asks Sinnot if she understands why she is here: "Oh, I understand all right. I understand the position of people like us in the British state." Superintendent Grace arrives from SO13 and dispels any hope that the prisoners will be transferred to Paddington Green. "I have to say I'm not personally confident that Sun Hill can cope with high security prisoners for more than a brief period," Monroe warns him. Carver observes to Grace's DS that "under the Act you can really take off the gloves, can't you?" "That's a bit of an unfortunate way of putting it," he is told. "Times have changed." Reading the list of names the prisoners want informed of their arrest, and the high-profile lawyer they've asked for, Grace declares that "they're out of luck on both counts. If they're allowed outside contacts at this time, I believe it will prejudice my enquiries. Alibis may be constructed, witnesses interfered with and evidence suppressed, OK?" "The prisoners are Sun Hill's responsibility," Monroe protests. "I can't abrogate their rights on your say-so." "No, but a senior officer can: superintendent or above. So why don't you get Charlie Brownlow on the blower?"

Boyden explains to the astonished Harris that they cannot have legal representation, and won't be getting out any time soon: "Under the Prevention of Terrorism Act, you can be held in police custody for up to forty-eight hours without being charged. Then, if the Secretary of State agrees, you can be held for a further five days." This contentious law was another legacy of the 1974 pub bombings, together with the conviction and release of the Birmingham Six. The IRA was as current an issue as ever in 1991, the year the Six were freed: a bombing campaign in Central London included a mortar attack on Downing Street in February that could have caused severe injury to the Cabinet if not for reinforced windows that had just been fitted.[34] While this two-parter sees the police dealing with the effects, the cause was about to be taken from them; the government was preparing to transfer powers for investigating the IRA from the Met's Special Branch to MI5, which already handled all other forms of terrorist activity. The handover was announced the month after these episodes aired and was followed by tense negotiations between the parties.[35] One can only imagine the mileage Wilsher and others could have gleaned from the politics of policing the War on Terror a decade later. Had it not been vanishing down the rabbit hole at the time, *The Bill* would have been the ideal vehicle to explore such issues. But terrorist plotlines weren't just out of step with the regime of the day, they were specifically *verboten*, out of a fear that real life would get there first and make an episode unshowable. That says something for the new ground rules created by 9/11: the sheer scale and visibility of the attack, and the existential threat posed thereafter. Decades of IRA terrorism in mainland Britain had got people 'used' to the idea, but what makes it such a potent topic for *The Bill* is that official institutions, like the army and the police, usually took the brunt. Already on the lookout for bombs in litter bins, West End police had a narrow escape when the IRA missed their section house and got a nearby ancillary building – again, a month after this episode aired.[36]

Discomfort begins to rise among the boys of Sun Hill as they too find themselves on the frontline of a war. "We are talking about dedicated revolutionary fanatics here," babbles Hollis, doing his best to alarm his colleagues. "If they can't shoot their way out, their comrades will be round with rockets and mortars, it's been done before. This mob's been known to hijack helicopters before now to blag their mates out. All I am doing George, is warning against complacency in the air and maximum danger." "All you're doing is going home to bed, the same as me." Stamp and Quinnan return from going "eyeball to eyeball with the terrorist scourge", the latter again accounting for the mess on his shirt: "Blood, brains, guts, monosodium glutamate, the Full Monty." Further up the chain the discomfort is of a different kind,

---

[34] Andrew, Christopher, *The Defence of the Realm: The Authorized History of MI5* (2009), p. 772

[35] Ibid, pp. 773-6

[36] *The Bill Podcast*: Former Met PC Kevin Holland Part 1, 2021

and the attitudes we expect from certain people are turned on their head, while keeping them entirely in character. Watching his back, the rule-bending Boyden is anxious about the treatment of the prisoners, telling Monroe that he has no idea how the interviews are being conducted: "A lot of what's going on here would be right out of order under normal circumstances." By contrast, the man who lives by the book is prepared to throw it away, based on bitter experience. "They're not suspected of anything normal. The rules are different in terrorist cases. You weren't in this station when a car bomb took it apart and killed one of our constables. You can't fight a war by the everyday rules." Grace reveals that PIRA's Active Service Units "got mountains of Kalashnikovs from Colonel Gaddafi in the mid-Eighties arms shipments." A recent series of attacks in the Home Counties has been connected to one such ASU, whose frontline troops are now in custody at Paddington Green. "What you've tripped over here looks like the support cell: long-stay players with deep cover who arrange transport and accommodation; store weapons and equipment." "They've lived normal civilian lives, waiting for the call to arms. Had a chance to soften up," says a hopeful Grace. "We get a clear run at it, keep them isolated – we can break 'em."

But these assumptions begin to fall apart in *The Wild Rover*, when a dissenting voice muscles in on the act: the wrecking ball that is Edward Roach, Esq. The lengthy recap that takes place for the benefit of him and Tosh, but really for the audience, suggests an anxiety not to leave new viewers at sea, even though there was only a single day between the two instalments when they were broadcast. At the same time, it demonstrates how far the two-parter had come since the early days of procedural cock-ups and church fetes. If Wilsher's *Cold Turkey* the previous year was a fifty-minute episode sawn in half, then this story is the clearest indication yet of the ground he is about to cover for the other side in *Between the Lines*. The unholy alliances between the police, the criminals and the intelligence services that came to dominate that series are given an airing here. The casting of Lynda Steadman, later to play Tony Clark's wife, as Julie Sinnot, together with guest appearances from Tom Georgeson and Siobhan Redmond in other episodes this year, enhance the sense of two programmes sharing the same DNA. While Sinnot and Harris are grilled yet again by SO13, Sun Hill CID are given the legwork of checking out their past lives and associates. The picture that emerges of these two terrorist masterminds is far from convincing: one chucked off a polytechnic course for late night partying and drug-taking, the other sacked after two days on a building site. "They're irresponsible, loud, piss artists – maybe druggies," Roach informs Grace. "If I wanted a couple to live here undercover, and provide support for terrorist operations, I'd want people who kept their head down and melted into the landscape, not walking disaster areas!"

His anxieties dismissed, Roach goes to Burnside and reminds him that if the case gets blown out years later on appeal, i.e. another Birmingham Six, "Sun Hill CID's prints will be on it." Against orders, Burnside reveals that the dead man, Joseph Pearce, was an Irishman who served in the British Army from 1967 to 1974, during the onset of the Troubles. "You don't have to tell me. I was in the Air Force at the time," says Roach, in another nod to Tony Scannell's real-life history. "Well he wouldn't be the only Irish soldier in the British Army who started to have doubts about his loyalties at the time of Bloody Sunday," notes Burnside. With the official ignorance of his governor, Roach begins to dig around Pearce's old haunts, and for the first time his own background is used to good effect in a story. Having ruled him out of a politically sensitive job in Belfast two years earlier, here it's his ticket into an Irish pub. He is barely inside before he's accosted by a man with a tin collecting "for the families of Irish political prisoners", the same worthy cause that we learnt in *Citadel* was pushed onto a young Richard Turnham; and like Richard, Ted duly pays up. The barman, an old contact of his, works both sides of the fence but doesn't want to know as soon as Pearce's name is mentioned. "Joe Pearce isn't bad news because anyone thinks he's a volunteer. He's bad news 'cos they think he's a tout! He's suddenly started spending a lot of time in the company of his old Army pals. Those still serving, I mean – and he's tried to do it on the quiet." The next day he meets Ted and reveals that three men came in after he left, asking about Pearce, who they have not met – and whose fate they are unaware of. "I know British soldiers when I see them. Is Army Intelligence tied up in this?" They want to set up a business deal that evening, and Roach decides to pose as the dead man.

Meanwhile, Grace makes a complaint about a Sun Hill officer "playing the wild rover" to Brownlow, whose eyes close in weary resignation when he learns which one. Here the story weaves its political themes with the long-standing subject of career politics in CID. Brownlow sees Burnside, asking him how he's finding his post as Acting DCI and stressing the importance of effective supervision. "Of course, support for subordinates is essential. But I'd hate to see an able man held back through misplaced loyalty. Believe me Frank, you can't save a man who's determined to drive his own career into the ground." With Harris beginning to talk after thirty-six hours in custody – "Who's he naming? His girlfriend, his Auntie Mary, the milkman?" – Roach meets Burnside and puts forward his own theory. The oddness of a hardened terrorist liaison panicking, making a run for it and literally losing his head has already been ascribed by one of the SO13 men to 'the Paddy Factor'. This was the working title for what became *The Long Good Friday*, and the film's key twist, in which a campaign of revenge seemingly conducted by rival gangsters turns out to be the work of the IRA, is cleverly inverted here. "When you know what you're looking for, all the evidence seems to fit in... There are soldiers on the ground looking for Pearce with something to sell. Now we're all assuming that automatic weapons mean terrorists, but what if there's a trade in them for *non*-political criminals? We all know the kind of scumbags who go in for armed blagging these days – they're all doped up to the eyeballs. Mention automatic weapons to those zombies, they go bandy." "So Pearce is the middleman, the armourer? It's all guesswork, Ted." "Up till now."

Learning of Roach's plan to buy the latest consignment, Burnside warns him, "If the wheels come off this one, and Brownlow does your legs once and for all, I'm going to have to help him. I am Acting DCI, I can't have my firm second-guessing SO13! It's etiquette – and politics. Self-defence is no offence." But on the proviso that "this really is all about pongoes flogging off equipment" he calls in help from the military police, who were about to nail Pearce for his sideline before he left the Army. That evening, in an upstairs room at the pub, Ted is introduced to his three mystery suppliers – and the spectre of extremism gives way to the more familiar rules of commerce. Ordered to frisk 'Pearce', one of the henchmen replies automatically, "Yes Sarge" and looks embarrassed. "It's no secret you're in the mob, is it?" says Ted. When he offers the boys a drink their leader accepts but insists, "They're too young." "A good sergeant's a mother and a father rolled into one, right? You see much action in the Gulf?" "Of a kind." "The Iraqis weren't shooting at us." "And the Yanks missed." "Brought back a lot of souvenirs?" "There was too much lying around to carry. Still," the sergeant adds, "if I'd known about the defence cuts I'd have filled a crate." Roach asks to see the goods before he pays and is taken to their car to inspect them; then armed police swoop in. Burnside points out that this result won't do either of them any favours – "No greater offence than being right too soon" – but for once, Ted has other motives besides getting the glory. He may be a policeman first and an Irishman second, but the latter still counts for something. In another pointed reference to the real events of 1991, he notes, "At least they didn't take fifteen years to sort this one out."

The use and potential misuse of ARVs may have been highlighted by Wilsher, but it's another author who explores that scenario in depth this year. In Tony Etchells' *Snap Shot*, Quinnan and Stamp are called out to a man accused by his neighbour of threatening him with a gun. They enter his flat, filled with military posters and memorabilia, and discover a display case of handguns and automatic rifles. "I collect replicas, all right?" reveals their twitchy owner, Gary Miller. "Replicas and militaria." The upstairs neighbour, who was broadcasting his music to the entire block, admits that Miller threatened to get a gun but didn't actually produce it. Tony wants to go, saying that if the music gets turned up again, "It's not our problem, is it? You'll have to see the council, Environmental Health, they'll sort him out." "He says noise makes him nervous," Dave clarifies once they have gone. "He reckons armed struggle's the only thing he understands." "He should feel right at home here then, shouldn't he?" They are called back to find Miller shouting up at his neighbour. After another round of promises, Tony is itching to get away and accepts a new shout, but Dave wants to stay: "He's out of his tree, he's drinking neat gin." "So are half the people on the estate!" The neighbour storms into Miller's flat to "sort him out" – and when Dave follows, he finds Miller holding a gun on him. They are both ordered out and Miller emerges, gun levelled. A call to CAD about a gunman prompts one from the Yard, asking if they want armed assistance. Tony and Dave try to cool the situation, the former advising that the ARV is not needed as they are only facing a replica. But as he is urging Miller to put it down, an ARV appears from nowhere and a stand-off develops. The man responsible is Conway, who tells Tony that "until we're certain this man is unarmed, I've told MP I want the ARV there fully deployed. We act on the assumption the gun is real, all right?"

Realising that this circus is only making things worse, Tony insists, "He's a berk!" "That's as maybe, but I'd rather be safe than sorry," says Donaghee, the lead ARV man. "Get down!" Tony is urged as he stands there trying to reason with Miller while the others take cover. They order him to drop the weapon as he begins waving it around. "Gary, stand still!" yells Tony. "He's going to shoot!" One of the officers opens fire, hitting Miller in the chest. An enquiry begins, headed by Superintendent Cochrane from MS-15. Tony maintains the ARV crew mishandled the situation and is prepared to make it official. "You nearly got yourself killed friend, it was real," Donaghee informs him smugly. "Nine millimetre semi-automatic, five live rounds, would have blown your brains out. Mind you, that wouldn't take a lot." Tony goes for him and the two have to be separated. There's a small but telling moment when Chapel, the officer who actually fired the shots, walks by with a mumbled, "Sorry." Regulations mean that he cannot be interviewed for twenty-four hours following the shooting, so everyone else is questioned first. The incident has been captured by a man with a camcorder, and Cochrane reviews the footage. Conway informs Tony of Miller's psychiatric history, admitting that "it's terrible that a man like that should have been facing armed officers." But he also tells him to stop dwelling on the ifs, buts and maybes. "Perhaps if you'd handled him differently, you'd have brought him in unharmed – and perhaps he'd have slaughtered half the street!"

It's revealed that Tony's warning cry of "He's going to shoot!" is what prompted Chapel to fire first – thinking it was for him, when it was for Miller. This echoes another real-life miscarriage of justice, the hanging of Derek Bentley in the Fifties: a policeman ordered his accomplice Christopher Craig to hand over his gun, Bentley called out, "Let him have it!" and Craig shot him. Because Craig was not yet an adult, it was only Bentley who got the noose. This ancient history would have been fresh in people's minds after the release of the film *Let Him Have It* in 1991. Like Bentley, Miller is a man of diminished mental capacity "and suddenly there are three people pointing semi-automatics at him! The ARV responded to the threat from Miller by trying to dominate the situation, only he thought that was his cue to be more threatening back!" But Tony's argument is in part a smokescreen for his guilt. Cochrane puts it in simple terms – "If you go tooled up for a shootout, you're going to find one" – and rejects Brownlow's suggestion that this applies to the ARV crew as well as Miller. The Chief Super advises Tony not to pursue his complaint as the report will likely exonerate them. "Doubts have been expressed about your handling of the domestic matter – doubts which, perhaps, you feel yourself." Even with his finger off the trigger, Tony ends up as culpable as Cryer was two years earlier. It was Bob who warned of the two kinds of copper that would be created by ARVs, "social workers in uniforms, and tooled up paramilitaries." Tony, who flirted with the latter as an AFO and so often complains that he is not the former, is revealed to be far closer to it than he knew. A beat copper at heart, he just doesn't have the patience to deal with those he views as hopeless cases. The baleful look on his face as Brownlow raises his limitations is proof that he knows them better than anyone. "I've heard from the hospital; Miller never regained consciousness. Nothing's ever clear-cut, is it Tony?" He stares back bitterly: "There's nothing more clear-cut than that, sir."

PUBLIC SERVICE

The familiar refrain, "We're not social workers", rings more false than usual during this year, given that the idea now has an active champion. The arrival in late 1991 of Sun Hill's fourth collator in three years illustrates the problems of a role that shackles an interesting character to a filing cabinet. Like his predecessor Cathy Marshall, the phlegmatic Ron Smollett, a copper from the old school, lasts only a year in the job before the baton is handed to Donna Harris – who, unlike the others is here to stay. In this twice-weekly era it was possible for the show's established writers to home in on certain characters and follow them for a while. It's Julian Jones who simultaneously guides Smollett and Cryer back towards active duty, as the two much-derided desk jockeys start to itch for the great outdoors. The way is paved for Ron's return to the big time in *The Taste*. Meeting a man whose flash sports car has broken down, he becomes suspicious about whether it is really his. Meanwhile, filling in as custody sergeant, Cryer gets embroiled in a dispute with Maitland over the correct application of PACE. Maitland finds Monroe outside and asks for his advice on how to resolve this thorny issue. Staring into the yard, Monroe declares, "What a poser" – just as Ron pulls up in the convertible. "You can't help it, but it makes you feel like a superstar in one of these!" "It's a shame it can't make you look like one." But in spite of all the jibes about "old RoboRon", he hits the jackpot, uncovering a scam involving a disqualified driver. He asks Cryer to put his name forward to Brownlow as home beat officer. "You've got the taste," observes their fellow veteran Tosh.

Ron's installation as the new home beat man feels like an attempt to get it right after Yorkie's stint on home beat in the hour-long era, which unlike in real life was mixed with other duties. He faces his first test in *Beggar My Neighbour*, when a tramp is found burned on a park bench after someone from the nearby Beckett Estate set fire to him. "The usual," says George after questioning passers-by. "The Three Wise Monkeys – except nobody's wise." Ron is reluctant to have Tosh by his side asking questions while he does his rounds on the estate: "They're just getting to know me out there." He gets on well enough with the black manager of the local community centre, but realises the latter has been holding back about drug dealers on the estate. "Because I won't play the white man?" he protests. "Naming names to keep you sweet? Don't lean on me, that's not the way we work together." After he has reluctantly handed over the details, he adds, "You know, maybe it was better when people like you and me just didn't talk to each other." On the way to raid a squat, Ron points out to the other PCs that the soft option of home beat is really the frontline of the frontline: "You go in here today then you're out of it, I'm the one who's got to answer the questions tomorrow." "Yeah, but how can you square knocking a door in with being Mr Community?" "Soft is the last thing I want to look around here." As the hammer is raised, a group of kids heckles Ron from nearby: "You're still a copper, in't you Smollett?" The hostility is amped up in Julian Jones's *Comeback*, in which Cryer make his long awaited return to the relief. It's a big day for Ron too, opening a police community office on the Kingsmead Estate. He enlists Dave and Cathy to help kit it out, insisting that the door remain open so people can see inside, even though it doesn't officially start until the next day. "Who does he reckon he is?" asks Dave once Ron has slipped outside. "It's a publicity job, that's all."

But when the area car is stolen and written off in a crash, Ron gets caught up in the investigation against his wishes. He reluctantly gives Brownlow the name of a youth who dropped into the centre and knows the driver who got away, on the assurance it won't be traced to him. As he locks up that night, petrol is thrown into the office and he has to escape via a side window as the building goes up in flames. In the hunt that follows in *Fireproof*, a piece of graffiti springs up saying 'Burn Pigs Out', but we see that Ron has made friends as well as enemies. "Everyone I've had in the shop this morning has been asking after you," says a concerned newsagent. A resident who told June that it was too dark for her to see much admits to Ron that she did see someone, but "I didn't want to tell that lady copper. 'Cos I know Jeff's black, and I'm not trying to say you're racist, I know you're all right Ron... well, things have happened in the past." In the mould of the racists she condemns, she obviously finds individual coppers OK when she gets to know them: justification for Ron's philosophy of getting up close to the public. But that also means getting close to the problem element. Another woman recognises the photo fit of the suspect as her daughter's boyfriend. The daughter does not share her fondness for their home beat officer: "He wants to pretend he's all nice so he can turn everyone in!" "That's his job, to catch people!" "To spy on us!" This tip-off leads to an arrest, Conway suggesting that "it vindicates all the work Ron's been doing on that estate, people really stood up to help him." "Maybe we've lost an office but gained a community," replies a hopeful Brownlow. Ron is given a gallon bottle of whisky by the grateful residents, assuring Conway that he will raffle it for charity – but adds that he'd rather have it than the commendation he is in line for.

There is seemingly no respite from – and no variety in – the parade of sink estates "007" is sent to on his missions of mercy. The grandmammy of them all may be Jasmine Allen, but through the Nineties there was also the Abelard, the Bronte, the Cockcroft, the

228

Copthorne, the Larkmead... to say nothing of the Bannister, the Fairways, the Matthew Arnold, the Tankeray, the Beckett, the Kingsmead... and probably half a dozen more. The only thing that distinguishes them is the new putdown each time one is mentioned – "I'd rather sleep on a bench than live in those flats", "You don't want a community police station, you want a fully loaded TSG van parked on that estate!" – and at times those one-liners feel like their sole *raison d'être*. Things are at their bleakest in Steve Trafford's two-parter *Well Out of Order/Into the Mire*, in which Ron's softly softly act comes in for severe criticism. "Look I'm working a twelve-hour shift today, we are running like mad just to keep still," protests Steve. "And he's up here swanning about, poncing cups of tea." After an assault on a shopkeeper at the Tankeray Flats, Meadows points out his team have pursued the criminal element there for months: "Whenever one of my lads is tailing some thief with a rucksack of car stereos back to the estate, someone from uniform turns up with a smiling community face and he dives for cover!" Brownlow and Conway maintain they must follow the long-term strategy of the community liaison panel. "So Ron Smollett's calling the shots now, is he?" Burnside complains. "I mean we all know if you go down that estate and ask the real community what they want, they'll tell you loud and clear: cuff 'em and stuff 'em!" Ron insists that if they go in mob-handed, six months' work will be down the drain. Meadows has put his objections on record, but "we're exercising restraint... Till the job comes completely unwrapped, when no doubt we'll be asked to go in and dig Ron Smollett out."

Following another vicious attack, on a community leader who loses the baby she is carrying, Burnside convinces Conway that they must go in hard – and the latter tells Ron ominously that they'll "have a chat in the morning." "How do you police a hellhole like this?" Tosh asks Burnside as they drive in. "You walk tall, carry a big stick and use it when you have to. You lose the streets to the local yobs and you can dream up all the murals and summer schools you like, but you won't win them back." Ron does win again, however, when a teenage couple come forward and admit that they know the attacker. He grabs the suspect and brings him in, much to the annoyance of Burnside. But in the next episode he learns of a wider strategy going on behind his back. Having found a man and his children squatting in a vacant flat, Ron visits the council's housing department with

Conway to discuss an area that "made Beirut look like the Ideal Home Exhibition." Bemused that seventy-two 'voids' have been left empty for months, awaiting repair works, they are told the truth. "The council intends to decant the occupants of Tankeray Flats and demolish. Until the money is available the project is on hold." "And in the meantime you'll let the whole place slide into the mire, is that the idea?" "That's not the intention, that may very well be the consequence." "I'm the Thin Blue Line down there," protests Ron. "I'm doing my best to create goodwill in the community and the rest of it, and now you're telling me the council's given up on the place! These 'occupants' that you intend to decant – I mean all right, they are not the solid citizens of Middle England, but most of them are decent people and they are sick of seeing their community going to the dogs!" The squatting epidemic turns out to be the result of a scam: a council repairman is letting people move into empty flats in return for private 'rent', most of which is pocketed by the same housing officer who Ron met that day.

Ron draws a distinction between the residents, mostly pensioners who "live in terror of going out", and the troublemakers, but this line is blurred in Tony Etchells' *Cold Shoulder*. The problems of social housing give way to those of anti-social housing, as Barry and Tony voice the debate over the Right to Buy scheme launched by the Conservative government a decade earlier, which gave people the ability to buy their council flat. "It's not something to be ashamed of you know, renting a council flat." "It's nothing to be proud of, either." "So now you've bought your own flat Tony, that makes you a decent person, does it?" "Why should people look after something if they don't own it? There is nothing wrong with people buying their flats, Barry." "There was nothing wrong with people renting them, either." Outside a housing block they find the victim of a stabbing, recognised by Jim as a notorious burglar, Mark Grant: "It couldn't have happened to a nicer feller." "Cresswell Court has moved away from traditional council management towards owner occupation," Brownlow observes at a planning meeting. "There's a residue of five or six problem families that think the rest of the neighbours are fair game. The mix of people is a contributory factor to the problem." The obvious suspect is Tony McKinnel, the son of a man broken into and assaulted a few months earlier by Grant, who got away with it;

but no-one is willing to implicate him. Amid a consensus that justice has been done, Meadows takes the unpopular stance: "Judge and jury now, are we Jim?" "All I'm saying is guv, he got what he deserved." "I've never understood that, 'got what he deserved', I never have done. Look, there's a seventeen year old lad lying in intensive care with his tripes hanging out," the DCI reminds his team. "Now if anyone thinks that's acceptable because he's a villain, or that two wrongs make a right, just say so and I'll give you something else to do."

Burnside suggests the police have let Grant walk over the estate for too long. On a visit Jim agrees, telling Meadows they're letting down people like McKinnel: "I mean look at this place – ninety five per cent decent people, the other five per cent you can't do anything with." "Them and us? We police by consensus Jim, not divide and rule." Meadows points out to the unmoved local publican the consequence of this race to the bottom: "Every man for himself, is that what you want?" When Grant wakes up, he claims a dozen people were watching as McKinnel approached and stabbed him. But he changes his mind, developing amnesia. McKinnel is brought in and lectured: "Justice is not a commodity, it's not something you buy like a council flat." "Privatised the prisons though, in't they? What he did to my dad – we won't tolerate people like that no more." Accused of "protecting an investment", he challenges Meadows: "So what's wrong with that? You've got a nice house, intcha? How many villains live where you live, eh? How would you feel if one of them moved in next door?" Brownlow suggests that, while he doesn't like it either, people are filling the gap left by the failure of the police. The show examined vigilantism many times, but rarely from such a specific angle – the upwardly mobile trying to distance themselves from the dregs. In a memorable ending, Meadows storms into their pub like an anti-hero at the climax of a Western, calling out the inhabitants of a town for their sins. "He's got your backing has he, to clear out the flats, get rid of the undesirables? A bit of stabbing here and there?" The landlord reluctantly orders McKinnel and his pals to leave, knowing the trouble that this moral gesture will cause him. "What happened to all the decent people, Frank?" Meadows asks his deputy as they too make an exit. "They bought their own flats, guv."

This unremittingly grim picture drew the ire of police as well as residents; *The Bill* lost one of its stand-ins for the Jasmine Allen when it was unwilling to include the more positive views of inner-city life requested by community officer Kevin Holland, the real life Ron Smollett.[37] But he later got them on side, and the relationship between show and police was far more co-operative than combative, which becomes overt on screen in the early Nineties. The activities of Ron can be seen as part of an effort to forge closer links with the Met. It was Julian Jones, who wrote so much for the character, whose 1991 episode *Without Consent* drew fire in high places. But, in a run of episodes this year that feel as if they were requested by the police to shine a light on certain issues, Jones's *Chicken* stands out as a throwback to those public information films of the Seventies that traumatised a generation by showing how juvenile pranks can escalate into tragedy. It builds to its powerful ending via a scene in which a classroom of kids laughs and jeers at a video on rail safety that a hapless BTP officer is trying to show them. The glimpse of a presenter who looks suspiciously like *It's a Knockout* compère turned convicted felon Stuart Hall makes the scene doubly macabre; perhaps those kids simply had judgement their adult peers lacked. With chants of "Boring!" they heckle their way through it until the bell goes and they scramble for the exit, barely pausing to take the safety leaflets offered. "First time I gave a talk here, a young lad at the back set fire to the curtains," says a sympathetic Ron. It's not just the youths, but the railway workers laughing at them as they race around in trolleys leading June a merry dance, who fail to see the funny side in the end. "It has been a problem in the area," a British Rail supervisor notes of the children's games. "It won't be any more," says Peters.

Railway pranks are a further source of trouble in *Fireworks*, by Duncan Gould, the writer who takes the lead on the 'public service' angle this year. The patrolling Tony is shaken by a massive bang from behind a fence and discovers two boys playing with unusual toys: detonators taken from the railway line. "The gangers strap them on the lines about a mile above where they're working," explains another BTP officer. "Then the train goes over it, it makes a bang and it warns the

---

37 *The Bill Podcast*: Former Met PC Kevin Holland Part 1, 2021

driver to slow down. The trouble is, the kids are always nicking them. We lost a hundred last week. They look harmless enough, until they blow your hand off. Thirty metres is a safe working distance." He and Tony march the two youths to their school, but then hear another bang from the primary next door. They rush over into the playground to find a six-year old girl with a bloodied face, caused by flying debris. "You hit it hard with a brick or something and it goes off. If you're too close, it sends the brick back in your face." Stamp tracks down the teen who is selling the detonators to other kids, corners him in a lift and adapts the caring approach of Smollett. Pinning the boy to the wall, he hisses a warning in his face, eyes bulging: "You'd better make up your mind what you're going to do, or you could end up with a face like hers!" Pushing him outside, he explains to a startled old lady, "Bit of community policing, madam." The school caretaker later calls Tony out to an unusual break-in, "More in the nature of a deposit than a withdrawal." He is shown a stack of detonators and says he knows who left them: "A bit of a face-saving tactic, in a manner of speaking."

Gould also delivers a story of an officer meeting trauma head-on, in the vein of *Fat'Ac* and *Chicken*, but this time the choice to put through the wringer is even more inspired. *All the King's Horses* opens with Steve hearing a crash round the corner, as Yorkie did in *Fat'Ac*, and rushing to the scene. Here we see, or rather don't see, an unexpected boon of *The Bill*'s police-only perspective: showing only the aftermath of what would be an expensive action sequence, not the moment itself. Steve discovers a timber lorry overturned outside a school, burying a child under debris. There is plenty of help on offer, but too many hands are part of the problem. Steve orders the over-zealous rescuers to move back and keep quiet; only then do they pick up where the cries of distress are coming from. He and Tony pull out a girl with minor injuries, then learn that a boy is missing too. Steve finds him and gets him breathing again, before handing him to the paramedics. As first responder he must compile witness statements for the accident report book, and goes with the boy to hospital; but en route, his heart stops again. "But he was all right! We had him..." a shocked Steve keeps repeating. The internal injuries from the crush are too severe and he dies soon after. Steve is left sitting numbly on a chair in casualty; this is not how the hero's story is supposed to end.

Another boy comes up to him hesitantly and admits the truth: that they were playing football and he kicked the ball over the fence. "And Paul said he'd go and get it, and he got it... but then the bell went, so he ran back across the road..." Steve comforts the tearful boy as they share in a guilt that is unfair on them both.

What serves as a powerful lesson on road safety to the child audience is also a test for the adults on screen. In the wake of the Phil Young debacle, the stumbling efforts to address mental wellbeing among the troops gain a little more momentum, but remain handicapped. Consoling the tearful Norika, Monroe is on solid ground; when it comes to fellow blokes he is all at sea. It's Conway, the stress counsellor you want only when the rest are on the phone to the Samaritans, who proves that he has learnt something from those bungled schemes of recent years. He gets the numbers of the officers involved so he can phone home and "let their other halves know they've had a stressful day." He advises Monroe to take the relief for a drink after the shift, and the bluff Northerner looks terrified at the prospect of being touchy-feely. "You don't have to hold their hands, Andrew; just show up and show them that you care!" Shrugging off other people's concern, Steve has gone into robot mode. "You seen one, you've seen 'em all," he tells Monroe glibly, refusing a request to talk to the mother; "nearly" saving her boy's life isn't good enough. As he compiles his accident report he becomes frozen, staring into space. The worried June tells Tony, who puts up his own shield of insouciance to deal with things like this, "The day you don't get upset about the death of a kid is the day you should quit." Ron agrees to have a word; but in the pub, his attempts at the "you did all you could" routine get nowhere. "Just go and play social workers with someone else, eh Ron?" barks Steve, rushing off to the toilets. Ron follows him in, knocking on the cubicle door, and is assured "I'm all right now." Only at the last moment does the police perspective become the viewer's alone. Tom Butcher brings a new, humane dimension to Steve as he slumps against the wall, his face streaked with tears; the hard man gets his turn.

Besides the unusual safety challenges, we get an insight into the range of extra jobs that fall within the police's scope. *Safety First* sees Cryer wading through the huge backlog of applications for shotgun licence renewals. "It's a pity the new Act didn't go further. If they made shotguns as hard to get as pistols and rifles, we wouldn't have every Tom, Dick and Harry wanting one," he declares, but is told, "It still has to be done – a security check on every shotgun keeper's home." He visits one such man who is a security consultant himself, warning him that his glass-fronted cabinet is no longer sufficient. "It needs to be a steel one. New police policy. It is a condition of granting and renewing a certificate now; it's in the Home Office guidelines." "It might be in the guidelines, but it's not in the Firearms Amendment Act," says the owner, Jones, highlighting a woolly piece of legislation. "All I'm required to do by law is to provide enough security to prevent access by unauthorised persons." He comes to Sun Hill to protest to Brownlow. "I know your views, Bob," says a sympathetic Monroe. "With respect sir, no-one can: until they've looked down the wrong end of a gun barrel." The Chief Super points out that Jones's stance is legally correct. "I wonder if things are going to be any easier when firearms licensing goes under civilian control," he muses. Jones maintains that "criminals will always get hold of guns." "Often by stealing them from legitimate owners," Monroe reminds him. He gets no assurances about the decision of the licensing branch, but Brownlow tells Cryer in private that he does not intend to oppose the renewal: "He is complying with the spirit of the Act." "How many others are going to take the same tack as Mr Jones?" asks Bob. "And then the more concessions we make, the more chances there are of a shotgun ending up in criminal hands."

The episode runs another storyline in tandem that proves his and Monroe's point. CID look into the history of a shotgun left behind after wounding a pawnbroker in a robbery. "I thought we were supposed to be able to trace each shotgun just like that now, sir," Jim says to Monroe. "Once we get all the new style certificates issued and everybody has to declare what guns they owned... it might be easier." Visiting a nearby gunsmith's to check its records, a hopeful Woods observes, "I'll be glad when we do have a record of every shotgun on a computer." "Cloud cuckoo land, mate," replies the clerk, leafing through his books. "Even if you did have time to keep up with the paperwork, you'd only have legally owned guns on record. Villains don't bother taking out licences, remember?" He himself sold the gun through the firm six years earlier; it was then sold back to them two years earlier and sold on to someone with dodgy connections, who claims he gave it to his brother but in fact "flogged it to a minicab driver last Christmas." Burnside tracks down this man and finds a garden shed full of weapons, which he rents to blaggers like the two who robbed the pawnbroker's. "You're going to need one of those steel cabinets for that lot," he declares as they are checked into custody. "Well we haven't got one of those anymore," Cryer observes, giving Brownlow a dark look. But the divide they cite between "legitimate" and illegitimate gun owners is more nuanced than the real law could manage at this time. It was in the early Nineties that the existing complaints and charges against one Thomas Hamilton proved no obstacle to the renewal of his handgun certificate. The powers that be always end up reacting to the worst, rather than guarding against it.

The above episodes give warnings on specific issues, but another by Duncan Gould widens the target. *We Should Be Talking* is one of those small masterpieces only possible in *The Bill*'s format: a weighty discussion about civic responsibility, condensed into one afternoon shift. George stops a man in a car suspected of a ramraid, while June finds a bloodied shoe left from the hit and run of a child who may be hurt somewhere. But their radios then go down, a division-wide problem caused by vandalism to a transmitter. June tries to talk to a witness who rushes away on a bus. "You'd better get on the Bat-phone love, no one'll give you the time of day round here," its driver warns her. But Cryer is seasoned enough to recall another approach, and puts it to Monroe: "We can do things in the old way for a while, like we did before we had radios." "You mean ringing in? I don't know if you'd noticed Bob, but they've done away with the TARDIS." "No I don't just mean ringing in, I mean getting the public to help us, letting us use their phones and that." "In London? Nowadays?" "Well people are still people." "OK Bob, but don't expect miracles. The old Blue Lamp approach doesn't cut much ice these days." Cryer enforces "some fire brigade policing", keeping the van at Sun Hill to respond to emergencies. The other old-timer, Ron, is also taken back to his youth: "Be just like before 1968 skip, eh? If you need any help, just ask the people. And I'll tell you something else, be a lot quieter. You won't get nearly as many rubbish calls and you'll be able to have as many cups of tea as you like." Sure enough, when June explains her situation, attitudes start to change. The newsagent she phones in from, suddenly concerned, tells her where the boy may live. Venturing onto one of Ron's familiar hostile estates, she gets a familiar hostile reception, until she explains she is working blind: "You and your mates must know this estate a great deal better than I do!" The woman she speaks to is galvanised into action, getting help from a friend. They find the boy with the aid of another child, torn away from his video games, who knows an out of the way spot to search.

On his way back, George spots another car of likely ramraiders, follows them to a pub and persuades the landlord to let him use his phone. He tries to stop them escaping and is nearly crippled as they back up their car with him hanging in the window. He is saved by a group who turn up with baseball bats, led by the landlord, and smash the windscreen. Though the car gets away, George is left bruised but intact. "I couldn't stand by and watch three against one, could I?" says the landlord. His faith borne out, Cryer observes that "people used to do it all the time, they knew you were on your Jack Jones." George spots the car driver he let go earlier, supposedly on an urgent business trip to Wales. Ron advises him to have a chat and read the man, not the PNC: "It's the job, being suspicious, talking to people." George questions him gently about the damage to his car and discovers that, though he has missed out on the ramraiders, he has found the driver who ran down the kid. The implication that technology has divorced the police from the public, who see their slick equipment and assume they can handle their own problems, is a further riposte to the ambitions of the security industry in *Citadel*: for telecommunications to fill the void in policing left by reduced manpower. But it's a message that could only be delivered at a certain point in history, in the early days of the digital revolution. To say that ship has sailed would be the understatement of all time. The almighty device as an extra limb for everyone, not just officialdom, is now taken for granted. So too are its curiously mixed blessings. The smartphones that have saved countless lives have also been used by the public and by police officers to turn crime scenes into their own personal content backdrops. Perhaps nothing has changed after all; to repurpose Bob's motto, people are still people.

THE AGE OF ANTIQUITY

While all around him go softly into that dark night, the grammar school ponce shows them how to make an exit: with as many waves as possible. Mike Dashwood's move to the Arts and Antiques Squad sets the template for another kind of departure – the transfer presented as a *fait accompli* at the beginning of somebody's last episode. *Part of the Furniture* opens with the man of the moment admiring his leaving gift. If a model policeman was the only suitable present for Bob Cryer at his anniversary do, then a classical figurine is all that will do for Dashers. "He didn't buy it!" Burnside corrects Mike, nodding at the hapless Jim. "Not after that Kim Reid fiasco. I happened to be in the local junk, erm, antique shop, and I spotted that. I thought it was appropriate, one way or the other." Mike nods approvingly: "It'll take pride of place on my credenza." "Yeah, well... suit yourself, Michael," says a bemused DI, and so begins another comic masterpiece from Christopher Russell. We learn that Mike got his posting to the new surroundings that have always eluded him simply by applying; the connoisseur of life's luxuries finally worked out his natural beat. Told by Cryer that he will miss him, Mike observes, "No-one upstairs is protesting too violently." Ted has already handed him a farewell wind-up, asking him to investigate a burglary that's "right up your street actually – fine furniture." When he learns that he is dealing with the theft of plastic chairs from a school, Mike is unfazed. Suspecting an inside job, he soon has the whole of CID chasing up leads for him. The trail points to a relief caretaker and his wife, who are selling on stolen goods from half the burglaries in the area. Their garage is filled with bricks: "What kind?" Mike asks Burnside. "The kind the third little pig used to build his house with, Michael – brick bricks."

Mike turns up to impart wisdom to his baffled sergeant: "Yellows – London stock. Over a hundred years old, Ted. Gangs nick these in bulk from derelict buildings, often owned by the council, then resell 'em – usually back to the same council." He gives him some more helpful lines of enquiry to follow: and in the best sight gag of the year, Ted raises the tempting brick in his hand behind Mike's back, before restraining himself. The second best comes minutes later during a raid on the suppliers, a massive brawl in which the camera turns into another officer, sending villains fleeing in its path. Burnside strolls through the chaos, men locked in punch-ups all around him, before delivering a sudden elbow jab to a thug, a la Rex Kramer beating up charity cases in *Airplane!* Having turned the entire ground upside down, Dashwood is safely out of it, enjoying farewell tea and biscuits with Brownlow. This is Mike in his element: not just conversing with the great and good but one-upping them. Agreeing that expertise in the antique world is sadly lacking, he notes, "Tell most policemen that you're looking for a lowboy and you get a very funny look." He outlines his new duties as part of the "knocker squad" that targets bogus callers to people's homes. "How about you sir, are you worth knocking?" "I beg your pardon?" "Are you an antique person?" He implies that the Chief Super may have a dodgy piece or two sitting around. Returning from their successful raid, Roach observes, "You should leave more often, Mike." Then the latter cheerfully reveals that the figurine Burnside bought for thirty quid is valued at three hundred in a catalogue: "Been a good day all round, hasn't it? See you in the pub." He leaves the rest of CID looking dumbstruck, but he has reckoned without the light touch of Derek Conway. Pushing a door into him, Conway wishes "all the best with the fine art, mate" – and Mike is left rattling the remains of his new investment in horror.

Mike Dashwood is another of those awkward fits like Taff Edwards or Tom Penny that made *The Bill* such a distinctive beast. As Jon Iles has observed, he was the fly in the ointment: the catalyst that got people moving, even if it was by getting their backs up. His exit spells the beginning of the end for the old guard in CID. First out of the door, Mike is back through it much faster than them, in a double header at the end of 1992, *Finders Keepers/Return Match*, in which he has become that bit more insufferable. Perhaps this is the fate of a guest character: to be painted in slightly broader strokes as they are now peripheral to the main cast. If anything the focus is on his old sparring partner Jim, onto an elderly couple hoarding stolen antiques. Thinking he has the big time to himself, he is horrified to realise he is still playing second fiddle. By now Dashwood has finished his transformation into the yuppie he always yearned to be, sporting a slicked back Gordon Gekko hairdo, although he still smokes his trademark cheroots. "No job's too big or too little," he replies to the suggestion that this is small fry for the Antiques Squad. "International art theft one day, granddad's silver watch the next – that's what gives the job such a buzz!" "Oh goody," Jim mutters as he trails after him, swing doors repeatedly shut in his face in one of the show's more obvious metaphors. "I'm off to New York this weekend – big conference on title of goods." "Well, if you need a lift to the airport..." Furious at Mike's suggestion that he is "getting a bit... parochial", Jim sends him packing. His own lack of knowledge soon becomes a problem, a familiar deer-in-headlight look creeping over him as he tries to work out the provenance of four hundred odd items either bought or bequeathed by dead relatives. Magnanimous, he comes back to Mike and apologises. Insisting that he take over, he offloads a disaster which Mike promptly turns into a triumph, involving no less than the Regional Crime Squad. "I'll send you a postcard," he promises the stony-faced Jim.

One episode later, Jim is looking into the theft of an antique doll collection when his personal nightmare pops up again: "Are you haunting me or what? Do you sit at Scotland Yard scanning our radio frequencies?" Mike is acting on information received from Burnside; "Dolls are a trend, all right? The theft thereof. Nobody made of china and under two feet tall is safe! If you've got a problem working with Michael Dashwood, just say so. I'll get someone else to take over, won't I Tosh? I'm not having Dashwood ending up in an alley with a sharpened peg doll in his back." Viv advises Jim he's "better off the job than losing it." "Who said I was going to lose it?" "You see, you rise to the bait," observes Tosh. "Me, I don't rise to anything anymore." Indeed, he remains tight-lipped as Mike patronises him: "I hope you appreciate the way I'm sharing everything with you, despite your siege mentality. I expect hostility from somebody as insecure as Jim, but not a man of your maturity." Mike is smacked in the face by a fleeing suspect; Jim, who got a bloody nose himself following up a lead for Dashers on his last day, erupts in rare joy at the sight of him dabbing at his shiner. But, courtesy of a tip-off from his snout Adrian – "What do you expect with the Antiques Squad, Lenny the Lip?" – Mike gets the location of the dolls. Again stealing a march on the rest of Sun Hill, he is kind enough to let Jim in on the action. They go in alone, "like the good old days." "What good old days?" grumbles Jim, the apprentice in CID when Mike tried and failed to grab a result behind Galloway's back five years earlier. Such glories are only possible now he is an outsider, not a regular; the whole point of the latter, from Carver to Roach to Burnside to Meadows, is that they stay thwarted. Having cast many actors from a comedic background, including Jon Iles himself, the show adheres to the sitcom rule: success is never as interesting as failure.

Realising from the drift around him that he is simply drifting, Jim lets his jaded attitude show in dealing with Mike's replacement, Alan Woods. The first genuinely new face in CID for three and a half years signifies the new breed of detective that would take over in the mid-Nineties. They're more straight-laced and professional than their forebears, who were firmly of the *Sweeney* generation, all shirtsleeves, sweat patches and whisky bottles. His distinguishing trait is "the bloke that plays rugby" in the same way his fellow Scot Greig was "that bloke with the clarinet" at first. But these sketchy backgrounds are still an improvement on the blank slates elsewhere; nothing much singles out Polly Page and Gary McCann, introduced this year too, save their rookie status. We are, perhaps, entering a period where the actors had to do what they could with interchangeable roles. Jim is given the task of easing in the new boy, to his obvious annoyance: "You've hardly transferred into the big time, mate." Alan is moving into the area with a new wife; learning that Jim is neither married nor divorced, he remarks, "Married to the job, eh? You've got the look." "What look?" "Dedicated." The big time is thrust upon them when they are called to an armed robbery. The culprit is a middle-aged woman running a meals on wheels service, extracting money from the banks by force after they refused her appeals for a loan. Jim, who has questioned a distraught cashier, is unimpressed at the defence that the gun was a hammer in a carrier bag: "She assumed you were willing and able to blow her head off! I mean that's the point of armed robbery isn't it, to put them in fear of their lives?" Rolling his eyes at this sermon, Woods ridicules the idea of a five-year sentence: "Och away, she'll get eighteen months' suspended and a nice spread in the local rag: the moped Robin Hood. You provide the burning sense of justice Jim, I'll provide a sense of proportion. I think we could make a good team."

But teamwork is thin on the ground a few episodes later in *Private Enterprise*, as Woods is courted by Brownlow for the rugby team. "You ought to get some of that," a watching Cryer tells Carver, before spelling out the one quality poor old Jim-Jim will never have in abundance: "Clout." Unaware that Alan is wincing at the idea when Brownlow's back is turned, Jim turns on the icy treatment. "Hey, what's the problem pal?" "Oh, no problem 'pal', it's just I ain't joined your fan club yet." They are reconciled when they get into a different kind of ruck, with a suspect, in which an entire storeroom is trashed. As they nurse their injuries, Woods reveals that his bad knee has gone, and with it any hope of leading the rugby team. "Put you out of favour with the nobs, that will." "That's OK by me," he sighs – and, just like Greig's short-lived musical talents, another gimmick is quickly shelved. But the points of similarity between the two Scotsmen are matched by their differences. Woods too is a stoic and rather unknowable figure – but despite being the elder of the pair, he's the junior in every other way. In *On the Record, Off the Record* they investigate a warehouse theft and find out that one of the employees has form for drugs and credit card fraud. "Do we pull him, or do we pull him?" asks an eager Woods, put in his place when Greig scolds him for being a little premature. When they speak to the security man, himself an ex-copper, Alan unwisely lets him know that someone at his firm has a record and gets a major dressing down: "You do not come out with confidential information like that to anyone, I don't care if he's an ex-commissioner! Is that understood? Make sure it is." As well as yielding most of the detective work to their superiors, the DCs start to make them look better by displaying the naivety that up till now was largely Jim's province.

Tom Cotcher's is not the only face this year that would become a familiar presence in CID. In a break with tradition, however, many returned as the same character slightly repurposed, not someone brand new. Martin Marquez has a cameo role as the Essex-based DC Pearce, minus the rank and first name he would acquire. Far more substantial is the role given to Gary Whelan, playing DS 'Ken' Haines, a Drugs Squad officer suspended over corruption charges who is found to have been set up. After the exit of Roy Galloway, it was seemingly mandatory for future DIs to be sourced from a past episode and then re-christened. After Tommy Burnside became Frank to avoid causing offence to a real Met officer, Ken Haines would return as Harry to take over from him – perhaps for the same reason, or maybe it just had a better ring to it. The one man who did come back as someone new was Russell Boulter, playing the wounded PC Trevor Gale in *A Blind Eye*; and yet, not *that* new. Gale may be a cheeky chappie at first, hoping to get a nurse's number as he lies in his hospital bed, but there's something familiar about the malevolent fury that descends on him when he realises that Tony helped put him there. "What exactly are you telling me, you just stood there watching? You're not a Catholic, are you? Shame. Couple of Hail Marys, few pints of lager, you'd feel a lot better. Go on, get lost, will you? And hey – try and pick up some real muggers next time."

There are more glimpses of the future in the number of scenes used to source the opening titles, including two from the same episode, *Hands Up*. Over many hundreds of appearances, their original context is easily forgotten – and memory is always a fragile thing. My earliest recall of *The Bill* is an episode where a youth absconds from a detention centre on the edge of woodland and is chased into it by a PC, with a shot of him splashing across wet ground. In adulthood it took time to narrow it down to Russell Lewis's *Not Waving*, from early 1992; little wonder, when my memory was telling me porkies. That building is in fact a nurse's housing block, spied on by a young man from what Steve deems the "nice honest travelling folk." When he escapes custody – "There was nothing I could do!" protests Roach, "But you do it so well," Burnside reassures him – Steve pursues the kid into the woods and into a canal, where the boy saves him from drowning. Another moment from that episode illustrates how things change when taken out of context, as Viv walks in on the rest of CID in Burnside's office, watching a video of a ramraid. This clip featured in Thames TV's celebratory montage of its back catalogue, in the final two minutes before it closed down as a broadcaster on New Year's Eve 1992. The fragments chosen make it look as if she has stumbled on a viewing of herself, with Burnside giving her a reproving glare for what she's doing on the tape! *The Bill* had earned its place in that line-up: one of the last great hits of a hit-making machine that had delivered time and again over the past twenty-five years. In the brave new world that was to follow, it wasn't just that opening ident of the London skyline that was lost to *The Bill*. Something of the guts, energy and innovation of Thames that marked the show's first eight years went with it.

Verdict: Another high-quality year for *The Bill* brings to a close an era of the show that got the ingredients exactly right. Both uniform and CID get plenty of meaty storylines, and that mixture of quirkiness and toughness that distinguished the programme is on full display. The only below-par element is the experimental title sequence that began in late 1991 and continues across this year, a weird disjointed affair that tries to cram in too many short, motionless clips of characters. Some programmes, however, are only worth watching for their opening titles; this is quite the reverse, a format that could have kept producing gold for a long time. The question posed in Volume 1, before the start of the half-hour era, over whether you could have too much of a good thing had been answered resoundingly over the next five years. But as the show acquires yet another episode per week from 1993 onwards, the same question rears its head, only amplified: can you have too, *too* much of a good thing?

BIBLIOGRAPHY

Andrew, Christopher, *The Defence of the Realm: The Authorized History of MI5*, Penguin, 2009

Colbran, Marianne, *Watching the Cops: a case study of production processes on television police drama "The Bill"*, A thesis submitted to the Department of Sociology of the London School of Economics for the degree of Doctor of Philosophy, September 2011

Cornell, Paul, Day, Martin and Topping, Keith, *The Guinness Book of Classic British TV – 2nd Edition*, Guinness Publishing, 1996

Crocker, Oliver, *Witness Statements – Making The Bill: Series 1-3*, Devonfire Books, 2020

Crocker, Oliver, *Witness Statements – Making The Bill: 1988*, Devonfire Books, 2022

Dann, Larry, *Oh, What A Lovely Memoir*, Devonfire Books, 2023

Kingsley, Hilary, *The Bill – The First Ten Years*, Boxtree, 1994

Lynch, Tony, *The Bill: The Inside Story of British Television's Most Successful Police Series*, Boxtree, 1991

Wheal, Elizabeth-Anne, https://elizabethannewheal.com/

Wilsher, J.C., *Paper Work: On Being a Writer in Broadcast Drama*, self-published ebook, 2022

ABOUT THE AUTHOR

Edward Kellett is a TV historian based in Eastbourne. His acclaimed *Reaching a Verdict: Reviewing The Bill* series of books have been published by Devonfire Books since 2023 and regularly appear in Amazon's Television History & Criticism Top 100 chart. Kellett also contributed a chapter examining *The Bill* and the police procedural for the book *New Waves: 1980s TV in Britain*, edited by Rodney Marshall and self-published through Amazon in 2024.

Edward's favourite exchange of dialogue from this period that was not quoted in the main text is from John Milne's 1990 episode *Carry Your Bags, Sir?*, when Brownlow learns from Conway that a man with an unresolved complaint against Sun Hill has been arrested for assaulting a police officer. "Whom did he assault?" "Hollis." "Oh, understandable. I suggest somebody has a word with Hollis, and explains to him the advantages of dropping the matter... I think we should get Bob Cryer to have a word. He can hit him too if necessary."

ACKNOWLEDGEMENTS

I would like to thank Oliver Crocker and Tessa Crocker for their help in preparing, proofing and formatting this book; Tony Virgo and J.C. Wilsher for their contributions to this volume, Tim Vaughan and Nigel J. Wilson for theirs to the previous one; Barry Appleton and Christopher Russell for their kind feedback, and along with J.C. Wilsher, for writing some of the best television ever made; and Sarah Went of *The Billaton*, without whom none of this would be possible.

On that note, I wish to extend special thanks to my mother, Marilyn Kellett: a woman who enriched the lives of everyone she came into contact with, and had an inspiring influence during her thirty-five year teaching career that cannot be measured. When she started to read through my debut effort, she told me confidently, "The first of many." I didn't expect that, seven weeks to the day it came out, and indeed seven weeks to the hour I was interviewed about it on BBC Radio, she would no longer be around to see them. I ended up reading some of my magnum opus to her on the final night. Now, in print as well as in memory, she can live on; and if anyone deserved that immortality, it was her.

AFTERWORD
By J.C. Wilsher
Writer, *The Bill* (1989-2001)

Legend has it that after the read-through for *Carry On Columbus*, Jim Dale told Barbara Windsor that it had been great to see so many old friends. When she pointed out that most of their original *Carry On...* co-stars were dead, Dale replied that he'd been referring to the jokes!

It was great for me to renew acquaintance with the half-forgotten lines, stories and characters of *The Bill* in Edward Kellett's account of the show in the early 1990's. As he says, this was the period of my most intensive involvement in it as a writer. Like Edward, for me those were the vintage years: half-hour episodes, lightly storylined if at all, with occasional two-parters, or situations developed across widely separated episodes which could also be viewed as stand-alone.

I loved the hit-and-run style of storytelling – the maxim was "start in the middle, get out before the end". My own metaphor was that *The Bill* didn't have a fourth gear – you kept your foot down, revving hard until the credits rolled. When I subsequently wrote for other series dramas, an hour or more long, I tried to write scripts with that pace and energy; it wasn't always welcomed.

Reading *Reaching A Verdict* reminded me of aspects of *The Bill* that the passage of time had obscured.

For a pre-watershed show, as it was in this period, it tackled difficult subjects and situations – including sex with minors, rape and other forms of violence against women and children – without compromise. It also portrayed police attitudes, language and behaviour which were a long way from what was being encouraged at Hendon training college – however, I was told by more than one ethnic minority viewer that the show wasn't realistic because it failed to reflect police racism and brutality.

Despite being self-consciously gritty, dark, and so forth, *The Bill* was often very funny, and I sniggered at some of the lines quoted here – and not just my own. Police Adviser Wilf Knight told me my scripts were funniest when I was trying to be serious – anyone who has spent time with police officers will recognise that as a characteristic copper's put-down.

The Bill was in the business of storytelling, whereas soaps and other formats were seen as "character-driven", and therefore more dramatically weighty. I met a woman at a party who knew one of the regular cast socially; she said she'd been to see him in a stage play "to see if he could act". I thought that was grossly unfair to the show and the cast; one of Edward Kellett's welcome acts of recuperation is to lay emphasis on the characters, and the considerable acting skill of those who brought them to life.

Like the other team members interviewed in Oliver Crocker's *Witness Statement* books, I look back on my time on the show as one of the happiest periods of my professional life. I was working with people who knew what they were doing, and they were trying to do it as well as possible – under constant time pressure. I remember propping up the bar of The William Morris, *The Bill's* Merton watering hole, with my Script Editor Tim Vaughan, and Production Scheduler Nigel Wilson. Nigel, within a thick haze of cigarette smoke, produced a crumpled envelope from his pocket, and on the back of it confidently worked out the running order for a string of imminent episodes, as yet unmade, and in some cases as yet unwritten by me and others.

For a lot of the time in those early years, I was too busy to realise how happy I was, but then as Joni Mitchell sang, "Don't it always seem to go on, that you don't know what you've got 'til it's gone?"

J.C. Wilsher, March 2024.

Paper Work: On Being a Writer in Broadcast Drama by J.C. Wilsher
Available from Amazon

ALSO FROM DEVONFIREBOOKS.COM

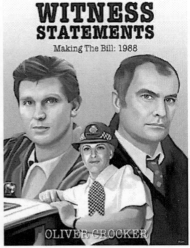

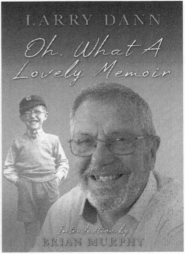